The Gospel in Christian Traditions

TED A. CAMPBELL

2009

OXFORD
UNIVERSITY PRESS

Oxford University Press, Inc., publishes works that further
Oxford University's objective of excellence
in research, scholarship, and education.

Oxford   New York
Auckland   Cape Town   Dar es Salaam   Hong Kong   Karachi
Kuala Lumpur   Madrid   Melbourne   Mexico City   Nairobi
New Delhi   Shanghai   Taipei   Toronto

With offices in
Argentina   Austria   Brazil   Chile   Czech Republic   France   Greece
Guatemala   Hungary   Italy   Japan   Poland   Portugal   Singapore
South Korea   Switzerland   Thailand   Turkey   Ukraine   Vietnam

Copyright © 2009 by Oxford University Press, Inc.

Published by Oxford University Press, Inc.
198 Madison Avenue, New York, New York 10016

www.oup.com

Oxford is a registered trademark of Oxford University Press

All rights reserved. No part of this publication may be reproduced,
stored in a retrieval system, or transmitted, in any form or by any means,
electronic, mechanical, photocopying, recording, or otherwise,
without the prior permission of Oxford University Press.

All scripture quotations (unless otherwise noted)
are taken from the New Revised Standard Version of the Bible,
copyright © 1989 by the Division of Christian Education
of the National Council of Churches of Christ in the USA.

Library of Congress Cataloging-in-Publication Data
Campbell, Ted.
The Gospel in Christian traditions / Ted A. Campbell.
   p. cm.
ISBN 978-0-19-537063-8
ISBN 978-0-19-537062-1 (pbk.)
1. Jesus Christ—History of doctrines. 2. Theology, Doctrinal. I. Title.
BT198.C26 2008
230.09—dc22   2008009345

9 8 7 6 5 4 3 2 1
Printed in the United States of America
on acid-free paper

to
Dale Marie

Foreword

Ted Campbell offers those of us involved in the life of Christian communities a rich gift in *The Gospel in Christian Traditions*. The gift is not like a fruit cake or a bottle of wine, something which we may or may not like the taste of. It is more like a set of tools or a box of mountain-climbing equipment: if we're carpenters or mountain climbers, his book equips us to pursue our vocations.

That vocation, generally speaking, is the work of Christian ministry and mission, and in particular, the part of that work that takes place beyond the boundaries of the local congregation. If we were exclusively focused on ministry and mission within one local congregation and the denomination to which it belongs, we might be able to get along reasonably well without dealing with the issues Ted Campbell addresses.

But as soon as we venture outside a single local church or denomination, we find ourselves having to interact and cooperate with Christians of other traditions. We may be in an interdenominational seminary. We may be involved in some work of compassion and justice from caring for the homeless to standing against an unjust war or trade policy. We may be engaged in evangelism and the making of new disciples and communicating with the unchurched. Our interaction and collaboration will eventually bring up differences and even tensions in our traditions, challenging us to find the common ground that unites us. A book like the one you are now reading is invaluable in this regard.

Of course, even if we stay within one congregation, we realize that our church and denomination is not an island, that we exist as part of this larger Christian movement, and that our boundaries are more permeable than ever, with more people than ever cross-pollinating and experiencing hospitality across denominational rims. So even within local churches and denominations, we need to get some sense of what gives coherence to the vast array of Christian communities—and the book that you are holding does just this.

This need for coherence intensifies, I think, in what many people call a postdenominational age. Although I don't think our denominations will or should go away, I do believe that the insularity, competition, and sectarian attitudes that have too often characterized the Protestant era can and should give way to a new attitude within and among denominations, across traditions and confessions.

First, within denominations, I believe we need a fresh appraisal of the core message that we all share so this core message can become increasingly primary and pivotal for us. Then, we can more freely maintain (or, if necessary, abandon or modify) our denominational distinctives as accents or spices or added features, because they are no longer seen as the language, main course, the basic product, or the raison-d'être of our community.

Second, among denominations, as we more clearly understand the core message or story that runs through all our traditions, we will find ourselves more wholeheartedly fulfilling the prayer of Jesus in John 17 and the ideal of Paul in Ephesians 4, so that our diversification will not lead to division, but rather unity. And as we together face the global crises and opportunities in which we all share, that unity will enhance the possibility of effective collaboration for the common good. To say the same thing in terms of my own work, the more we share a generous orthodoxy, the more we can help the world see that everything must change—and all things can become new—in light of the gospel.

Of special interest to me is Ted Campbell's explanation of centrifugal and centripetal forces at work in our denominations across generations. As someone involved both in the renewal of existing institutions and in the development of new congregations and movements, I see these dynamics at play constantly. I even see centrifugal and centripetal forces at work in my own spiritual biography and ministry over time. Having this language will help many people, I believe, make better sense of behavior patterns that have up to now been baffling.

In these pages, Ted Campbell offers us not just a scholarly (but accessible) consideration of the core message of our faith, but he also demonstrates what we might call a neo-ecumenical methodology for this postdenominational era. If the old ecumenism to some degree sought unity through some combination of interinstitutional communication and interinstitutional mission, and if it to some degree avoided the content of our faith for fear that dogma would divide (some would debate this, I'm sure), this book invites us to discover at the heart of our dogma a treasure that we all share. Perhaps, having more clearly affirmed that common treasure, our communication and missional collaboration will become much more authentic and sustainable.

All this must be done from a certain posture or tone, and that is another gift of this volume: Ted Campbell's tone models not a critical or suspicious hermeneutic but an irenic one, one characterized by a kind of second naiveté. The time is ripe, I think, for us to receive this gift.

From institutional headquarters in New York or Geneva or Rome or Istanbul to coffee shops and living rooms and classrooms everywhere, it is a good thing when people consider the gospel that was announced and embodied by Jesus, proclaimed by the apostles, and handed down, generation by generation, to you and me. Aided by this helpful text, let us do so, in humility and love and joy, together.

—Brian McLaren
Laurel, MD

Preface

This book grows out of a trajectory of research in Christian doctrine and my own involvement in ecumenical dialogue, specifically, as a United Methodist representative to the Faith and Order Commission of the National Council of the Churches of Christ (NCCC) in the USA (1992–2002), a participant in ecumenical-Pentecostal dialogue sponsored by the NCCC, a participant in Eastern Orthodox and Methodist dialogue on Christian spirituality, and more recently as a member of a dialogue team between The United Methodist Church and the Episcopal Church in the United States (from 2006 to the present time). My earlier engagement with the work of the NCCC Faith and Order Commission resulted in a study of doctrine taught in specific Christian confessional traditions (*Christian Confessions*, 1996). At the conclusion of that work, I asked what doctrines might be described fairly as having been shared between most Christian traditions. I envisioned developing this material into a larger study of commonly shared Christian teachings, but I became convinced along the way that the first step in such a larger project would be to document critically the basic Christian narrative, the "good news" or "gospel," as it has been professed and received across confessional traditions and in the ecumenical movement. This book is the result of that study.

The research on which this book is based has been carried out at three institutions: Garrett-Evangelical Theological Seminary (Evanston, Illinois), Claremont School of Theology (Claremont, California), and Perkins School of Theology, Southern Methodist University (Dallas, Texas). I am grateful for the institutional and research support that

xii   PREFACE

each of these schools has afforded. The staff of Bridwell Library at SMU have helped time and again with critical issues, and this unique library has proven to be a treasure of resources for this project: envision a blue Georgian room where no computer clicking is allowed and whose bookshelves are endowed with the complete range of the *Patrologia Latina*, *Patrologia Graeca*, and the *Corpus Christianorum*.

I also wish to express thanks to the following persons who have offered comments and suggestions for this project: Dr. Bradley Nassif (North Park University), Dr. Jeffrey Gros, FSC (Memphis Theological Seminary), Dr. Mark Stamm (Perkins School of Theology, Southern Methodist University), Rev. Virgil Matthews (Midland, Texas), Dr. Bart D. Ehrman (University of North Carolina at Chapel Hill), Dr. Denis Fortin (Andrews University Theological Seminary), Dr. Sondra Wheeler (Wesley Theological Seminary), Dr. Douglas M. Strong (Seattle Pacific University), Mr. Émile Landry (Houston, Texas), and Mr. Theo Calderara (Oxford University Press, New York). I am deeply grateful to Dr. Brian D. McLaren, who has offered the foreword to the book.

All scripture quotations (unless otherwise noted) are taken from the New Revised Standard Version of the Bible, copyright © 1989 by the Division of Christian Education of the National Council of Churches of Christ in the USA.

Some musical works whose words appear in this book have been used by permission of the copyright holders. These include the following:

> "O Church of God, United" (1953) by Frederick B. Morley; copyright © 1954, renewed 1982 by The Hymn Society (administered by Hope Publishing Co., Carol Stream, Illinois, 60618); all rights reserved; used by permission.
>
> "The Blood Will Never Lose Its Power" (1966) by Andraé Crouch, copyright © 1966, renewed 1994 by Manna Music, Inc., 35255 Brooten Road, Pacific City, Oregon 97135/ASCAP; all rights reserved; used by permission.
>
> "Lord I Lift Your Name On High" (1989) by Rick Founds, copyright © 1989 Maranatha Praise, Inc./ASCAP (administered by Music Services); all rights reserved; used by permission.
>
> "Breath of Heaven (Mary's Song)" by Amy Grant and Chris Eaton, copyright © 1992, Age to Age Music, Inc./Riverstone Music (both administered by The Loving Company)/SGO Music Ltd. (administered by Bug Music); all rights reserved, used by permission.

This book is dedicated to my wife, Dale Marie (Fick) Campbell. We once lived in a Lincoln College flat behind the Oxford University Press bookstore on the High Street, Oxford, at a time when the Press was celebrating its five hundredth anniversary (1978), so there is a certain bond between us and the venerable institution whose North American branch is publishing this book. I could say that Dale Marie has been a consistent source of help and inspiration for this and other projects, which would be very true. But the great gift I have been given is to be with her, and for this I am most profoundly grateful.

Contents

Foreword, vii
  Brian D. McLaren
Preface, xi

Introduction, 1

1. The Gospel in Proto-Orthodox Christian Communities, 13
     I Corinthians 15:1–11: The Transmission
       and Reception of the Gospel, 14
     The Gospel in Early Christian Catechesis and Creeds, 19
     The Gospel and the Canon of Christian
       Scripture in the First through Fourth Centuries, 24
     The Meaning of the Gospel in
       the Earliest Christian Communities, 28

2. The Gospel in Ancient Christian Churches, 31
     Ancient Christian Churches, 31
     The Gospel in the Creeds, 32
     The Gospel in the Liturgy, 39
    The Gospel in the Liturgical Year, 46
     The Meaning of the Gospel in the
       Traditions of Ancient Christian Churches, 49

3. The Gospel in Protestant and Related Churches, 55
     Protestant and Related Churches, 55
     The Gospel in Creeds and Doctrinal Statements, 58

The Gospel and the Unity of Scripture, 63
The Gospel in Protestant Worship, 65
The Meaning of the Gospel in the Traditions
 of Protestant and Related Churches, 70

4. The Gospel in Evangelical Communities, 75
Evangelical Communities and Churches, 75
The Gospel in Evangelical Doctrinal Statements, 82
The Gospel in Evangelical Worship, 87
The Gospel in Evangelism and Training Media, 94
New Signs of Affirmation of the Gospel, 96
The Meaning of the Gospel in Evangelical Communities, 97

5. The Gospel and the Ecumenical Movement, 101
The Ecumenical Movement, 101
The Gospel as the Ground of Scripture and Tradition, 104
The Apostolic Faith in the Ancient Creeds, 106
The Gospel in Ecumenical Liturgical Renewal, 107
The Meaning of the Gospel in the Ecumenical Movement, 109

6. The Mystery of the Gospel, 111
Three Clusters of Meaning, 111
Some Responses to Issues, 117
The Gospel and Criteria for Christian Unity, 121
The Mystery of the Gospel, 124

7. A Methodological Afterword, 127
Historical and Ecumenical Study, 127
Doctrine and Doctrinal Reception, 129
Commensurability and Mutual Understanding, 132

Notes, 137
Bibliography, 177
Index, 191

The Gospel in
Christian Traditions

Introduction

Christ has died,
Christ is risen,
Christ will come again.
—Memorial Acclamations in the Eucharist

Between a quarter and a third of the earth's six and a half billion people can be identified as members of Christian churches.[1] But is there a common message or "gospel" that has been received and proclaimed in the Christian churches that count more than two billion people as their members? And what does the gospel mean in these widely differing, indeed divided, Christian traditions? The purpose of this book is to examine these questions by considering communal texts and practices that demonstrate how Christian traditions have understood and transmitted the gospel ("good news"), the most basic Christian message that Christian churches today have inherited from ancient Christian communities.

Despite the wide diversity represented in the New Testament literature, New Testament texts presuppose at specific points that there was a common understanding in early Christian communities of the church's basic proclamation (*kerygma*) of God's saving work in Christ (the "good news" or gospel, *euaggelion*).

> Now I would remind you, brothers and sisters, of the good news that I proclaimed to you, which you in turn received, in which you also stand. . . . Whether then it was I or they [others who

> had proclaimed the message], so we proclaim and so you have come to believe (I Corinthians 15:1 and 11).[2]
>
> I am astonished that you are so quickly deserting the one who called you in the grace of Christ and are turning to a different gospel—not that there is another gospel, but there are some who are confusing you and want to pervert the gospel of Christ (Galatians 1:6–7).[3]
>
> Beloved, while eagerly preparing to write to you about the salvation we share, I find it necessary to write and appeal to you to contend for the faith that was once for all entrusted [or "handed on"] to the saints (Jude 3).[4]

As the first chapter will show in more detail, the Christian message was expressed prior to the writing and long before the canonization of the New Testament in a particular group of early Christian communities. This message or gospel served as the basis for the development of Christian creedal formulae and as a criterion for defining the canon of Christian scriptures in the early Christian centuries in the communities that came to be regarded as orthodox, that is, the groups that I and others call "proto-orthodox" Christian communities.[5] These early proto-orthodox Christian communities transmitted the gospel to historic Christian churches that exist today, not only ancient churches (Orthodox, Catholic, and Assyrian churches) but Protestant, Anglican, and Evangelical churches as well (the understanding of the gospel in these groups of churches will be the subject of chapters 2, 3, and 4).

The assertion of a common Christian faith has been one of the key goals of the ecumenical movement, the movement that has sought to make visible the essential unity of Christian churches. The presupposition of the ecumenical movement is that Christian unity is a gift and cannot be created by the churches. But because the churches remain visibly divided, the ecumenical movement seeks to make visible the essential unity that is given as a gift of grace. To describe a common Christian gospel in a broad ecumenical framework is possible today because careful discussions between Christian churches in the twentieth century began to clarify the meaning of beliefs and practices shared between them. A particular strand of the ecumenical movement, the Faith and Order movement, has sought to deal directly with issues of doctrine and church practices that have historically divided Christian churches. The Faith and Order movement sponsored ecumenical conversations that explored and sought to resolve these divisive issues by examining historic uses of language, by interpreting historic statements about the Christian faith in their originating contexts, and by reaffirming the Christian gospel discerned in ancient statements of Christian faith. Chapter 5 will show how the Faith and Order movement has dealt with the issue of what constitutes the Christian gospel shared between Christian churches that have been visibly divided in the past.

But although ecumenical insights deeply influenced Christian historical scholarship and theology through the 1970s, they have had far less influence on theological and historical scholarship since that time. Studies of early Christianity in recent decades have emphasized the diversity of early Christian communities rather than the common threads that link early Christianity with the teachings of surviving Christian communities.[6] In the same period, that is, since the 1970s, studies of Reformation and later Western Christianity have emphasized the distinct character of denominational and ethnic Christian traditions rather than common ties between Christian traditions separated at the time of the Reformation.[7] These developments in scholarship since the 1970s are consistent with the emergence in the same period of postmodern interpretations of cultures, interpretations that have consistently emphasized the particularities of cultures and traditions in contrast to both traditional and Modernist claims about broader cultural unities. Postmodern scholarship has consistently found incommensurability where traditional and Modernist scholarship claimed commensurability.[8] The challenge that postmodern scholarship raises for such a study as this book offers is the challenge of finding contemporary methods of historical and theological interpretation that can adequately demonstrate critical points of unity or commensurability between traditions without denying well justified claims of differences and diversity in ancient as well as modern Christian traditions. A sketch of such a methodology is given later in this introduction and is taken up in more detail in chapter 7.

For the purposes of this introduction I note four critical issues for discerning a common Christian gospel in recent decades. Discerning a common Christian gospel today is a critical issue because, in the first place, contemporary studies emphasizing the diversity of early Christianity have sometimes created the impression that the traditional view of Jesus taken by Christian churches was a relatively late development, one that was imposed and enforced by secular political authorities in the fourth century and thus not in continuity with the earliest forms of the Christian message. Even though the demonstration of wide diversity in itself does not warrant the claim that there were no forms of unity in beliefs and practices, the well documented diversity of early Christian communities has been taken, at least in popular culture, to denote the absence of significant unity in teachings and practices in early Christian communities. This is represented, for example, in Dan Brown's *The Da Vinci Code* (2003) in which a fictitious scholar claims that the canonical gospels were accepted as scripture by a secular political process in the fourth century and that extracanonical gospels such as the "Gospel of Mary" may represent the most accurate historical account of Jesus.[9] In its popular form, this relies on some patently erroneous claims—for example, the notion that the emperor Constantine or the Council of Nicaea had something to do with the canon of Christian scripture. It leaves readers with the impression that the understanding of Jesus maintained by traditional Christian churches relies on later documents, especially when readers are unaware of the chronology of the composition of the New Testament and other early Christian literature, the process of canonization of the New Testament, and—perhaps most important—the existence of earlier narratives about Jesus embedded within the earliest New Testament writings.

In contrast to this currently popular point of view, critical studies of oral traditions underlying the New Testament literature (studies undertaken from the 1930s) insisted that a foundational narrative about Jesus (the gospel) was handed down before the writing of the canonical gospels and that the canonical gospels expanded upon this earlier narrative.[10] Moreover, ecumenical scholarship (since at least the 1960s) asserted that the unity of Christian communities today relies on continuity with the gospel message that was expressed both in the New Testament literature and in the earlier oral traditions that were transmitted in early Christian creeds and liturgy.[11] Chapter 1 will show how the oral traditioning of the gospel narrative shaped not only the writing of the canonical gospels and other New Testament texts but also shaped the processes by which New Testament scriptures were recognized as having canonical authority. The case needs to be made in response to contemporary representations of Jesus that the gospel affirmed and received in historic Christian churches stands in continuity not only with the New Testament literature but also with these earliest strands of gospel tradition that lay behind the development of the New Testament. To show the grounds for this claim of continuity of the gospel message on the part of historic Christian churches is one of the objectives of this book.

Discerning a common Christian gospel today is a critical issue because, in the second place, some contemporary studies of Christian theology presuppose that there is no fundamental agreement as to the basic meaning of the Christian faith. This point of view builds on well documented claims of wide diversity in early and later Christian communities. A sign of this is the tendency in the study of Church history in the last two decades to refer to "Christianities" rather than "forms of Christianity" or the variety of "Christian traditions."[12] Claims of widespread diversity in Christian teachings and practices can be pressed to the point where they are no longer documented historical claims but simply the presupposition that there is no essential unity between divided Christian communities. When taken as a presupposition, these claims implicitly challenge conclusions reached by ecumenical scholarship in the twentieth century and beyond.

David Kelsey's study of the nature of theological education, *To Understand God Truly* (1992) has an example of this trend:

> There is no one "core" or "basic" or "essential" material theme or doctrine, nor any one pattern of them, that is the Christian thing. The generally accepted conclusion of historical studies is that there never has been. There is not even a past, perhaps originating, "essential" or "core" construal of the Christian thing from which Christians have departed in different ways and to which they might return.[13]

Kelsey was influenced in this claim by studies documenting the wide diversity of early Christian communities—he cites Robert Wilken's study of *The Myth of Christian Beginnings* (1981). And he was not alone in making such a claim: other studies of Christian theology have similarly taken claims of diversity to imply a lack of unity in historic Christian communities or a lack of commensurability between the doctrinal claims that Christian communities make about their most central and definitional beliefs and practices.[14] Contemporary theological studies, moreover, often proceed by a method that emphasizes the thought of individual theologians more than teachings affirmed by and received in Christian communities (churches). This consistent focus on the thought of individual theologians and its complementary lack of focus on the claims of Christian communities has, I believe, an inherent effect of marginalizing claims about unity in central Christian teachings.[15] Moreover, it could also be that contemporary theologians have been exposed to the persistent sense of malaise and a lack of centeredness in older Protestant and Anglican churches (more on this in what follows).

This is not to deny that there are threads of contemporary Christian theology that acknowledge specific forms of continuity in doctrine and practices and deal directly with communally affirmed and communally received Christian teachings and practices. Karl Barth's *Church Dogmatics*

(1932–1968) incorporated extensive reflection on specific Christian doctrinal texts (especially Reformation and post-Reformation dogmatic texts), and the German ecumenical theologian Edmund Schlink's *Ökumenische Dogmatik* (1993) offered an elaborate systematic theology grounded in ecumenical dialogue between Protestant, Catholic, and Orthodox traditions. It is important to note for the purposes of this study that both Barth and Schlink took the gospel message to be the heart of the Christian faith as affirmed doctrinally.[16] Contemporary Catholic dogmatic theology has continued to make claims of continuity and unity, for example, in the *Introduction to Christianity* by Cardinal Ratzinger, now Pope Benedict XVI.[17] In the United States, a cluster of contemporary theologians including George Lindbeck, Ellen Charry, Bruce Marshall, and William Abraham have offered contemporary theological interpretations grounded in corporately affirmed doctrinal materials and their researches have found significant grounds for unity between Christian traditions.[18] Thus, theological studies that proceed on the presupposition that there is no substantial historic consensus in the Christian faith represent only one strand of contemporary theological reflection, but their concern is pervasive enough to warrant a critical response.

The present work is not indeed a work of systematic theology, because its methods are primarily historical and ecumenical, but I hope that it will be relevant to these contemporary theological issues, because they themselves make historical claims and appear to contradict claims that have been made by ecumenical groups. I offer here an historical and ecumenical justification for claims of unity and commensurability by delineating a core sample, through highly varied strata of Christian tradition, which focuses on the most basic common teaching of historic Christian communities, the gospel message. Other areas of unity and commensurability in central Christian teachings need to be demonstrated, but it seems appropriate to begin with the most constitutive of Christian teachings.[19]

In the third place, another contemporary reason for a renewed discernment of the basic Christian message, the gospel, at the beginning of the third Christian millennium has to do with the particular crises faced now by old-line Protestant and Anglican churches in the United States and elsewhere.[20] A series of divisive issues—such as the issues of whether churches should ordain gay and lesbian persons, and whether clergy should be authorized by churches to perform unions of gay and lesbian persons—have divided these churches in recent decades. Since the 1990s, these issues have been raised to *status confessionis*, that is, to the level of teachings or practices that must be communally and explicitly affirmed (or condemned) for the sake of the unity of the church. These issues have forced the churches to consider what the most fundamental ground of their unity as Christians is.

How is the discernment of the gospel relevant in this situation? On the one hand, those who see specific positions on human sexuality as definitive of Christian unity—and who thus may see these issues as grounds for division within church bodies—maintain that the gospel has to do with salvation from sin. The churches, on their view, cannot endorse or permit that which the Christian scriptures identify as sin, and St. Paul's letter to the Romans names homosexual relationships as an instance of sin from which the gospel offers salvation (Romans 1:26–27). On the other hand, those who do not see particular positions on sexuality as necessary for Christian unity maintain that the nucleus of the gospel message contained within the Christian scriptures, historic creeds, and liturgies does not specify that homosexual acts or relationships should be considered as impediments to Christian unity (or to ordination). As an analogy, they point out with that there are parallel practices condemned as sin in the Christian scriptures (for example, the remarriage of divorced persons, a practice condemned by Jesus' own words: Matthew 5:31–32, 19:7–9; Mark 10:4–12; Luke 16:18), which many churches have come to allow in specific cases. The issue is not, strictly speaking, what constitutes sin, but is rather how tight or specific a definition of sin and of the gospel is necessary to define Christian unity or to serve as grounds for the division of Christian communities.

When Anglican and Protestant churches in the past faced similarly divisive issues—for example, the highly divisive issue of slavery in the United States—they were able eventually to come to consensus, though not without divisions that lasted for a century or more.[21] In these past conflicts, consensus was reached on the basis of strong confidence in basic Christian teachings and practices maintained by these churches, including preeminently their confidence in the gospel message itself. But although the framework of fidelity to historic Christian teachings and practices remains in place in the formal doctrinal standards, prayer books, and hymnals of these churches, the denominations face these newly divisive issues now with far less confidence in unitive Christian practices and teachings than they held in the past. Protestant and Anglican sermons, originally devised as the preeminent means of explaining the gospel message, have been utilized for decades now as means for offering inspirational messages or commentaries on contemporary issues, often offering little substantial reference to communally affirmed doctrine that could build confidence in a Christian community's most central message. Catechetical processes in the churches in the same period have likewise failed to instill confidence in the commonly held message of Christian communities. The lack of sustained teaching and preaching on unitive Christian doctrines and practices has lent considerable fire to the claims of denominational conservatives that the leadership of the denominations, especially when they press for progressive changes, are motivated more by secular concerns than for fidelity to the Christian message itself.

One might have hoped that the foundation of ecumenical reflection on the central meaning of the Christian faith that had developed through the twentieth century would have helped the churches in this situation. But a number of factors—denominational retrenchment in the face of declining membership and declining resources, theological formation that minimizes the importance of corporate expressions of faith (see the previous points), and perhaps these divisive issues themselves—seem to have shifted the focus away from the strong ecumenical commitments that characterized these churches fifty years ago. This comes at a time when old-line Protestant churches most critically need the ecumenical witness that points to the heart of the Christian message. This situation is especially ironic as it comes at a time when the most ancient Christian communities (Eastern and Oriental Orthodox, Catholic, and Assyrian churches) have entered into very significant ecumenical relationships with each other,[22] the Catholic Church has worked vigorously to strengthen ecumenical relationships with other churches,[23] and some Evangelical churches have become involved in ecumenical dialogue.

This leads to a fourth reason why discerning a common Christian gospel is a critical issue today, because many churches that originated in the context of Evangelical movements are now seeking to relate themselves to the broader communities of Christian churches throughout the world.[24] From the late nineteenth century through the middle of the twentieth century Evangelical churches and other ecclesial organizations (such as evangelistic associations) defined their unity, for the most part, by criteria unique to their own denominational traditions or by criteria established by their own independent congregations or associations. This typically meant that they defined themselves doctrinally against old-line Protestant and Anglican churches and against each other.

Since the 1970s, however, many Evangelical and Pentecostal churches have come into significant dialogue with each other and with other churches. In 1977 a group of Evangelical theologians issued "The Chicago Call: An Appeal to Evangelicals." This document not only called for

Evangelical engagement with critical social issues (as the earlier, Chicago "Declaration of Evangelical Social Concern" had done in 1973), it also called for Evangelicals to appropriate the heritage of the whole Christian tradition, and to work with other Christian churches for the unity of the whole church.[25] Contacts between Evangelical groups and other churches inevitably raised issues of what practices and beliefs are necessary to define Christian unity.

Since the 1970s, various groups of Evangelicals have engaged directly in dialogue with Catholics and with Eastern Orthodox Christians. The Catholic Church participated in dialogues with Pentecostal churches and with representatives of the Charismatic movement beginning in 1972. A series of extensive reports document their most important conclusions, including areas of agreement and areas of continuing disagreement.[26] Between 1977 and 1984, Catholic and Evangelical leaders held a series of meetings focusing on issues of Christian missions. Their work led eventually to a lengthy summary report laying out areas of common teaching and mission as well as concerns stated on both sides of the dialogue.[27] In addition to Catholic-Evangelical dialogue, informal dialogues between Evangelical and Eastern Orthodox Christian leaders have been undertaken since the 1980s. The Society for the Study of Eastern Orthodoxy and Evangelicalism was formally constituted in 1990 and has sought to expand the scope of these dialogues.[28]

A specific instance of new liaisons between Evangelicals and Catholics can be seen in the publication *First Things*,[29] which has provided a new platform where Evangelicals and Catholics (and others) can engage critical theological and ethical issues. The issue of abortion has been particularly critical as a common concern for Catholics and Evangelicals in recent decades, and this is reflected in *First Things,* but the publication has provided a broader forum for Evangelical-Catholic dialogue as well. In 1994 *First Things* published "Evangelicals and Catholics Together: The Christian Mission in the Third Millennium," a manifesto of concerns common to Evangelical and Catholic churches.[30] Another sign of new liaisons can be seen in the Center for Catholic and Evangelical Theology, founded in the early 1990s, which sponsored *In One Body through the Cross: The Princeton Proposal for Christian Unity* (2003),[31] a proposal for a new way forward for ecumenical dialogue on the part of sixteen Catholic and Protestant theologians. The Center's work has been carried on by way of its periodical *Pro Ecclesia.*

Another sign of this contemporary engagement in ecumenical dialogue came in a working group of the Faith and Order Commission of the

National Council of the Churches of Christ in the USA in the 1996–2000 quadrennium. I served as a coleader of this group with Dr. Gilbert Stafford of the Church of God of Anderson, Indiana. This working group focused on dialogues that explicitly paired newer and typically American-born church traditions (such as the traditions of Seventh-day Adventist, Holiness, and Pentecostal churches) with older Christian traditions. So, for example, the group heard a dialogue between Holiness and Eastern Orthodox church representatives on the subject of Christian worship and a dialogue between Anglican and Seventh-day Adventist representatives on eschatology.[32] The method developed in these dialogues has become part of the framework of ecumenical discernment that I have utilized in this book.

Yet another instance of Evangelical Christians moving towards dialogue with other Christian traditions can be seen in the contemporary "emergent church" phenomenon. This involves a new cluster of Christian groups nurtured, for the most part, in conservative Evangelical communities who are now seeking spiritual depth and "a generous orthodoxy" in contrast to the restrictive definitions of Christian faith offered by conservative Evangelicals in the past.[33] For this reason, the "emergent church" phenomenon can be described as "post-Fundamentalist" or even "post-Conservative.[34] The phenomenon is encapsulated in the whimsical subtitle of Brian D. McLaren's *A Generous Orthodoxy*:

> Why I am a missional + evangelical + post/protestant + liberal/conservative + mystical/poetic + biblical + charismatic/contemplative + fundamentalist/calvinist + anabaptist/anglican + methodist + catholic + green + incarnational + depressed-yet-hopeful + emergent + unfinished Christian[35]

McLaren could be simply confused, but his quest for "a generous orthodoxy" reflects his own movement from contemporary Evangelicalism towards the common Christian tradition. The discernment of a common gospel is crucial to the broad movement on the part of Evangelical churches to connect themselves to older Christian traditions.

With these concerns in mind, then, I ask in this book if it is possible at the beginning of the third Christian millennium to discern a common Christian gospel between three groups of churches:

> ancient Christian churches (including Eastern and Oriental Orthodox churches, the Catholic Church, and the Assyrian Church of the East; the subject of chapter 2),

Protestant and related churches (including Waldensian, Moravian, Lutheran, Anglican, Reformed, and Methodist churches; the subject of chapter 3), and

Evangelical churches (including Baptist, Holiness, Pentecostal, and Adventist churches, and some of the contemporary Evangelical megachurches; the subject of chapter 4).[36]

I ask if a common gospel can be discerned that stands in continuity with the proclamation of the early proto-orthodox Christian communities and that is received and proclaimed in the range of Christian traditions represented within each of these contexts. Insofar as all of these communities claim the distinction of being "Christian" communities and claim, in some way, that what they intend or mean by the term "Christian" should be mutually comprehensible between them, it is critical to discern a common or communally shared gospel. This is an inescapable issue for those communities that claim the name of "Christian," and it would be impossible if it were not for a solid foundation of dialogue, understanding, and resources provided for by biblical, historical, and ecumenical scholarship in the twentieth century.

The methods used in this book involve the examination of texts and practices that reflect what Christian communities have taught as the gospel as it is received and professed in Christian communities today. Commensurate with this method, the conclusions reached make claims about what Christian churches have taught and teach today about the essence of Christian faith, the gospel. Although historical and descriptive evidence may not answer all the questions about the central meaning of Christian gospel, the concerns raised earlier—claims or at least presuppositions about Jesus in contemporary culture, the claims made (or not made) by contemporary theologians, issues about what constitutes the center of Christian unity in old-line Protestant denominations, and the movement of Evangelical communities to identify themselves with the broader Christian tradition—warrant a critical historical and ecumenical examination of the claims that churches have made about the nature of Christian faith.

The focus in this work is consistently on Christian doctrine, understood as corporate consensus on what Christians teach as communities and the ways in which these teachings or doctrines have been received in the churches.[37] It examines a particular core sample that extends through all of the strata of Christian tradition present in the churches mentioned above and focuses on the transmission and reception of the gospel message through these historic strata. It attempts to demonstrate shared meanings of the gospel by way of careful study of texts, linguistic study, communal practices, and by the results of careful dialogue between Christians of widely varying traditions. Further methodological definitions and observations are made in chapter 7, "A Methodological Afterword."

I offer the following in my role as an historian whose work bears relevance (I hope) to the work of doctrinal and systematic theology and to ecumenical studies. I offer this as a United Methodist theologian concerned with my own church's attempt to grapple with issues of fundamental or essential unity in the faith. I offer this as an individual interpreter—my words obviously do not have the status of communally affirmed or communally received teachings, but I have attempted through these words to give voice to a crucially important core of Christian teachings that needs to be recognized in contemporary church life and in contemporary theological reflection.

1

The Gospel in Proto-Orthodox Christian Communities

Christ died for our sins
in accordance with the scriptures,
he was buried,
he was raised on the third day
in accordance with the scriptures.
—The gospel message transmitted by Paul,
I Corinthians 15:3b–4

The "gospel" refers to the proclamation of the "good news" about Jesus Christ on the part of Christian communities.[1] Subsequent chapters will show that the term "gospel" could be capable of wider meaning, for example, when Protestants take "the gospel" to mean both the message about Jesus Christ and the message about human salvation that results from Christ's work, or when Evangelical communities take "the gospel" to mean all of this and the particular experience that believers have when they affectively appropriate the gospel message. This chapter will discuss the "gospel" in its simpler sense, that is, the message or good news of God's work in Jesus Christ, although it will be clear even at this point that the gospel narrative is seldom told or recited without making a connection to human salvation.

A critical study of the Christian gospel as it has been received in Christian traditions must begin with the very earliest Christian texts. The development of early Christianity was not a simple evolution from Jesus to the apostles to subsequent Christian churches; it involved a cluster of highly varied communities that held very significantly differing visions of what Christian faith or life might mean.[2] Within the scope of New Testament literature itself there is abundant evidence of diverse communities, and there are explicit references in the New Testament literature to other communities regarded as schismatic, heretical, or otherwise dangerous. What this chapter examines, then, is the gospel message as it was transmitted and received in a specific range of Christian groups identified here as "proto-orthodox" communities, in the period between the first and the fourth centuries C.E. As the term suggests, these are the communities (or churches) that in retrospect were regarded as being in continuity with historic Christian churches. This chapter examines within this range of early Christian communities a consistent expression of the gospel from the earliest decades of the Christian movement, commencing with a very primitive expression of the gospel given in I Corinthians 15:1–11.

I Corinthians 15:1–11: The Transmission and Reception of the Gospel

Since at least the 1930s, New Testament scholars have identified a number of passages, especially in the Pauline literature, which include earlier Christian statements of belief.[3] Although some of these passages simply echo words or phrases from earlier Christian formulae, some passages include more complete statements with formulae explicitly indicating the transmission (the "handing-on") of an earlier tradition. One of the most complete of these expressions of the Christian gospel, with introductory formulae, is given in I Corinthians 15:1–4, and is as follows:

> Now I would remind you, brothers and sisters, of the good news [gospel; *euaggelion*] that I proclaimed to you, which you in turn received, in which also you stand, through which also you are being saved, if you hold firmly to the message that I proclaimed to you—unless you have come to believe in vain.
>
> For I handed on to you as of first importance what I in turn had received
>
>> that *Christ died for our sins*
>>   *in accordance with the scriptures,*
>> and that *he was buried,*
>> and that *he was raised on the third day*
>>   *in accordance with the scriptures* . . .

> Whether then it was I or they, so we proclaim, and so you have come to believe [I Corinthians 15:1–4, 11].⁴

This passage is introduced by two formulae indicating an oral tradition that had been "handed on" or "proclaimed" by one person or community and "received" by another community: "Now I would remind you, brothers and sisters, of the good news [*euaggelion*, 'gospel'] that I proclaimed to you, which you in turn received . . ." (vs. 1) and then "For I handed on to you as of first importance what I also received . . ." (vs. 3a). The statement of the gospel or "good news" then follows in the words quoted earlier in italics. After these words and an added series of testimonies to Christ's resurrection, there follows a concluding formula, "Whether then it was I or they [others who had proclaimed the message about Christ], so we proclaim and so you have come to believe" (vs. 11). It is very important to note the second-person plural in these passages, consistently missed in English-language translations in which "you" can be misinterpreted as a singular pronoun. The act of handing on an oral tradition was a communal act, not an act of individual communication.

The New Testament documents explicitly claim that the message about Jesus Christ was first proclaimed and handed down in primitive Christian communities orally before the New Testament documents themselves were written down. This is represented most literally in Luke's account of the day of Pentecost in Acts 2, when Peter, ". . . standing with the eleven, raised his voice and addressed them, 'Men of Judea and all who live in Jerusalem, let this be known to you and listen to what I say'" (Acts 2:14). He then proceeded to announce the good news about Jesus Christ (vss. 15–36).

But Peter's sermon in Acts 2 was recorded many decades after the event and was framed by Luke's carefully written narrative of the early Christian community. The words recorded in I Corinthians 15, by contrast, were written down by the decade of the 50s C.E., and are framed by the mechanism by which oral traditions were guarded and transmitted in the ancient world. Transmitting texts orally subjected them to the constant possibility of mutation, but safeguards were devised in oral cultures to protect texts. Four of these safeguards, all of which appear in the New Testament texts referring to oral traditions predating the texts of the New Testament themselves, are as follows.

- An oral text was uttered in an assembly with witnesses present who could vouch for its accuracy. In the passage from I Corinthians cited above, Paul states that "whether it was I or they," referring to other witnesses who had also heard the message about Christ, "so we proclaim and so you have come to believe" (vs. 11). The intervening verses (5–10) give a series of witnesses to the resurrection. In the passage from the Acts of the Apostles cited above, Peter stands "with the eleven" apostles, who serve as witnesses to his proclamation. Cf. II Timothy 2:2, ". . . what you have heard from me through many witnesses [NIV, 'in the presence of many witnesses'] entrust to faithful people who will be able to teach others as well."[5]

- The oral text was often introduced by a solemn formula, essentially an oath, utilizing technical language indicating that it had been accurately handed down and received, and it was often followed by a parallel solemn assertion of its accuracy. Two distinct introductory formulae are given to the I Corinthians 15 passage cited earlier (I Corinthians 15:1 and 3) and they are paralleled by those introducing Paul's transmission of the tradition of the supper in I Corinthians 11:23, "For I received from the Lord what I also handed on to you, that . . ." The term translated "I handed on" (*paredoka*) which appears in both of these passages (I Corinthians 11:23 and 15:3) is the basis for the Greek word for "tradition" (*paradosis*) and is part of the technical terminology that often accompanied such formulae of tradition.[6]
- In some cases, following the transmission of an oral text, blessings were pronounced on those who would accurately hand down the tradition, and anathemas (curses) pronounced on those who transmitted the tradition inaccurately. The most prominent example of this is the conclusion to the Revelation to John (Revelation 22:18–19) which Fundamentalist Evangelicals have taken as referring to the entire text of the holy scriptures since the Revelation traditionally appears at the conclusion of printed and bound versions of the Christian Bible. The author of the epistle to the Galatians pronounces a double anathema on anyone who "proclaims to you a gospel contrary to what you received" (Galatians 1:8–9).
- Apart from the oral texts themselves, there were sometimes given general exhortations to "hold fast" or preserve accurately the texts that had been handed down in this way. Examples of these exhortations can be found in II Thessalonians 2:15, "stand firm and hold fast to the traditions [*paradoseis*] that you were taught by us, either by word of mouth or by our letter," and in II Timothy 4:1b-2a, "I solemnly urge you: proclaim the message" or "word."

Although blessings and curses do not appear in the passages from I Corinthians examined here, the other elements of the ancient culture of "handing on" and "receiving" oral traditions are present in this passage.

The very early nature of these words, even with respect to other New Testament materials, should not be missed. Commenting on I Corinthians 15:3b–5 in a comprehensive survey of scholarship on *The Historical Jesus*, Gerd Theissen and Annette Merz describe a nearly universal consensus of New Testament scholars that "The derivation and age of the formula [in I Corinthians 15] point to the earliest period, close to the events themselves."[7] This passage gives, then, an instance of the "good news" or gospel as it had been proclaimed orally in the earliest Christian communities before the gospels or even the epistles of the New Testament were written down.

What is transmitted in the words of I Corinthians 15:3b–4 seems simple enough. Three short phrases affirm Christ's death, burial, and resurrection.[8] But these brief affirmations bear theological content. The word "Christ" itself bore multivalent religious meanings by the end of the intertestamental period, suggesting "the anointed" one and the messiah of prophetic speculation.[9] Christ's death is said to be "for our sins" (vs. 3b) and this phrase links the narrative of Christ's work with God's work of forgiveness. The repeated phrase "in accordance with the scriptures" links the narrative of Christ's work with the narrative of God's acts and of God's people in the Hebrew scriptures.[10]

I note one further matter about I Corinthians 15:3b–4, and that is the claim that these words were transmitted "as of first importance." By the time these words were written down in the first epistle to the Corinthians, Paul recognized that they encapsulated the most critical datum of the faith with which he was concerned and he appeals to this datum as the basis for unity in the factious Corinthian community. This is consistent with the solemn introduction and conclusion to the passage that he gives, and it clarifies the sentiment he expressed early in the letter, "For I decided to know nothing among you except Jesus Christ, and him crucified" (I Corinthians 2:2). Whether Paul had access at this early point to oral versions of the longer narratives of Christ's crucifixion recorded in the canonical gospels is debatable; what is clear is that he knew the kernel or core of the Christian message as it was transmitted in the oral tradition which he himself re-transmitted in the epistle. The expression "as of first importance," then, is the apostle's recognition of the priority of this kerygma,[11] this basic assertion of the Christian gospel as he had received it and transmitted it to the Corinthian congregation as the ground of their communal identity and unity.

The passage in I Corinthians 15:1–11 examined here offers the most explicit memory of the primitive Christian gospel cast in a solemn formula of transmission. But other passages in the New Testament echo the memory of this primitive message. Two passages from Paul's letter to the Romans will show this. In these passages Paul refers to the simple content of the Christian faith as the acknowledgment that Jesus is "Lord" and the belief that God raised Jesus from the dead.[12] In Romans 4:24b–25, Paul wrote that faith, or possibly righteousness (justification)

> . . . will be reckoned to us who believe in him who raised Jesus our Lord from the dead, who was handed over to death for our trespasses and was raised for our justification.

A similar echo of the kerygma can be heard in Romans 10:9:

> . . . because if you confess with your lips that Jesus is Lord and believe in your heart that God raised him from the dead, you will be saved.

Similar passages encapsulating the gospel message were embedded in the second-century literature that followed the New Testament writings. For example, in the letter of Ignatius of Antioch to the Philadelphians (written in the decade of the 110s C.E.), this formula appears:

> But the gospel possesses something distinctive, namely, the coming of the Savior, our Lord Jesus Christ, his suffering, and the resurrection. For the beloved prophets preached in anticipation of him, but the gospel is the imperishable finished work.[13]

Shorter and more formulaic expressions of the gospel message about the death and resurrection of Jesus—very much like the passages cited above from the New Testament book of Romans—appear very consistently in the early second century literature that followed the New Testament, specifically, in I Clement, the letters of Ignatius of Antioch to the Ephesians, Magnesians, Trallians, Romans, Philadelphians, and Smyrnaeans, the letter of Polycarp to the Philippians, and the Greek letter attributed to Barnabas.[14] The transmission of this primitive gospel message lay behind and shaped the writing of the New Testament literature (including the literary genre of gospel) and served as a criterion for the discernment of the Christian canon of scripture (see later in this chapter).[15]

The Gospel in Early Christian Catechesis and Creeds

The previous section has examined the transmission of the primitive Christian gospel as it was embedded in the letter of the apostle Paul to the Corinthians. But this gospel was not only embedded the New Testament scriptures; it continued to be transmitted orally in the early centuries of the Christian community. Later Christian writings show a number of forms in which it had been transmitted and received in proto-orthodox communities. The letter of Ignatius of Antioch to the Smyrnaeans, written in the decade of the 110s C.E., begins with a commendation of the "unshakable faith" of the Smyrnaeans, who believed in common with Ignatius that Jesus Christ:

> . . . is truly of the family of David with respect to human descent, Son of God with respect to the divine will and power, truly born of a virgin, baptized by John in order that all righteousness might be fulfilled by him, truly nailed in the flesh for us under Pontius Pilate and Herod the tetrarch (from its fruit we derive our existence, that is, from his divinely blessed suffering), in order that me might raise a banner for the ages through his resurrection for his saints and faithful people, whether among Jews or among Gentiles, in the one body of his church.[16]

In this case, Ignatius' statement of the Christian faith was directed against early Christian communities who doubted or denied the literal human suffering of Jesus Christ, and this concern to refute docetic views of Christ would remain a strong incentive for the statement of the Christian gospel in the second century.

Irenaeus of Lyons, who wrote in the decade of the 180s C.E., associated the proclamation of Christ with baptism, as can be seen from this simple formula that appears at the beginning of his treatise on *The Demonstration of the Apostolic Preaching*:

> . . . we have received a baptism for the remission of sins
> in the name of God the Father
> and in the name of Jesus Christ the Son of God
>
> > *who was incarnate*
> > *and died*
> > *and was raised again*
>
> and in the Holy Spirit of God.[17]

In this passage and in a longer passage from Irenaeus cited in the next paragraph, the essential elements of the gospel message are located within a larger framework, namely, that of the trinitarian formula used for baptism. Associated with baptism, the trinitarian formula derives most directly from Matthew 28:19, although there were "binitarian" formulae (invoking God the Father and Jesus Christ) in earlier New Testament materials, such as I Corinthians 8:6, ". . . yet for us there is one God, the Father, from whom are all things and for whom we exist, and one Lord, Jesus Christ, through whom are all things and through whom we exist."[18] Similar "binitarian" and trinitarian formulae appear in the Christian literature of the early second century.[19]

Early in his treatise *Against Heresies,* Irenaeus offered a more elaborate account of the gospel received in the church in a trinitarian framework, beginning with a solemn formula of transmission and concluding with a similar formula claiming fidelity to the message about Jesus Christ as the ground of the church's unity:

> The church, indeed, though disseminated throughout the
> world, even to the ends of the earth, received from the apostles
> and their disciples the faith
>
>> in one God, the Father Almighty, the Creator of heaven and
>> earth and the seas and all things that are in them;
>> and in the one Jesus Christ, the Son of God, who was
>> incarnate [or "enfleshed"] for our salvation;
>> and in the Holy Spirit, who through the prophets
>>
>>> preached the economies,
>>> the coming,
>>> the birth from a virgin,
>>> *the passion,*
>>> *the resurrection from the dead,*
>>> and the bodily ascension into heaven of the beloved
>>> Son, Christ Jesus our Lord,
>>> and his coming from heaven in the glory of the
>>> Father to recapitulate all things . . .[20]
>
> Since the church has received this message [*kerygma*], however it has preached this faith, [and] no matter how it has been dispersed through the world, it guards it [the message] diligently as inhabiting one household . . .[21]

This passage is complex and bears some explanation. The content of the transmission given here is set in a trinitarian framework, as can also be seen in the previous passage quoted from Irenaeus. However, the narrative of Christ's life is placed not under the article on the Son, as it would appear in other versions of the churches' creeds but, rather, under the article on the Holy Spirit, where it is said that the Spirit inspired the prophets who had foreseen the various events of Christ's life. In this roundabout way, the tradition given by Irenaeus confirms the teaching of the doubled phrase "in accordance with the scriptures" in the earlier version of the tradition embedded in I Corinthians, and in the case of the tradition in Irenaeus, all of the events of Christ's life are understood as the fulfillment of the prophetic tradition of the Jewish scriptures. Irenaeus's account of the signal events in Christ's life does not include a reference to Jesus' burial (which I Corinthians 15:4 does include), and in place of the early claim that "Christ died," it refers to Christ's "passion" or suffering. The tradition in Irenaeus expands on the tradition in I Corinthians by adding references to the "dispensations" of God, Christ's "advents," his birth "from a virgin," his ascension, and his future manifestation.

These tradition passages were crucial for Irenaeus's argument against those he identified as heretics. He admitted that the heretics could produce their own versions of the Christian scriptures, but Irenaeus maintained that the heretics had departed from the orally transmitted gospel that he gave in the passage quoted here.[22] In this case, he trusted the orally delivered gospel more than written scriptures as a sign of continuity with the apostolic faith.

Irenaeus's tradition represents the Christian message as he had heard it in his native Asia Minor and as he transmitted it in southern Gaul where he served as bishop. Another form of the tradition is given by the North African writer Tertullian, shortly after 200 C.E. Writing in Latin against the teacher "Praxeas" (whose identity has been long disputed), Tertullian cites what he calls a "rule" (*regula*) of faith. Although his introduction to this "rule" is linked to his narrative against Praxeas, his conclusion is cast as a formula of tradition:

In fact, we always, and now all the more so, believe, as instructed by the Paraclete, who leads into all truth,

> that there is in fact one God,
> but that under the dispensation which we call "economy"
> there is also a Son of this one God, his own Word,

> who proceeded from him,
> through whom all things were made, and without
> whom nothing was made:
>
> [We believe that] this One was sent by the Father
> into the Virgin and was born from her, man and
> God, son of man and son of God, and was named
> Jesus Christ.
>
> [We believe that] *he suffered, that he died and was
> buried, according to the Scriptures, and was
> resurrected by the Father* and ascended into heaven
> to sit at the right hand of the Father, and will come
> to judge the living and the dead.
>
> Who from there sent out, in keeping with his promise, the
> Holy Spirit the Paraclete, from the Father, the Sanctifier of
> the faith of those who believe in the Father and the Son and
> the Holy Spirit.
>
> That this Rule has come down from the beginning of the Gospel,
> even before all former heretics, not to speak of Praxeas of
> yesterday, will be proved as well by the comparative lateness of all
> heretics as by the very novelty of Praxeas of yesterday.[23]

As with the tradition transmitted by Irenaeus, the tradition transmitted by Tertullian is cast in a trinitarian framework, but in Tertullian's version the specific material about the life of Jesus is placed under the second article (about the Son) rather than the article about the Holy Spirit. This would become the consistent form of later Christian creedal statements. In some respects Tertullian's version of the cardinal events of Christ's life comes closer to that of I Corinthians 15:3b–4, because it explicitly mentions Christ's death and utilizes the expression "according to the scriptures" to link the events of Christ's life with the teachings of the Jewish scriptures.

The Latin recension of the document that has been historically called *The Apostolic Tradition* (from the third or fourth centuries C.E.) includes an interrogatory form of the rule of faith associated with baptism.[24] The candidate for baptism was asked to profess each of the articles of the tradition before being immersed. Although the first article is missing from the Latin recension, it is assumed as in the following translation:

> [Do you believe in God the Father Almighty?]
> Do you believe in Christ Jesus, the Son of God,

> who was born of the Holy Spirit and the Virgin Mary,
> *and was crucified under Pontius Pilate, and was dead and*
> *buried, and rose again the third day, alive from the dead,*
> and ascended into heaven, and sat down at the right hand of
> the Father, and will come to judge the living and the dead?

> Do you believe in the Holy Spirit, in the holy church, and in the resurrection of the body?[25]

Although briefer and set in an interrogative form, this version of the tradition in its structure closely parallels that given in Tertullian. A similar form of the gospel tradition is given in Origen (from the early third century in Alexandria).[26]

These instances of the traditioning of the gospel in Irenaeus, Tertullian, Origen, and the Latin recension of the *Apostolic Tradition* show that this process of orally handing on and receiving the Christian message, which began before the New Testament scriptures were written, continued as a very active process in Christian churches throughout the Mediterranean world in the early Christian centuries alongside the transmission of the New Testament documents. That it was associated with preaching and the teaching of new converts to the faith seems clear from the passages cited earlier in this chapter and from the interrogatory form of the affirmation given above from the Latin recension of the *Apostolic Tradition*. Augustine of Hippo refers to this process when he describes in his *Confessions* the conversion and profession of faith of the Neoplatonic philosopher Marius Victorinus:

> Eventually the time came for making his profession of faith. At Rome those who are about to enter into your grace usually make their profession in a set form of words which they learn by heart and recite from a raised platform in view of the faithful . . .[27]

Augustine himself gives almost the complete text of the baptismal creed as he knew it (the "set form of words" in the preceding quotation) in his treatise *De Fide et Symbolo* ("On the Faith and the Creed").[28] The Latin tradition of the gospel developed eventually into the baptismal creed that was utilized throughout the Western church and came to be called "the Apostles' Creed" (*symbolum apostolorum*), reflecting a belief that the apostles themselves gathered after the day of Pentecost and composed this creed under the inspiration of the Holy Spirit.[29] But versions of this baptismal creed remained in use in Greek-speaking churches in the Eastern Mediterranean as well, and these would become the basis for the Nicene Creed.

The quotations of the gospel tradition and the growing creedal traditions given earlier in this chapter show that although there were important differences in the wording of these forms of the tradition, central elements remained tenaciously embedded in them. Jaroslav Pelikan commented:

> A study of the creedal phrases in Irenaeus, Tertullian, and Hippolytus [i.e., the Latin recension of the *Apostolic Tradition*] shows there was great variation not only between one Christian writer and another, but between one quotation and another by the same writer, suggesting that the texts of the creeds themselves were far from uniform and that an author adapted and elaborated the texts to suit his purposes. Two elements remain constant through the citations, and one or both of them may safely be said to have formed the outline of most creeds: Father, Son, and Holy Spirit; the life, death, and resurrection of Jesus Christ. These were, according to Origen, "the particular points clearly delivered in the teaching of the apostles"; apostolic continuity, he argued, did not preclude discussion of other issues, but this central content was not negotiable.[30]

The fact of this "central content" handed on from one generation in the church to another lies at the heart of this study of the gospel in Christian traditions. The gospel cannot be a vague expression in this regard. It refers to the central teaching about Christ's life, death, and resurrection that was at the heart of the earliest Christian message, transmitted from generation to generation, and proclaimed in the churches.

The Gospel and the Canon of Christian Scripture in the First through Fourth Centuries

The preceding discussion has shown, first, that the Christian gospel was transmitted in an oral tradition before the writing and the canonization of the Christian scriptures and then, second, that Christian communities continued to transmit the gospel in oral forms alongside the written Christian scriptures. In the first four centuries C.E., a series of movements such as Marcionitism, Valentinianism, and Montanism forced the proto-orthodox Christian communities to define more carefully their own criteria for unity among their churches.[31] Continuity with the apostolic gospel was a primary criterion for orthodoxy, but along with it there developed an understanding of the Christian scriptures that were to be read as authoritative or "canonical" scriptures in the churches.

One critical criterion that helped define a canon of scripture for proto-orthodox Christian communities was their affirmation of the Jewish scriptures that Christians would come to call the Old Testament.[32] The early Christian message recorded in I Corinthians 15:3b–4 asserts twice that the saving work of Christ was "in accordance with the scriptures," and this expression also appears in the "rule of faith" as given by Tertullian above and then in the text of the Nicene Creed. Similarly, the gospel message recorded in a formula of transmission by Irenaeus (see earlier) places the work of Christ under the article on the Holy Spirit, asserting that the Spirit had inspired the scriptures that foretold Christ's coming. All of these texts indicate the understanding of proto-orthodox communities that their gospel stood in continuity with the Jewish scriptures that Christians would call the Old Testament. In contention with such second-century groups as Marcionites and Valentinians, proto-orthodox Christian groups claimed this continuity with the Old Testament and claimed that the one God who created the material universe was also "the Father of our Lord Jesus Christ" (Romans 15:6). The New Testament writings also asserted continuity with the Jewish scriptures, most prominently in the motif of the fulfillment of prophecy. Moreover, continuity with the Old Testament became a criterion by which the canon of New Testament scriptures was discerned in the early Christian centuries.[33]

Beyond the recognition of Old Testament scriptures as being in continuity with the Christian gospel, proto-orthodox Christian communities began to recognize an authoritative or canonical body of Christian literature, what today is called the New Testament. The literature of the New Testament canon takes the primitive Christian proclamation as a datum. Paul appeals to it, for example, in resolving a conflict within the Corinthian congregation concerning the nature of the resurrection, and it is at this point that he offered the kerygma in the form in which it is considered above, just as he offered the narrative he had received of the Lord's Supper (I Corinthians 11:23–26) in resolving an issue concerning appropriate participation in the supper as the Corinthians celebrated it. The literary form of "gospels," including the canonical gospels in the New Testament, expands on the narrative of the early Christian proclamation of Christ's life, death, and resurrection, adding additional material about Jesus' life and sayings.[34] Although earlier collections of material about Jesus (for example, the so-called Q source) may have existed prior to the writing of the canonical gospels, a "gospel," properly speaking, is defined by the narrative of Christ's life, death, and resurrection contained in the apostolic message as it had been transmitted orally prior to the composition of written gospel books.

The recognition of a body of Christian writings as authoritative for proto-orthodox Christian communities came as a result of a long process extending from the second through the fourth centuries C.E., but this process was grounded in the sense that some writings reflected more faithfully the apostolic faith that was already a datum when the process of canonization began. The New Testament canon was defined beginning in the middle of the second century through conflicts with Marcionites, Valentinians, and other groups that claimed their own authoritative scriptures and utilized, in the case of the Marcionites, different versions of Christian scriptures than those read in other churches. These were all Roman groups, and the first list of Christian scriptures approved to be read in churches, the Muratorian fragment, comes from the vicinity of Rome in the same period (the 150s and 160s C.E.). This document shows that even by this time proto-orthodox churches regularly read from the four gospels in the present New Testament canon and from a collection of the letters of Paul.[35] Although the process of canonization of the New Testament books extended into the fourth century C.E., three criteria were consistently used to judge which scriptures should be read in churches.

- The scriptures read in proto-orthodox communities affirmed the reality of Christ's life, death and resurrection transmitted in the primitive kerygma. In the case of Valentinians and other second-century groups, Jesus' resurrection could be treated as a merely spiritual event, and in many cases it was the words of Jesus rather than the narrative of his life that characterized the scriptures utilized in these communities.
- The scriptures read in proto-orthodox communities referred to and affirmed the Jewish scriptures that Christians now call the Old Testament. In the case of Marcionites, Valentinians, and other groups, the "Father of Jesus Christ" was seen as an entirely different deity, an "alien god" not to be associated with the God described in the Jewish scriptures.
- The scriptures read in proto-orthodox communities affirmed that the one God is the creator of the material world. In the belief of Valentinians and some other groups, an "alien god" had created the spiritual realm only, and the material realm was the creation of a demiurge or secondary deity.

These criteria were closely intertwined. The apostolic kerygma maintained that the death and resurrection of Christ was "in accordance with the scriptures" and so connected the narrative of Christ's work with the Old Testament. The Old Testament, in turn, maintained that the one God is the creator of the material universe, and so the Christian scriptures understand Christ as the agent of God in creation (e.g., John 1:3) and as taking on literal human "flesh" (John 1:14; cf. I John 1:1).

It cannot be claimed that proto-orthodox communities consistently maintained the scriptures intact or unaltered from the ways in which they were originally written down. Bart D. Ehrman has shown evidence of "orthodox corruptions" of the Christian scriptures, that is, cases where the criteria listed above appear to have been re-written into earlier documents, including documents now received as canonical scripture in Christian churches.[36] This shows the cumulative force of the criteria of canonization laid out earlier in this chapter: these criteria were not only utilized in retrospect to determine which works were to be regarded as canonical or orthodox; they actually affected the writing, revision, and transmission of the Christian scriptures as well as their canonization.

It was not until 367 C.E. that Athanasius, the bishop of Alexandria in Egypt, gave a definitive list of New Testament books answering to the canon of New Testament books utilized in Christian churches today.[37] Although the basic list of New Testament books read in churches had been agreed on since the middle of the second century, as illustrated in the Muratorian fragment, there had been disputes and discrepancies about the canonical books between Christian communities up until the time of Athanasius' letter. Many churches, for example, did not read the Revelation to John the Divine as canonical scripture. Even after the time of Athanasius, some disputes continued, for example, about whether the Epistle to the Hebrews should be read as canonical scripture in the churches.

The point should not be missed, however, that the gospel narrative transmitted in the early Christian kerygma and then in various forms of the creed was not only something included within the text of the New Testament. It was indeed included within the New Testament text, for example, in the crucial passage in I Corinthians 15 examined at the beginning of this chapter. But the gospel narrative existed before the writing of the canonical gospels and shaped the latter, and it was also transmitted apart from the text of the New Testament. In this way it became a principal criterion by which the text of the New Testament was established and by which the New Testament writings continued to be interpreted. Thus

Frances Young comments on the use or "performance" of scripture by the late second-century bishop Irenaeus of Lyons:

> [P]roper performance of scripture for Irenaeus depends in the end not on canons of interpretation offered by the scriptures themselves, nor on a sense of context within the flow of an overarching narrative history, but rather on "the plan of salvation," on what we might call the Christian kerygma, on a framework belonging to the particular community which designates these books as authoritative, a framework related to these books but "extra" to them, a framework passed down openly in a tradition guaranteed as ancient and reliable, but honed and refined by theological argument, modified by controversy, thought through in a systematic way to meet the needs of the times.[38]

The gospel narrative, the Christian kerygma, then, was a decisive factor that shaped the proto-orthodox Christian communities as they interpreted the Christian scriptures and as they eventually determined which writings should be received as authoritative or canonical. It is in this sense that Jaroslav Pelikan could speak of the "interdependence of Scripture, tradition, and creed."[39] The next chapter will take up some of the ways in which the gospel narrative was expressed in the creedal tradition of ancient Christian churches that persist into the present time.

The Meaning of the Gospel in the Earliest Christian Communities

What did the gospel mean, then, in these early, proto-orthodox Christian communities? The material considered in this chapter exposes a cluster of interrelated meanings, many of which are tied closely to the ancient cultural contexts and specifically to the Jewish religious and cultural context in which these meanings were embedded.

In the first place, the gospel transmitted in proto-orthodox communities denotes the simple narrative, the story that involves the death, burial, and resurrection of Jesus. As the story is retold, the death and resurrection are the most crucial points: mentioning the burial of Jesus appears to be simply a way of reinforcing the reality of Jesus' death and making the resurrection correspondingly more dramatic. What was critical for the primitive Christian community was to believe ". . . in him who raised Jesus our Lord from the dead, who was handed over to death for our trespasses and was raised for our justification" (Romans 4:24b–25).

As this passage from Romans shows, the simple narrative of Jesus' death and resurrection was understood as revealing God's work of redemption. The use of the terms "Christ" in I Corinthians 15:3 and the term "our Lord" in Romans 4:24 (or "the Lord" elsewhere) evoke a rich variety of meanings already present in the earliest strata of Christian traditioning of the gospel narrative. The claim that Christ died "for our sins" (I Corinthians 15:3) evokes both the servant songs of Isaiah (especially Isaiah 53:1–7) and the Jewish sacrificial cultus associated with forgiveness of sins (cf. Leviticus 4:1–7:27). There appears to be no stratum of the Christian message that stands apart from these religious meanings. That is to say, the Euhemeran view favored by the Enlightenment, the view that Jesus was simply a human being to whom divinity was later (and wrongly) ascribed, flies in the face of the earliest texts (oral and written) about Jesus.

The gospel narrative is expanded in canonical "gospels" (Mark 1:1, "The beginning of the good news ['gospel'] of Jesus Christ, the Son of God") but the basic narrative structure focusing on Jesus' death and resurrection remained in place. In fact, a disproportionate amount of space is given to the concluding week of Jesus' life in each of the canonical gospels, as contrasted with collections of sayings about Jesus such as the Gospel of Thomas. Deeper meanings for the gospel narrative are expounded in the canonical gospels, for example, by the use of titles ("Son of God," "Son of Man," "the Word," "the Lord") and by the interposition of the narrative of the supper into the gospels, opening up the sacrificial and paschal meanings of the gospel which were celebrated in the eucharist (discussed in the next chapter).

The use of the gospel narrative in various forms of the *regula fidei* alongside the books that came to be read as Christian scriptures provided a continuing norm for the life and teachings of Christian communities. Thus the claim that Christ's death and resurrection were "in accordance with the scriptures" was a norm that affirmed the validity of the Old Testament scriptures for proto-orthodox Christian communities and validated the proto-orthodox teaching that the one God who was associated with Jesus Christ was the same one who created the material world, thus ruling out the claims of Marcionites, Valentinians, and others who maintained that the creator must be a demiurge or lesser deity. The affirmation of the Jewish scriptures in this way identified Israel as God's people but also bore the seeds of Christian supercessionism in the claim that reading the

Jewish scriptures in the light of the gospel was the truest reading of them, perhaps the only true reading of them.

The role of the gospel narrative in norming the composition and canonization of the Christian scriptures set the stage for the liturgical exposition of the Jewish and Christian scriptures in the cycle of the Christian year, which the next chapter will consider. It also set the stage for the Protestant argument that the gospel itself is the heart of the Christian scriptures and the key to understanding the whole Bible (chapter 3).

2

The Gospel in Ancient Christian Churches

He suffered death and was buried.
On the third day he rose again
in accordance with the Scriptures.
—The Nicene Creed, fourth century C.E.

Ancient Christian Churches

This chapter considers how the primitive Christian gospel has been handed down and received in the churches that grew from the ancient proto-orthodox communities described in chapter one and that still exist today, namely, the Catholic, Eastern Orthodox, Oriental Orthodox,[1] and Assyrian churches.[2] These churches proclaim the Christian gospel in the form in which it had been transmitted in the early Christian rule of faith that became the baptismal creed in various forms.[3] They affirm the Old Testament scriptures and with these acknowledge only one God as the creator of both the material and spiritual worlds, although they would later differ over the inclusion of specific apocryphal or deuterocanonical books within the canon of the Old Testament. They accept the canon of New Testament scriptures that had prevailed among proto-orthodox communities. They are governed by bishops who represented the continuity of teachings and practices with the earlier Christian communities.

Although these four communities of ancient Christian churches entered into ecumenical understandings with each other in the last half of the twentieth century, they do not yet share full communion with each other. Ecumenical dialogue between these traditions has clarified what they all hold as being central to the faith that they share with each other, and these elements of common faith and practice shared by the ancient Christian communities have to be critical elements in the discernment of a common Christian message today. Chapter 5 will discuss broader ecumenical relations that these churches have, for example, with Protestant and Evangelical churches. This chapter focuses on the ways in which the ancient Christian communities affirm the Christian gospel.

How, then, do the ancient Christian churches reflect the gospel received from the primitive and proto-orthodox Christian communities of antiquity? What follows examines three primary expressions of the gospel in ancient Christian churches: the affirmation of the gospel in the use of historic creeds (preeminently the Nicene Creed), the affirmation of the gospel in liturgy (preeminently in the eucharistic liturgy but also in other traditions of worship), and the affirmation of the gospel in the celebration of Easter and the evolving cycle of worship through the Christian year.

The Gospel in the Creeds

All of the ancient Christian churches considered here affirm the Christian faith utilizing versions of the Nicene Creed, that is, the creed of the Council of Nicaea (325 C.E.) as revised subsequently in the fourth century. These revisions are customarily associated with the First Council of Constantinople (381 C.E.) and for this reason the received form of the Nicene Creed is often referred to as the "Nicene-Constantinopolitan Creed," although the records of the assembly in 381 do not include the text of the creed.[4] More commonly called the Nicene Creed, this is the most universally used creed in Christian churches today. The text of this creed is as follows:

> We believe in one God,
> the Father, the Almighty,
> maker of heaven and earth,
> of all that is, seen and unseen.
>
> We believe in one Lord, Jesus Christ,
> the only Son of God,
> eternally begotten of the Father,
> Light from Light,

true God from true God,
begotten, not made,
of one Being with the Father.
Through him all things were made.
For us all (man) and for our salvation
he came down from heaven:
by (the power of) the Holy Spirit
he became incarnate from the Virgin Mary,
and was made man.
For our sake he was crucified
under Pontius Pilate;
he suffered (death) and was buried.
On the third day he rose (again)
from the dead
in accordance with the scriptures;
he ascended into heaven
and is seated at the right hand of the Father.
He will come again in glory
to judge the living and the dead,
and his kingdom will have no end.

We believe in the Holy Spirit,
the Lord, the giver of life,
who proceeds from the Father.
Who, with the Father and the Son,
is worshipped and glorified,
who has spoken through the Prophets.

We believe in one, holy, catholic,
and apostolic church.
We (acknowledge) confess one baptism
for the forgiveness of sins.
We look for the resurrection of the dead,
and the life of the (world) age to come. Amen.[5]

The Nicene Creed was directed, in the first place, against the teachings of Arius and his followers who maintained that Christ was a created being, one who, although preexisting the rest of the creation, had an origin in time: "there once was when he was not."[6] In support of monastic spirituality, Arius and his followers emphasized the humanity of Christ as a model for the Christian monk facing temptation and overcoming it.[7]

Those who objected to Arius' view of Christ could not reconcile Arius' subordination of Christ with the church's worship of Christ, a practice which can be traced to the very earliest proto-orthodox Christian communities[8] and which was noted by persons outside Christian communities (such as the Roman official Pliny the Younger) as a characteristic practice of the Christians.[9]

In contrast to Arian teachings, the Nicene Creed affirms that Christ is "Light from Light, true God from true God, begotten, not made, of one Being with the Father." In response to further controversies over the divinity of the Holy Spirit, the Creed's affirmation of the Holy Spirit was amplified (after the first Council of Nicaea) to include an affirmation of the complete divinity of the Holy Spirit, confessed to be "the Lord, the giver of life, who proceeds from the Father; who, with the Father and the Son, is worshipped and glorified, who has spoken through the Prophets." The controversies with which the Nicene-Constantinopolitan Creed was concerned were not primarily about philosophical perspectives or about terms like "substance"; they were controversies about fundamentally religious claims about what is ultimate, what is to be valued above all else, what is (and is not) to be worshiped. And in this matter the unique and fierce logic of ultimates prevailed. Ultimates, by their very nature, do not allow of compromise. If Christ is worshiped as divine, then Christ is fully, completely God. If Christ is created, then Christ is less than fully God and worship of Christ would amount to worship of the creation, that is, idolatry. The same logic applied to the Holy Spirit, and so each of the persons of the divine Trinity was confessed to be co-equal as God.

At the heart of the Nicene Creed is its affirmation of the ancient Christian message about Jesus Christ:

> he suffered (death) and was buried.
> On the third day he rose (again)
> from the dead
> in accordance with the scriptures

Christ's death, burial, and resurrection are affirmed, and the phrase "in accordance with the scriptures" comes directly from the earliest expressions of the gospel tradition, as in I Corinthians 15:3-4.

Moreover, the received version of the Nicene Creed affirms in each of the three "articles" on the three persons of the Father, the Son, and the Holy Spirit, that it is the one God, the God of the Old Testament and thus the God of Israel, who is confessed.[10] The first article states that the

Father is the "maker of heaven and earth, of all that is, seen and unseen." The expression "seen and unseen" refers to a distinction between the material world (that which is "seen") and the spiritual world (that which is "unseen"; cf. Hebrews 11:1–3). Rejecting the cosmology of those ancient Christian groups who claimed that the true God created only the spiritual realm, this article affirms that the one God has created both the spiritual and the material worlds and in this respect allies itself solidly with the teaching of the Jewish scriptures. The second article affirms that Christ "rose (again) from the dead in accordance with the scriptures." In this case, the Creed repeats the precise words that were used in the traditioning of the gospel in I Corinthians 15:4, affirming that the work of God in Jesus Christ is continuous with the work of God recounted in the Jewish scriptures. The third article affirms that the Holy Spirit "has spoken through the Prophets," confessing in this way that the Holy Spirit is also the one celebrated as God in the Old Testament.

The authority of this creed as an expression of common Christian faith does not rely solely on the fact that it was approved by a council of bishops. As mentioned above, the text of the creed does not appear in the documents that have come down from the assembly in 381 that Orthodox and Catholic Christians recognize as the second Ecumenical Council. That assembly was itself composed almost entirely of Eastern bishops and so it was hardly "ecumenical" in the sense of representing the inhabited world (*oikoumene*) of Christians. As an expression of common Christian faith, the authority of the Nicene Creed relies on its having been consistently used as a means of teaching the faith and proclaiming the faith on the part of Eastern and Western Christians in the centuries after it was formulated. That is to say, the creed was "received" in the churches,[11] especially as it was consistently used as a way of teaching the faith (catechesis) and of professing the faith at baptism and in the eucharist.

Chapter one shows how ancient Christian communities had used a "rule of faith" epitomizing the Christian gospel as a way of teaching the faith and as a means of affirming the faith at baptism. From the fourth century the Nicene Creed came to be used in this way, although as it was received and used in churches the actual text used might be the older version from the assembly of 325, the later version associated with the assembly of 381, or some variation of these. For example, the bishop Theodore of Mopsuestia in Asia Minor gave a series of ten catechetical lectures in the early 400s C.E. on the original version (325 C.E.) of Nicene Creed. He concluded this series by exhorting the catechumens,

> It behooves you now to remember carefully the words that have been spoken to you in order that by keeping without modification the creed of the religion of the fear of God you may truly receive the happiness of the future benefits . . .[12]

By the late 400s, the Nicene Creed was so regularly used at baptism in the Eastern churches that an Eastern Roman emperor (475 C.E.) could state that it was this creed "into which we and all the faithful before us were baptized."[13] This was not the case in the Christian West, where the Apostles' Creed remained in use as the most consistent instrument for Christian catechesis and for baptismal profession. Even so, there is evidence that by the time of Charlemagne the Nicene Creed was utilized alongside the Apostles' Creed in Latin churches as a means of teaching the faith.[14]

The Nicene Creed eventually came to be the creed recited by Christian congregations, Western as well as Eastern, in the celebration of the eucharist. In Eastern churches this came about originally as a result of the christological controversies of the fifth century C.E. Those identified as heretics by the councils of Ephesus (431 C.E.) and Chalcedon (451 C.E.) vigorously asserted their consent to the earlier expression of orthodoxy given in the Nicene Creed in the previous century. The *Ecclesiastical History* of Theodore the Reader states that a "Monophysite" patriarch of Antioch (one who did not accept the teaching of the Council of Chalcedon on the two natures in the one person of Christ)[15] in the early 500s insisted on the recitation of the creed at every service, and around the same time a Monophysite patriarch of Constantinople ordered similarly that the creed should be said in every service there.[16] After the election of a patriarch of Constantinople in 536 C.E. who assented to the teachings of Ephesus and Chalcedon, a chronicle reports that an assembly of laity and clergy together recited the creed "according to custom."[17] Thus the practice of reciting the creed in the eucharistic liturgy originated with leaders opposed to the teachings of Chalcedon, but the practice was quickly taken up by those who supported the Chalcedonian teaching, and has become the universal custom of Eastern Christian churches.

In Western churches the use of the creed in the eucharistic liturgy also came about in response to christological issues, but in this case it was in response to Arianism early on, then subsequently to the rise of adoptionist teaching in Spain in the eighth century C.E. that provoked the church to initiate the regular recitation of the creed in the liturgy. The adoptionist teaching, which arose in areas controlled by Muslims, maintained that Jesus Christ was a human being who was "adopted" or chosen by the divine Word to be Son of God. In response to this teaching, Latin Christian leaders began to insist that the Nicene Creed, with its full affirmation of the divinity and eternal sonship of Christ, should be regularly recited in churches, and the reforms of the Carolingian period insisted on the recitation of the Creed.[18]

It was in fact at the time when the Nicene Creed came to be regularly recited in the Western eucharistic liturgy that the Western church allowed a critical alteration to the Creed. This was the addition of the words "and the son" (*filioque*) to the Nicene Creed's statement about the Holy Spirit, who is said in the Western version from this period to proceed "from the Father *and the Son*." This was directed against the adoptionist teaching that prompted the regular recitation of the Creed: to say that the Spirit "proceeds from the Father and the Son" emphasized the equality of the Son with the Father. Eastern Christians objected to the addition since it was not part of the original Nicene Creed that had been received in the churches.[19] This provoked a very serious division between Eastern and Western churches, especially over the issue of whether a church such as that of Rome could alter the Creed as received. However, it was not (as has been very often taught) the ground for the mutual condemnations and excommunications of church leaders in 1054 C.E., and probably only one among the many cultural as well as theological grounds for the eventual division of Eastern and Western churches in the Middle Ages. Moreover, the issues raised by the *filioque* clause were thoroughly considered by Eastern and Western Christians in the twentieth century, as a result of which the Catholic Church no longer sees *filioque* as a barrier to unity between Eastern and Western churches[20] and Orthodox churches are considering the extent to which it should remain a barrier to visible unity.

Before concluding this section by considering how the Nicene Creed is utilized in ancient Christian communities today, it may also be important to recognize that the Nicene Creed was itself cited in subsequent Christian doctrinal statements. It was in fact the "Definition of Faith" of the Council of Chalcedon (451 C.E.) that first definitively attributed the received form of the Nicene Creed to the assembly or council of Constantinople of 381 C.E. The "Definition" begins by reciting "The Creed of the 318 fathers at Nicaea" and "the same of the 150 saintly fathers assembled in Constantinople,"[21] that is to say, both versions of the Nicene Creed, the original version of 325 C.E. and the subsequent received text that was attributed to the council of Constantinople in 381 C.E. Similarly, the third council of Constantinople, 680–681 C.E., also begins its "Exposition of the Faith" by affirming both of these versions of the Nicene Creed, and the last of the seven ecumenical councils, the second council of Nicaea, 787 C.E., recites the received text of the Nicene Creed.[22] The pattern of beginning a new definition of faith by reciting one of the ancient creeds would be followed by many Protestant and related churches.

Eastern Orthodox churches today recite the Nicene Creed at every celebration of eucharist (the Divine Liturgy) and their liturgies for daily prayer include the recitation of the Nicene Creed at two different times daily. In the Liturgy of St. John Chrysostom, the most frequently used eucharistic liturgy in Eastern Orthodox churches, the Nicene Creed is recited following the readings of scripture, congregational prayers, and the sharing of the peace, and just before the beginning of the anaphora, the eucharistic prayer. Before the congregation says the creed together, a deacon says, "The doors! The doors!" (a reference to the need for watching the doors of a Christian church during the ages of persecution), and then "In wisdom let us attend."[23] Most Oriental Orthodox churches, including the Coptic, Ethiopian, West Syrian, and Malankara Syrian churches, say the Nicene Creed in the eucharistic liturgy in the received form, that is, in the same way in which it is said by Eastern Orthodox churches (i.e., without the *filioque* clause).[24]

The Armenian Apostolic Orthodox Church belongs to the family of Oriental Orthodox churches, but in the Armenian Church a different form of the Creed is recited. This version of the Creed contains the most distinctive expressions of the original version (325 C.E.) of the Nicene Creed (in the English translation of Archbishop Nersoyan, "God of God, light of light, very God of very God, begotten and not made; of the selfsame nature of the Father . . .") but adds some phrases ruling out specific ancient heresies (for example, "By whom he took body, soul and mind and everything that is in man, truly and not in semblance," directed against Apollinarianism). It includes the anathemas attached to the original (325 C.E.) Nicene creed and its statement on the Holy Spirit includes more material than the original Nicene Creed (it has statements affirming the "one catholic and apostolic [holy] church" and affirming one baptism for the forgiveness of sins) but less than the received form of the Nicene Creed (it does not include any statement about the procession of the Holy Spirit from the Father or from the Father and the Son).[25] This Creed is recited in the Armenian liturgy following the readings of scripture and the sermon, and it is the custom of some Armenian congregations to join hands while chanting the creed as a sign of unity in the faith.

In the Catholic Church the Nicene Creed is recited at every Sunday mass and at masses celebrating major feasts, following the scripture lessons and the homily, and before the beginning of the eucharistic rite proper. In the Catholic Church, the Nicene Creed is said according to the received text but with the *filioque* clause as indicated above.[26] It is customary for Catholics to bow as a sign of reverence for Christ's incarnation during the words "by (the power of) the Holy Spirit he became incarnate from the Virgin Mary, and was made man." The Catholic Church also utilizes the Apostles' Creed at baptism, as a means of teaching the faith, and at mass in some countries. Thus by the solemn recitation of the creeds, the ancient churches reaffirm the core of the Christian gospel that had been proclaimed from the earliest moments of the Christian community.

The Gospel in the Liturgy

There has been increasing recognition in recent decades of the central role that worship plays in the teaching and reception of doctrine. The assertion *lex orandi lex credendi*, "the rule of prayer is the rule of faith," is often cited as a way of summarizing the importance of worship for the establishment and interpretation of doctrine.[27] Jaroslav Pelikan called the Divine Liturgy of Eastern Orthodox churches "the church's preeminent confession of faith."[28] This section considers how liturgy—especially the eucharistic liturgy—also serves as a way of proclaiming the Christian gospel.

Chapter one began with an examination of the primitive Christian gospel wrapped in the formulae of tradition in I Corinthians 15:1–4. But there is another passage in I Corinthians that utilizes a nearly identical formula of traditioning, and that is the narrative of the supper given in I Corinthians 11:23–25:

> For I received from the Lord what I also handed on to you, that the Lord Jesus on the night when he was betrayed took a loaf of bread, and when he had given thanks, he broke it and said, "This is my body that is for you. Do this in remembrance of me." In the same way he took the cup also, after supper, saying, "This cup is the new covenant in my blood. Do this, as often as you drink it, in remembrance of me."

The same technical terminology of handing on and receiving an oral tradition that was used in I Corinthians 15:1 and 3 is used in I Corinthians 11:23: the tradition was "received" and "handed on," and again the term "you" (denoting those to whom the tradition was delivered) is in the plural. Close parallels in the synoptic gospels (Mark 14:22–24; Matthew

26:26–28; Luke 22:17–20) to the narrative embedded in this formula show how the same oral tradition had been handed on and received in other communities. As with the tradition of the gospel in I Corinthians 15:1–4, this passage also transmits one of the most primitive strands of Christian tradition. And just as the kerygma of I Corinthians 15:3–4 proclaims Christ's death, burial, and resurrection, Paul follows the brief narrative given earlier with this comment (I Corinthians 11:26):

> For as often as you eat this bread and drink the cup, you proclaim the Lord's death until he comes.

When Christians subsequently followed Christ's instruction ("Do this . . .") by celebrating "the Lord's supper" (I Corinthians 11:20) or eucharist, they engaged in a distinct act of proclamation intimately tied to the primitive kerygma.[29] This celebration became the customary pattern of Christian weekly worship. The words "For as often as you eat this bread and drink the cup" suggest that it was already the normative practice in the Corinthian congregation to which Paul's letter was addressed. This section considers how the eucharist functions as a way of proclaiming the Christian gospel in ancient Christian churches.

The deeper meaning of eucharist for early Christians cannot be understood apart from its context in ancient sacrificial cultus and, in particular, the Passover ritual that was the context of the eucharistic meal. Jesus' words and actions handed down in the passage cited earlier and in its parallels in the synoptic gospels were recognizably part of the Passover ritual but the words were altered so that they point to the significance of Jesus' own life and work: "this is my body that is for you," "This cup is the new covenant in my blood."[30] In the context of the Passover meal, these words identified Jesus' own work with the signal moment of God's work of redemption on behalf of Israel. Early Christians did not miss the sacrificial context and meaning of Jesus' words and actions, and New Testament texts frequently allude to sacrificial and Passover meanings associated with Christ's work. In I Corinthians 5:7, for example, Paul wrote, "Clean out the old yeast so that you may be a new batch, as you really are unleavened. For our paschal [Passover] lamb, Christ, has been sacrificed." The author of Ephesians exhorted Christians to ". . . live in love, as Christ loved us and gave himself up for us, a fragrant offering and sacrifice to God" (Ephesians 5:2). The letter to the Hebrews understood Christ's work as the fulfillment of the sacrificial cultus of Israel, perhaps reflecting a historical context immediately after the destruction of the temple in Jerusalem and the cessation of the sacrificial rites that were conducted in it: "But when

Christ had offered for all time a single sacrifice for sins, 'he sat down at the right hand of God . . .'" (Hebrews 10:12).

Although the death of Jesus Christ is the moment of Christ's life that is most often associated with sacrifice, the ancient context suggests a more elaborate nexus of meanings. In ancient cultures, sacrifice was not simply the killing of an animal.[31] A sacrifice involved at least three distinct elements:

1. An offering was made from the best of a person's possessions (the "first fruits" of one's fields, or the firstborn of one's flocks), representing the offering of oneself to the deity.
2. That which was offered (grain or meat) was transformed by burning (cooking). This was a mysterious process to ancient people, and they often took the burning and the smoke of the sacrificial fire as a sign of divine acceptance of an offering: "an offering by fire of pleasing odor to the LORD" (Leviticus 1:9 and 13).
3. Worshipers and priests together partook of the offered and cooked grain or meat as a ritual meal. This was taken as a sign of restored fellowship between worshipers and the deity. Sometimes it was imagined that the deity also partook of the feast.

Early Christians understood Christ's life (including his death) as his offering to God: Paul took Christ to be "our paschal lamb" (I Corinthians 5:7), and the paschal lamb in the Jewish context was offered to God before it died.[32] They understood Christ's resurrection as a sign of divine acceptance of Christ's offering: the reference to Christ as "a fragrant offering and sacrifice to God" in Ephesians 5:2 draws an analogy between Christ's resurrection and the rising smoke of a sacrifice, suggesting that Christ's resurrection was understood as the sign of divine acceptance. The early Christians understood the eucharistic meal itself as a sign of renewed fellowship with God and with each other, and they understood it to be a way of proclaiming God's self-offering in Jesus Christ. The eucharist was understood as a deep mystery in which Christ's whole work, Christ's self-offering, was celebrated. It is in this sense that the eucharist proclaims Christ "until his coming again."

All of the ancient Christian communities—Eastern Orthodox, Catholic, Oriental Orthodox, and Assyrian—celebrate eucharist as the normative weekly pattern of Christian worship. The ancient churches developed distinctive forms of liturgy in different cultures, and most maintain traditions of worship in ancient languages (including Greek, Latin, and Syriac) although the Catholic Church since the 1960s has allowed vernacular translations of the mass, and some Eastern Orthodox churches have also developed vernacular-language services. Despite differences in cultures and languages, and despite the fact that these elements are ordered differently in the various ancient church traditions, there are certain elements that appear consistently in the eucharistic celebrations of all the ancient churches.

1. The congregation offers praise to the divine Trinity—Father, Son, and Holy Spirit—throughout the service.
2. The Holy Scriptures (Old and New Testament) are read aloud, with special reverence attached to the reading of the gospel. In Orthodox churches, there is a special procession with the gospel book.
3. The congregation offers prayers on behalf of the community and the world.
4. The congregation honors and commemorates (but does not worship) Christian saints. They may address "prayers" to saints, but these "prayers" are not understood as taking the place of prayers addressed directly to God (see the previous item), and are understood as being equivalent to addressing one's concerns to a living Christian friend.[33]
5. The Nicene Creed is said (or sung) by the congregation.
6. Worshipers are summoned to raise their hearts and minds in thanks and praise to the creating and redeeming God and to join with the angelic host in their heavenly songs.
7. Christ's institution of the supper is recounted.[34]
8. The death and resurrection of Christ are explicitly remembered (this and the previous item are referred to as the *anamnesis*; see the text following on this point).
9. The priest and congregation pray for the coming of the Holy Spirit.
10. The elements of bread and wine are consecrated by prayer and are shared with the worshipers.
11. The people are blessed and dismissed.

In almost all of the ancient Christian communities, a tone of reverence is set by the use of candles and lamps and by burning incense, the smoke of which is seen as rising like the prayers of believers before God. In addition to these, other elements such as hymns, songs, chants, or particular forms of prayer may be utilized in the service depending upon particular cultures, traditions, and seasons. Worshipers may use such gestures as making a sign of the cross, holding one's hands up in prayer, bowing, and prostrations. They may show respect and honor by lighting candles in front of images of Christ and of the saints or they may light candles to represent their own particular prayers. Although preaching was not a consistent part of worship in ancient churches through the Middle Ages, since the sixteenth century it has become customary in Catholic churches to have a sermon or homily following the reading of the scriptures, and this practice is now observed in many Eastern Christian churches as well.

As rituals for the eucharist developed, the eucharistic prayer came to incorporate an explicit recollection or memory (anamnesis) of Christ's saving work, item eight in the list of elements given above. The *Apostolic Tradition* includes a version of the eucharistic prayer from the third or fourth centuries C.E. in which Christ's work is recounted in terms reminiscent of the early kerygma and the early creeds:

> You sent him from heaven into a virgin's womb; and conceived in the womb, he was made flesh and was manifested as your Son, being born of the Holy Spirit and the Virgin. Fulfilling your will and gaining for you a holy people, he stretched out his hands when he should suffer, that he might release from suffering those who have believed in you.
>
> And when he was betrayed to voluntary suffering that he might destroy death, and break the bonds of the devil, and tread down hell, and shine upon the righteous, and fix a term, and manifest the resurrection, he took bread and gave thanks . . . [the institution narrative is given here]
>
> Remembering, therefore, his death and resurrection, we offer to you the bread and the cup . . .[35]

As difficult as it may be to imagine that the narrative recounted in I Corinthians 11:23–25 was not (or not always) connected with the celebration of the supper in early Christian communities, Paul F. Bradshaw points out that the passage given above from the *Apostolic Tradition* is the earliest text of a eucharistic prayer that explicitly includes the institution narrative. Some very ancient forms of the eucharistic prayer do not include this (for example, the eucharist liturgy of Addai and Mari used by the Assyrian Church of the East),[36] and Bradshaw concludes that it may have been only from the middle of the fourth century that the institution narrative was regularly included.[37] By the fourth century, at least, the institution narrative was regularly recited along with the remembrance of the death and resurrection of Christ. However, even when the anamnesis did not include the institution narrative, it typically included the gospel narrative, the account of the death and resurrection of Jesus Christ.

This form of remembrance or anamnesis can be seen in the Liturgy of St. John Chrysostom, a eucharistic liturgy from the fifth century C.E., which is the most commonly used liturgy in Eastern Orthodox churches today:

> Remembering this saving commandment [to eat the bread and drink of the cup] and all those things which have come to pass for us: the cross, the tomb, the resurrection on the third day, the ascension into heaven, the sitting at the right hand, and the second and glorious coming.[38]

A similar remembrance of the work of Christ from the Western church in the Middle Ages was preserved in the Tridentine mass:

> Holy Trinity, accept the offering we here make to thee in memory of the passion, resurrection, and ascension of our Lord Jesus Christ . . .[39]

The next chapter will show that similar forms of anamnesis were preserved in Anglican and Protestant liturgies for the eucharist.

Although the anamnesis makes this most explicit, the message of the gospel, of God's work in the life and death and resurrection of Jesus Christ, lies at the center of the eucharistic celebration of ancient Christian communities. This fact may be difficult to discern by other Christians due partly to the issue of languages: it is easier to understand when, for example, the mass or the divine liturgy is said in a modern language. It is partly a result of the very different cultures in which worship and devotion are expressed. In fact, one of the issues faced by the ancient Christian communities themselves is the need for better training (catechesis) for persons in their own communities, for whom ancient languages and cultures may also seem quite alien. In some respects, the difficulties in understanding are a result of genuine theological and doctrinal differences, for example, over "prayers" addressed to saints or how Christ is present when Christians celebrate eucharist. This is a point at which, as chapter 7 will show, cultural and linguistic and genuinely theological boundaries present formidable barriers to understanding between Christian communities, and these existing barriers to understanding call for sustained study and exposure in order to understand what really happens, in this case in the eucharistic liturgies of the ancient churches. But by attentive and sympathetic observation, it is possible for other Christian communities to discern that the eucharist as it is celebrated in these ancient Christian communities has at its core the celebration of Christ's saving work instituted by Christ himself, and each part of the celebration, understood in its own context, expresses the mystery of God's work of redemption in Jesus Christ.[40]

There are other acts of worship in Orthodox and Catholic churches that reflect the transmission and reception of the ancient Christian message. Issues about Mary, the Mother of Jesus, have been closely bound up with issues about Jesus Christ himself, and devotion to Mary often conveys the mystery of the gospel in the ancient Christian communities. For example, the following prayer addressed to Mary in the evening prayer services of Eastern Orthodox churches expresses the mystery of the gospel message. In this prayer, Mary is addressed as *Theotokos,* the "God-bearer" or "Mother of God," the one who gave birth to one person, Jesus Christ, who is both God and human:

> The mystery of all eternity,
>   unknown even by the angels:
> God made man, by union without confusion,
> And revealed to those on earth through you,
>   O Theotokos.
> He voluntarily accepted the cross for us,
> By which he resurrected the first created man,
> Saving our souls from death.[41]

Again, this may be a point that warrants sustained discernment, because it does involve significant theological differences (whether "prayers" should be addressed to Mary or other saints) and differences in manners of expressing devotion, but from the perspective of the ancient Orthodox and Catholic communities, the point of honoring the Blessed Virgin is to point beyond her to the mystery of God's redemptive work in Jesus Christ to whom she gave birth, that is, to point to the gospel.

Beyond the liturgies performed in the churches, Christians of the ancient church traditions developed other settings and genres in which the narrative of the Gospel could be retold and reexperienced. In Eastern Christian churches in particular national contexts, traditional songs associated with Christian festivals are often sung in churches before the celebration of the liturgy. Similarly, the later Middle Ages in Latin Christianity saw the development of carols, songs originating in popular culture, often associated with major feasts (such as Christmas carols). Late medieval passion plays in the Latin West rehearsed the key elements of the gospel narrative. Personal piety in the Western Middle Ages emphasized devotion to the wounds and suffering of Christ, hence the prominent use of the image of Christ crucified (the crucifix) in medieval Western Christian culture. Personal devotion to the humanity of Christ led to the popularity of pilgrimages to the places associated with Christ's human life in Palestine and the forbidding of Christian pilgrimages to Palestine on the part of Muslim leaders was a trigger event leading to the Crusades. Emphasis on the humanity of Christ continued in the *Devotio Moderna* movement, beginning in the fourteenth century and represented in Thomas à Kempis' devotional classic, *On The Imitation of Christ* (ca. 1418). The *Devotio Moderna* movement would influence the spirituality of early Protestant Reformers, including Luther and Calvin.

The Gospel in the Liturgical Year

The preceding sections have examined the ways in which the traditions of ancient Christian communities—Catholic, Eastern and Oriental Orthodox, and Assyrian—express the Christian gospel by the use of historic creeds, especially the Nicene Creed, and in the celebration of eucharist as it focuses the community on the work of Christ. A third way in which the ancient Christian communities express the gospel is in the cycle of the Christian year, which focuses their communities annually on the celebration of the signal events of Christ's birth (Christmas), Christ's revelation to the world (Theophany or Epiphany), and Christ's passion, death, and resurrection (Lent, Holy Week, and Easter). The full cycle of observance of the Christian year was a development of ancient and early medieval Christian communities and it grew from the annual celebration of Easter in ancient Christian communities.

According to the canonical gospels, the events of Christ's death and resurrection occurred in conjunction with the Jewish celebration of Passover.[42] The coming of the Holy Spirit occurred on the day of Pentecost, which was the Jewish Feast of Weeks (Acts 2:1). Early Christians continued to mark time by such festivals: many years after the Pentecost event recorded in Acts 2, Paul "was eager to be in Jerusalem, if possible, on the day of Pentecost" (Acts 20:16) and he later wrote to the Corinthians that "I will stay in Ephesus until Pentecost" (I Corinthians 16:8). When Paul wrote, "For our paschal [Passover] lamb, Christ, has been sacrificed. Therefore let us celebrate the festival..." (I Corinthians 5:7b–8a), it is barely possible that he meant "let us celebrate the festival" in some merely spiritual or symbolic way, but the most natural reading of this text is that he encouraged Christians to celebrate the Passover festival which even then was in the process of being transformed into the Christian celebration of Easter. A Christian sermon that survives from the second century C.E., the "Paschal Homily" of Melito of Sardis, draws elaborate parallels between the work of Christ and the Jewish celebration of Passover, showing that in his time (around the 170s C.E.) the Christian celebration of Easter was still intimately tied to the Jewish celebration of Passover.[43] The word for "Easter" used in ancient churches is *Pascha,* the same word used in the New Testament for "Passover"; so in the passage cited earlier from I Corinthians 5:7, the New Revised Standard Version has "For our *paschal* lamb, Christ, has been sacrificed . . ." The great festival of Easter, then, grew from the Jewish celebration of Passover as early Christian communities adapted Passover customs to celebrate the resurrection of Jesus Christ.

Historical texts from around 200 C.E. show how the Christian Passover was being celebrated at that time. The African Christian writer Tertullian referred to separate Christian celebrations of Easter ("pascha": at this point, this denoted the "Christian passover" celebrating Christ's death and resurrection) and Pentecost. The most appropriate time for baptisms, he stated, was on the Friday before Easter (later usage would refer to this as "Good Friday"), but the day of Pentecost might also be appropriate.[44] He indicated that Christians normally fasted and prayed kneeling as a sign of penitence and mourning in the season leading up to Easter, but they rejoiced and prayed standing up in the fifty-day period from Easter through the day of Pentecost.[45] He suggested in one place that Christians observed a full month of fasting prior to Easter.[46]

A little more than a hundred years after Tertullian's time, the first Council of Nicaea (325 C.E.) established formal rules for determining the date of Easter (though controversies over calculating the date of Easter remain to the present time), and set the period of fasting before Easter as forty days, recalling the temptation of Christ in the wilderness.[47] This fast did not imply that Christians went entirely without food for forty days: they abstained from food from sunup to sundown each day and they ate after sundown, as Muslims would do in the fast of Ramadan. By the time of the Council of Nicaea, the celebration of Easter involved a vigil beginning on Saturday evening and continuing past midnight until the announcement of the resurrection and the beginning of the Easter festival. These customs—the forty-day fast of Lent, the celebration of the three-day period (the "triduum") from Good Friday through Easter Sunday, culminating in the Easter vigil and the celebration of the resurrection on Easter morning, then the celebration of Pentecost seven weeks after Easter—became the common practice of all the ancient Christian communities.

The feast of Christ's resurrection remains the central, most solemn feast of the Christian year in Orthodox, Catholic, and Assyrian churches, the preeminent means by which these communities celebrate the Christian gospel, the death and resurrection of Jesus Christ.

The Lent-Easter-Pentecost events form a cluster of celebrations focused around Easter. Another cluster developed around the celebration of the birth and revelation of Christ to the world, but this cluster developed somewhat later than the Easter-related festivals. Some Egyptian communities in the third century C.E. celebrated Christ's baptism on the equivalent of 6 January in the Egyptian calendar, and by the middle of the fourth century Egyptian Christian communities regularly celebrated 6 January as both the baptism and the birth of Christ.[48] From some point in the fourth century, Western Christians began to observe the twenty-fifth of December as the birth of Christ, perhaps as a Christian response to the popular Roman pagan festival of Saturnalia which in the late third century had been celebrated on that date.[49] Eventually 6 January came to be a celebration of the revelation ("epiphany" or "theophany") of Christ to the world and from that point was associated with the narrative of the visit of the Magi to the infant Christ. In Eastern churches, the feast of Epiphany on 6 January still holds status as a more significant church festival than the celebration of the nativity of Christ on 25 December, and in the Armenian Church, only 6 January is celebrated (there is no separate celebration of Christmas). From the sixth century C.E. a season of preparation for the celebration of Christmas and Epiphany developed; this season is now known as Advent, because it looks forward to the coming (*adventus*) of Christ.

By the eighth century C.E. the pattern of the Christian year was firmly fixed, as is evident in such documents as the Gelasian Sacramentary, which gives the full cycle of feasts in the Christian year as celebrated in the Western church in that century. With the development of the cycle of the Christian year, the churches annually celebrated from early winter through the springtime the gospel in the festivals of the birth, life, death, and resurrection of Christ, and the celebration of the coming of the Holy Spirit on the Day of Pentecost, seven weeks after Easter. These celebrations fell into two main groups: the Advent-Christmas-Epiphany cluster, celebrating the coming of Christ and his revelation to the world, and the Lent-Easter-Pentecost cluster, celebrating Christ's passion, death, and resurrection, and then the gift of the Holy Spirit. Following these traditions, the ancient Christian communities celebrate the gospel narrative of God's work in Jesus Christ in their annual cycle of celebrations. But, then again,

Sunday had been celebrated to commemorate Christ's resurrection since very early in the church's life, and Christians also employed a Friday fast in remembrance of Christ's passion and death. In this way, every week offers a commemoration of the gospel message about Jesus Christ's death and resurrection, and each week plays out on a small scale the church's larger annual commemoration of the gospel.

An important development in regard to the Christian year was the composition and collection of worship materials specific to particular seasons. The Easter sequence *Victimae paschali laudes,* composed in the eleventh century by the German poet and biographer Wipo, conveys a particularly clear understanding of both the paschal meaning of Christ's sacrifice and the note of victory over the powers of death. The poem begins:

> Let Christians offer their sacrifice to the paschal victim;
>> The lamb has redeemed the sheep;
>> the innocent Christ has reconciled sinners to the Father.

These verses convey the meaning of Christ's death as fulfilling the role of the Passover (paschal) sacrifice. The poem also contains the words:

>> Death and life engaged in wondrous combat.
>> The captain of life, once dead, now reigns alive![50]

Here the text conveys the understanding that Christ's death and resurrection constitute the defeat of the powers of death and evil. The poem, which became a standard Easter hymn in the Western church, then, transmitted both the ancient understandings of Christ's work as the fulfillment of the Passover sacrifice and the moment of God's victory over evil.

The Meaning of the Gospel in the Traditions
of Ancient Christian Churches

This chapter has examined three particular ways in which the ancient Christian communities receive and affirm the apostolic message of the gospel. In solemnly teaching and reciting the ancient creeds, preeminently the Nicene Creed, they receive and transmit the kernel of the primitive Christian message about the death and resurrection of Jesus Christ. In the weekly celebration of eucharist, they again celebrate and proclaim Christ's work. In the annual cycle of the Christian liturgical year from Advent through Christmas-Epiphany through Lent and the great festivals of Easter and then Pentecost, they recurse through the saving events of

Christ's incarnation, suffering, death, and resurrection. The gospel in the first place continues to denote in ancient churches the simple narrative of Jesus' life, death, and resurrection. But what else does the gospel mean as it is received and transmitted in the ancient Christian churches?

Embedded in the creeds, the simple narrative of the works of Christ took on additional meaning as a norm by which heterodox teachings could be addressed by the churches. This was not novel in itself, because the Gospel narrative had been used in this way even in its earliest appearances: Paul cited it in I Corinthians 15 as a way of refuting disputes about the nature of the resurrection in the Corinthian community. In all versions of the Nicene Creed the gospel narrative is embedded in a trinitarian framework that had been elaborated (especially in the second article of the creed) to refute Arianism. In the received form of the Creed (the Nicene-Constantinopolitan Creed), it is used in the same way to refute the pneumatomachian teaching that would not admit the equality of the Holy Spirit with the divine persons of the Father and the Son. In the Athanasian Creed (only utilized in the Western church), the gospel narrative in a trinitarian framework is used to refute heretical teachings about the divine Trinity in an even sharper way, including anathemas against those who depart from defined teachings.[51] These anathemas, along with recognition of the later character of the Athanasian Creed compared to the basic form of the Apostles' Creed and the Nicene Creed, would become grounds for some Protestant and related churches not to include the Athanasian Creed among confessional affirmations or in liturgical use (see chapter 3).

Moreover, as it is embedded in the historic creeds used in the ancient Christian churches, the gospel was inseparably linked to the affirmation of one God, the same God described in the Jewish scriptures who is affirmed as the creator of the material universe. The Nicene Creed retains the words "in accordance with the scriptures" that had come down from the earlier tradition in reference to Christ's resurrection. It affirms that the Father is the creator of "all things, seen and unseen," parallel to the way in which the Apostles' Creed affirms the Father as the "creator of heaven and earth." The Nicene Creed affirms that the Holy Spirit "spoke through the prophets" and in each of these ways the creedal tradition in the ancient churches affirms the unity of God, continuity between God's actions in Jesus Christ and God's acts in the history of Israel, and the goodness of the material world which God made. In contention with Marcion, Valentinus, and other teachers, this affirmed that Christ's acts were not to save humans out of the material creation but, rather, that God had entered into the material creation—God's own good work—in the person of Jesus Christ.

The use of sacrificial language in the eucharist as it is celebrated in ancient Christian churches opens up a range of meanings associated with the gospel. If the simple phrase "Christ died for our sins in accordance with the scriptures" by itself suggested the servant songs of Isaiah or the sin offerings described in the Hebrew scriptures, placed in the context of the eucharist it suggests the identification of Christ's work with the passover sacrifice. But whether Christ's work is associated with sin offerings or the paschal sacrifice, it is crucial to understand that in the context of ancient sacrificial cultus, not only in Israel but in the ancient world more broadly, sacrifice had a very wide range of meaning including the simple act of making an offering to God, signs of the divine acceptance of the offering, and restored fellowship represented in a shared meal. Sacrificial language would become problematic later in the church's experience when sacrifice itself became a culturally unfamiliar practice and especially when, as a result of this unfamiliarity, it came to be associated almost exclusively with the killing of an animal victim. Part of the richness of the sacrificial meanings of the gospel embedded in the celebration of eucharist in ancient churches is the way in which sacrificial meanings of the gospel point to the significance of Christ's whole life—not just his death—as his offering.

This implication of the sacrificial meaning of the gospel is consistent with the patristic understanding of Christ's whole life as a "recapitulation" and thereby a sanctification of every aspect of human life. Irenaeus of Lyons had written that Christ "passed through every stage of life, restoring to all communion with God," and thus "God recapitulated in Himself the ancient formation of man, that he might kill sin, deprive death of its power, and vivify" human beings.[52] This notion of Christ as the prototypical human being[53] opens up the rich notion of Christ's work making possible the divinization or "deification" of every aspect of humanity, a central theme of Eastern Christian spirituality.

In the next place, the gospel narrative provides a framework in the ancient Christian churches through which the scriptures are interpreted through the cycle of the Christian year. It must be remembered that the Bible as a bound volume would have been very rare through the Middle Ages and the only consistent exposure that laity and most clergy and members of religious orders had to the scriptures came by way of the readings in the liturgy. Since these were arranged according to the cycle of the Christian year, the gospel narrative thus functioned to order the way in which the scriptures were heard by Christians. Late in the Middle Ages, the genre of the postil (Latin, *Postilla*), a commentary on the scriptures arranged according to the lectionary, gave bishops and other preachers (e.g., itinerant Dominican and Franciscan preachers) ways to frame sermons consistently following this pattern. When homilies or sermons became the norm in Catholic churches from the sixteenth century (simultaneous with the development of seminaries), they focused on the reading of the scriptures according to this cycle. Specific prayers and songs associated with the liturgy and with forms for daily prayer in Catholic and Orthodox churches reinforce the interpretation of the scriptures according to the narrative of the gospel structured according to the Christian year. This overarching sense of the meaning of scripture as centering on the events of Christ's life, death, and resurrection would set the stage for the Protestant understanding of the gospel as the center of and the key to the Holy Scriptures.

It is possible for the gospel message to be hidden or obscured in the ancient Christian communities, just as the next chapter will show that it has become quite possible for the gospel message to be obscured and even neglected in Protestant churches. Protestants in the past have exaggerated as a standard trope the corruptions of late medieval Catholicism, and critical misunderstandings arose at the time of the Reformation, for example, the belief that Catholics worshiped saints, or that Catholics believed that salvation is by works. For centuries, Eastern Christianity was very little understood by Protestants; it could be either romanticized or castigated when not well understood. There may have been an element of truth in the claim that, by the time of the Reformation in the sixteenth century, many laypersons in Catholic and Orthodox churches were poorly catechized, sermons were not regularly preached in parish churches, and the religious life of lay Christians had in many cases come to focus on such practices as the cult of the saints.[54] However, very similar critiques can be made of adherents of old-line Protestant churches today (chapter 3) and in fact it is a critical problem faced by contemporary Evangelical churches that have in many cases succeeded in attracting large numbers of adherents but have not always been so successful in the deeper formation of Christians (chapter 4).

But the gospel is deeply and thoroughly embedded in the culture of ancient Christian churches, as this chapter shows; indeed, the gospel lies at the heart of the ancient churches. It is not only to be seen in their formal creeds and doctrinal statements, but in the regular worship practices in which these churches engage from week to week and throughout the cycle of the Christian liturgical year. The depth of the understanding of the Christ-event in ancient Christian communities is a gift that comes with the difficulty of communicating these deeper meanings to modern persons unfamiliar, for example, with ancient languages, ancient sacrificial cultus, and in general with the cultures in which many of these meanings are embedded. The reforms of the Second Vatican Council have provided strong resources for Catholics in addressing these issues, for example, by the introduction of vernacular languages and culture-specific forms of worship, by the development and use of the *Catechism of the Catholic Church* (1992), and by the development of rich resources for adult catechism associated with the Rite of Christian Initiation for Adults. Chapter 5 will show how Catholic and Orthodox understandings of scripture and tradition and Catholic work in liturgical renewal have contributed to a renewed sense of the meaning of the gospel in the ecumenical movement more broadly and in Protestant churches in particular.

3

The Gospel in Protestant and Related Churches

The true treasure of the church
is the most holy gospel
of the glory and grace of God.

—Martin Luther, Thesis 62 of the
"Ninety-Five Theses," 1517

Protestant and Related Churches

The principal Lutheran confession of faith, the Augsburg Confession, was addressed to the Holy Roman Emperor Charles V in 1530.[1] It opens by noting dissensions and divisions over issues of Christian doctrine and practice, and expresses the wish:

> ... to unite the [divided parties] in agreement on one Christian truth, to put aside whatever may not have been rightly interpreted or treated by either side, to have all of us embrace and adhere to a single, true religion and live together in unity and in one fellowship and church, even as we are all enlisted under one Christ.[2]

This was written before Christian states went to war with other Christian states. Just seven years later, caught in the fire of inter-Christian carnage, the conciliatory tone of the Augsburg Confession had given away to the harshest condemnations, indeed, to outright curses pronounced between

Catholic and Protestant communities.[3] In the wake of centuries of division between these churches since the time of the Reformation, Protestant and Catholic communities in the twentieth century have had to work hard at the project of discerning the common faith they share with each other and with other Christian communities as well. This chapter examines the transmission and reception of the common Christian gospel in Protestant and related church communities.

A common theme of the reforming movements of the late Middle Ages as well as the Reformation age was the reform of the church by the return to the primitive gospel message. One of the early leaders of the Czech Reformation, Matthias of Janow, expressed in 1393 his concern for a return to the simplicity of the gospel in the following words:

> I am persuaded that, if unity and peace are to be restored to Christendom, the weeds must be uprooted (Matt. 15:13), the gospel stated in a concise and concentrated form on earth (Rom. 9:28), and the church of Jesus Christ led back to its basic source. For this it will suffice to retain just a few apostolic definitions.[4]

Lutheran churches have often taken the title "Evangelical Lutheran" to express their conviction that the gospel (Latin, *evangelium*) is the foundation of a Christian church.[5] The gospel was, according to Martin Luther's Ninety-Five Theses, "the true treasure of the church,"[6] and his own eloquent explication of the meaning of "gospel" is as follows:

> ... the *euangelion*, the gospel, neither is, nor can be, anything other than the proclamation of Christ the son of God and of David, truly God and man. By his death and resurrection, He has conquered sin, death, and hell for us and all who believe in Him. The gospel may be proclaimed in few words or in many; one writer may describe it briefly and another at length. If at length, then many of the works and words of Christ will be set down, as in the case of the four evangelists. Those who write it briefly, like Peter or Paul, say nothing of Christ's works, but tell succinctly how He conquered sin, death, and hell by His own death and resurrection on behalf of those who believe in Him.[7]

In this passage, Luther makes it clear that what he understood by the gospel was the proclamation or announcement of God's work in Jesus Christ, especially in Christ's death and resurrection.[8] Luther went so far as to claim in the Small Catechism that in the establishment of Reformation churches, "... the gospel has been restored ..."[9] However, the term "gospel" had a twofold meaning for Luther and many subsequent Protestant teachers. It did denote the basic proclamation of God's acts in Jesus Christ, but, as the passage quoted here shows, it also denoted God's work in Jesus Christ as it brings about the redemption of those who have believed and have been baptized. That is to say, "gospel" denotes in Protestant and related communities both God's decisive acts and the application of those acts to Christians. Luther understood the expression "believe in," as he explicated the Apostles' Creed, as involving belief that Christ's work is applied "to me."[10]

By the awkward expression "Protestant and related churches" in this chapter, I denote a wide range of churches that were influenced by the Protestant Reformation of the sixteenth century. In the text following in this chapter, I will have specific reference to the following churches or families of churches influenced by the Protestant Reformation:

The Waldensian Church (now in a union with Methodist churches in Italy)
The Moravian Church
Lutheran churches
Reformed churches (including Presbyterian and Congregational churches)
Anglican churches
Methodist churches
Union churches and churches that resulted from twentieth-century unions influenced by the Ecumenical Movement (such as the Church of South India, the Church of North India, the United Church of Canada, and the Uniting Church in Australia)

Some of these—most notably, churches of the Lutheran and Reformed traditions—originated straightforwardly at the time of the Protestant Reformation in the sixteenth century. Anglican churches were organized independently of the Catholic Church in this period, though Anglicans can claim distinct institutions and traditions that predated the century of the Reformation and many Anglicans do not want to identify themselves as "Protestants." Some of the church traditions considered in this chapter originated long before the Reformation: this is the case with the Waldensian Church of Italy (now in a union with Italian Methodists) and the Moravian Church, which originated in the Czech reforming movement of the fifteenth century and was subsequently restructured in the eighteenth century. I will also have reference to the Mar Thoma Church, which traces its origins to the apostolic age and in many ways reflects its origins as an ancient Eastern Christian church, although it was strongly influenced by Anglicans from the eighteenth century. Other church traditions considered in this chapter such as that of Methodist churches originated after the time of the Reformation but reflect central doctrinal tenets and practices of the Reformation churches.

The Gospel in Creeds and Doctrinal Statements

In the first place, Protestant and related churches have affirmed the gospel as it has been handed down in historic Christian creeds, as the previous chapter has shown with respect to the ancient Christian churches. The Mar Thoma Church uses only the Nicene Creed in the form in which it has been received and transmitted in Eastern Christian churches, that is, without the *filioque* clause. Most of the churches that emerged from the European Reformation of the sixteenth century affirmed both the Nicene Creed (in its Western form with the *filioque* clause) and the Apostles' Creed, and in some cases they also affirmed a third creed that had developed in the Latin West, the so-called Athanasian Creed.[11]

The *Book of Concord* (1580), the principal collection of Lutheran dogmatic documents, gives the full texts of the Nicene Creed, the Apostles' Creed, and the Athanasian Creed at the very beginning of the volume, before any of the specifically Lutheran doctrinal statements included in the book.[12] The Formula of Concord (1577), which enunciated Lutheran consensus in doctrine and is a key document in the *Book of Concord*, also refers to these three creeds as "the unanimous, Catholic, Christian faith and confessions of the orthodox and true church . . . "[13] Similarly, within the Thirty-Nine Articles of Religion of the Church of England, article 8 affirms the three creeds.[14] This affirmation of the creeds passed into the usage of global Anglicanism, although some Anglican churches (such as the Episcopal Church in the United States) omit the reference to the Athanasian Creed in the eighth Article. The Second Helvetic Confession (1566), utilized very broadly by Reformed churches, affirms the teachings of the ancient creeds in this way:

> And, to say many things with a few words, with a sincere heart we believe, and freely confess with open mouth, whatever things are defined from the Holy Scriptures concerning the mystery of the incarnation of our Lord Jesus Christ, and are summed up in the creeds and decrees of the first four most

excellent synods convened at Nicaea, Constantinople, Ephesus, and Chalcedon—together with the creed of blessed Athanasius, and all similar symbols; and we condemn anything contrary to these.[15]

The Moravian doctrinal statement called "The Ground of the Unity" (most recently revised in 1995) names the Apostles' Creed, the Nicene Creed, and the Athanasian Creed in that order as the first of ten historic doctrinal statements that are claimed by the Moravian Church as consonant with its faith, and their liturgical books (at least since the 1960s) include both the Apostles' Creed and the Nicene Creed (the latter without the *filioque* clause).[16] Similarly, a contemporary ecumenical statement of the Waldensian Church affirms "the great symbols or confessions of the ancient church," and names specifically the Apostles' Creed, the Nicene Creed, and the Athanasian Creed.[17] The historic creeds, then, are given a position of priority among the doctrinal statements of Protestant churches, and the gospel narrative stands at the center of these creeds for Protestant and related church as it does for the ancient churches considered in the previous chapter.

Patterns of catechesis in these churches also show the central place that the gospel narrative holds in their communities. Anglican and Lutheran churches consistently utilize the Apostles' Creed as the basic means by which Christian doctrines are taught in their catechisms. Luther's Small Catechism (1529), the catechism consistently used by Lutherans for teaching the faith before confirmation, devotes an entire section to the Apostles' Creed by which the most fundamental Christian doctrines are taught and learned.[18] The catechism of the Book of Common Prayer teaches the complete text of the Apostles' Creed to those being trained for the profession of their faith.[19]

Anglican and Lutheran churches also use the historic creeds in their forms of weekly and daily worship. Luther's Small Catechism instructs Christians to say the Apostles' Creed as well as the Lord's Prayer every morning and evening and Lutheran eucharistic services include the Nicene creed.[20] The Anglican Book of Common Prayer (in its classic 1662 version) has Christians recite the Apostles' Creed at baptism and then at daily morning and evening prayer on most days.[21] The Prayer Book uses the Nicene Creed in its eucharistic service,[22] consistent with the practice of ancient churches noted in the previous chapter. Historic Anglican usage according to the 1662 prayer book also utilized the Athanasian Creed at morning prayer on specific holy days in the year, but this practice was discontinued by those Anglican churches that have removed the Athanasian Creed from Article 8 of the Thirty-Nine Articles.[23]

Although churches of the Reformed tradition (including Presbyterian and Congregational churches) affirmed the doctrines of the ancient creeds, as seen in the quotation given above from the Second Helvetic Confession, they did not use the Nicene Creed in worship in the sixteenth century but consistently utilized the Apostles' Creed both in eucharistic services and in services intended solely for preaching. Thus, a eucharistic service from 1525 used by the early reformer Ulrich Zwingli included the Apostles' Creed, said antiphonally by men and women in the congregation.[24] Martin Bucer's Strasbourg Liturgy of 1539[25] and John Calvin's Geneva liturgy of 1554 both included the Apostles' Creed,[26] and in fact the basic outline of Calvin's *Institutes* follows the structure of the Apostles' Creed as it had been used in Christian catechesis.[27] It was not until the seventeenth century that English Puritans would offer eucharistic services in the Reformed tradition with the option of saying the Nicene and the Athanasian creeds, here reflecting their indebtedness to the liturgy of the Church of England.[28]

Beyond the use of the historic creeds in catechesis and worship, Protestant and related churches also affirm in their formal doctrinal statements the substance of the gospel by way of the doctrines taught in the historic creeds, often explicitly using the language of the creeds. The Augsburg Confession (1530) cites the Nicene Creed at the beginning of its first article of faith, on the divine Trinity: "We unanimously hold and teach, in accordance with the decree of the Council of Nicaea . . ."[29] The Augsburg Confession also cites the Apostles' Creed in asserting that Christ "will return openly to judge the living and the dead, etc., as stated in the Apostles' Creed."[30] Similarly, the Anglican Articles of Religion affirm the doctrine of the Trinity and the doctrine of the two natures in the one Person of Christ following the language of the Nicene Creed and the Definition of Faith of the Council of Chalcedon.[31] Reformed doctrinal statements affirm the teachings about the divine Trinity and about Jesus Christ utilizing the language of the historic creeds including, for example, the assertion in the Nicene Creed that Christ is "of one substance" with the Father.[32] Even Anabaptist theologians of the Reformation age, such as Balthasar Hubmaier and Dirk Philipsz, affirmed the traditional language of Nicene and Chalcedonian teachings.[33]

A distinctive use of ancient creedal material can be found in the Moravian Easter Litany, which has functioned as the principal doctrinal statement of the Moravian Church since the time when that church was renewed and reorganized in the eighteenth century. The Easter Litany (1749) follows the wording of the Apostles' Creed and expands it as an act of praise on behalf of the community.[34] Historic Moravian practice since the eighteenth century has been to utilize the Easter Litany as part of a service often held outdoors in a church's graveyard at sunrise on Easter morning.

Methodist churches followed doctrinal and liturgical traditions inherited from the Anglicanism of John and Charles Wesley. However, in revising the Book of Common Prayer and the Thirty Nine Articles of Religion for American Methodists, John Wesley omitted the Anglican article affirming the three creeds and he omitted the use of the Nicene Creed in the eucharistic liturgy, leaving Methodists only the Apostles' Creed among the historic creeds. Moreover, Methodist use of the Apostles' Creed from the eighteenth century omitted the phrase "he descended into hell," which Methodists (mistakenly) took as meaning that Christ went to the place of eternal punishment reserved for reprobate sinners.[35] Nevertheless, the Apostles' Creed was formally affirmed by Methodist churches and has been very regularly utilized by Methodist congregations.[36] Under the influence of the ecumenical movement, Methodist churches came to use the Nicene Creed in the twentieth century, and some Methodist hymnals now place the Nicene Creed in the first position among statements of faith to be communally affirmed.[37] Also in response to ecumenical concerns, Methodists in the late twentieth century began to offer the option of using the Apostles' Creed with the expression "he descended to the dead."[38]

Consistent with their use of the historic creeds, the principal doctrinal statements distinctive of Protestant and related churches affirm the gospel narrative of God's decisive acts in Christ's life, death, and resurrection even when they do not explicitly cite the creeds. The Augsburg Confession sets the pattern for subsequent Protestant doctrinal statements about Jesus Christ in its article on "The Son of God":

> . . . there is one Christ, true God and true man, who was truly born, suffered, was crucified, died, and was buried in order to be a sacrifice not only for original sin but also for all other sins and to propitiate God's wrath. The same Christ also descended into hell, truly rose from the dead on the third day, ascended into heaven, and sits on the right hand of God, . . .[39]

Very similar wording is employed in the Anglican Articles of Religion, although the Anglican Articles divide this passage from the Augsburg Confession into three separate articles affirming Christ's incarnation and death, Christ's descent into hell, and Christ's resurrection from the dead.[40] The Westminster Confession of Faith (1646) includes similar words.[41] The Methodist revision of the Anglican Articles has the articles on the incarnation and death of Christ and on Christ's resurrection, but omits the Anglican article on the descent of Christ into hell, consistent with the Methodist custom through the twentieth century of omitting the clause about Christ's descent into hell in the Apostles' Creed.[42]

Within these Protestant confessions of faith, sacrificial language is used to explain the meaning of Christ's work. The statement from the Augsburg Confession quoted above, for example, states that Christ "was truly born, suffered, was crucified, died, and was buried in order to be a sacrifice not only for original sin but also for all other sins and to propitiate God's wrath."[43] This associates Christ's sacrifice with the whole sequence of events in Christ's life up to his death and burial, although it does not explicitly affirm the resurrection as part of Christ's sacrifice. Very similar language was used in the Anglican Articles of Religion (articles 2 and 21), and although the title of a subsequent article speaks "Of the One Oblation of Christ Finished upon the Cross" (article 31), the article emphasized the expression "finished upon," that is to say, the crucifixion was the last aspect of the sacrifice of Christ and there was to be no liturgical continuation of the oblation.[44] In the Westminster Confession, which follows and expands on the items of the Anglican Articles, sacrificial language is minimized (it is removed from the statement about Christ's life, death, and burial) although there is a statement that "by his perfect obedience and sacrifice of himself" Christ accomplished the reconciliation of "those whom the Father hath given unto him."[45] In these statements, every aspect of Christ's work with the exception of the resurrection is seen as a significant element of Christ's sacrifice. Protestant doctrinal statements, represented in Anglican article 21 referred to earlier, went to great lengths to emphasize the once-and-for-all, completed nature of Christ's sacrifice, in opposition to what they understood to be the Catholic claim that Christ's sacrifice was offered again (or brought to completion) in the mass.[46]

Protestant doctrinal statements also reflect an interpretation of Christ's death and resurrection that emphasizes God's victory over evil through these signal events. Luther's Small Catechism teaches believers to say that Christ:

> has redeemed me, a lost and condemned creature, delivered
> me, and freed me from all sins, from death, and from the power
> of the devil, not with silver and gold but with his holy and pre-
> cious blood and with his innocent sufferings and death . . .[47]

The words of this passage from the Small Catechism regarding Christ's conquering death and hell are incorporated into the Heidelberg Catechism, utilized by Protestant Union churches.[48] Similarly, the Small Catechism states that one of the effects of baptism is that it "delivers from death and the devil . . ."[49] This is consistent with what Luther himself said about the meaning of the gospel quoted at the beginning of this chapter: among other things, the gospel denotes the good news that "By his death and resurrection, [Christ] has conquered sin, death, and hell for us and all who believe in Him."[50] The First Helvetic Confession, affirmed by Swiss Reformed churches in 1536, asserts that Christ "has overcome and conquered death, sin, and the whole power of hell . . ."[51]

The various uses of the historic creeds shown earlier here—formal affirmation of ancient creeds, their use in worship and catechesis, the affirmation of their most critical content in formal doctrinal statements—show the consistent intention on the part of Protestant and related churches to affirm the faith that had been handed down from the apostolic age and that had been encapsulated in the primitive rule of faith and in the creeds affirmed by ancient Christian communities.

The Gospel and the Unity of Scripture

One of the persistent themes of the reforming movements of the sixteenth century was the use of the Christian canon of scripture as the primary criterion for the knowledge of salvation and for the reform of the church.[52] As chapter 1 has shown, the canon of Christian scripture was itself defined by proto-orthodox understandings of the gospel. Protestant Reformers saw the gospel as the central message that provided the unity of the whole Bible. So Martin Luther referred to scripture (both the Old and New Testaments) as "the swaddling clothes and the manger" in which the Christ child is found:

> Here [in the scriptures] you will find the swaddling clothes and the manger in which Christ lies, and to which the angel points the shepherds [Luke 2:12]. Simple and lowly are these swaddling clothes, but dear is the treasure, Christ, who lies in them.[53]

Consistent with this focus on Christ as the central meaning of the scriptures, Luther insisted that the scriptures are to be interpreted in the light of Christ: "Scripture is to be understood not contrary to, but in accordance with Christ. Therefore Scripture is to be referred to him, or else we do not have what represents Scripture."[54] It is in this sense that Protestant doctrinal standards could speak of the scriptures as "containing" the gospel, sometimes identified as "the Word of God." Thus the original "protesters" (*protestantes*) at the Second Diet of Speyer (1529) asserted that "We are determined by God's grace and aid to abide by God's Word alone, the Holy Gospel contained in the biblical books of the Old and New Testaments."[55] In both of Luther's statements and the statement of the protesters at the Second Diet of Speyer, the gospel is understood to be the message about Jesus Christ that lies at the center of the canonical scriptures. Indeed, the protesters at Speyer identify "the Word of God" not with the whole of scripture but with "the Holy Gospel" that is "contained" within the scriptures.[56]

This notion of the gospel as the central meaning of the Christian scriptures is consistently stated in Anglican and Reformed doctrinal statements. The Anglican Articles of Religion assert that "The Old Testament is not contrary to the New: for both in the Old and New Testament everlasting life is offered to Mankind by Christ..."[57] Similarly, the Westminster Confession states that in the Old Testament, the "covenant of grace" through Christ was offered by way of "promises, prophecies, sacrifices, circumcision, the paschal lamb, and other types and ordinances..." and in the New Testament the same covenant of grace is offered by the preaching of the Word and the sacraments.[58]

As Protestants developed their ways of the interpreting the Bible, they elaborated a theory of interpretation often encapsulated under the expression "the analogy of faith" (*analogia fidei*). The term itself is from Romans 12:6, "We have gifts that differ according to the grace given to us: prophecy, in proportion to faith..." but the expression translated "in proportion to faith" could also be rendered "according to the analogy [Greek, *analogian*] of faith."[59] As a principle of biblical interpretation, this term came to have two closely related meanings. The first is that the scriptures are their own best interpreters. This was often explained as signifying that if the meaning of a scriptural passage is unclear, it should be understood according to the meaning of clearer passages of scripture, so the Reformers and Protestant theologians spoke of the "perspicuity" or clarity of the scriptures.[60] In a second sense, however, the term came to denote the principle that the Bible must be understood in the light of its central message about salvation in Jesus Christ. So the Reformed theologian Guillaume du Buc (Bucanus) of Lausanne asserted that the analogy of faith meant "the constant and unchanging sense of Scripture expounded in open [or "clear," *apertis*] passages of Scripture and agreeing with the Apostles' Creed, the Decalogue, and the Lord's Prayer."[61] In this particular sense, the "rule of faith" which was the gospel narrative embedded in the Apostles' Creed continued to norm the church's understanding of the scriptures similar to the ways in which it had normed the development and interpretation of the canon of scripture in the earliest Christian centuries.

It is not clear that this latter understanding of the "analogy of faith" was uniformly affirmed by Reformation churches because the expression seems in some cases to have only the first meaning given earlier, namely, the principle of interpreting less clear passages of scripture in the light of passages whose meaning is clearer. Nor is it clear that this principle of Biblical interpretation was affirmed explicitly in corporate dogmatic or doctrinal statements on the part of Reformation churches. However, it does reveal a critical presupposition of the Reformation's understanding of Biblical authority, namely, that the meaning and authority of the whole Bible rests on its transmission (through all its parts) of the gospel narrative, the message of God's redemptive work in Jesus Christ. And this is consistent with the claims of Luther and other early Reformers cited earlier that Christ is the center of the scriptures, "the swaddling clothes and the manger" in which Christ is found. It is in this sense that a report on *The Catholicity of Protestantism,* offered by Free Church (that is, non-Anglican) leaders to the Archbishop of Canterbury in 1950, could claim that one of the key principles of Protestantism was "the setting up of the primitive Rule of Faith as the standard of all Church life and Christian belief."[62]

The Gospel in Protestant Worship

The preceding sections of this chapter have examined the Christian gospel expressed through the use of historic creeds among Protestant and Anglican churches, the Mar Thoma Church, and the Moravian and Waldensian churches, both in eucharistic services and in some cases in services for daily morning and evening prayer. The preceding discussion has also noted the distinctive contribution of the Moravian Easter Litany as the most significant historical doctrinal statement of the Moravian Church, expressed in the church's annual Easter ritual.

The age of the Reformation brought some critical changes in forms of Christian worship in Western churches, Catholic as well as Protestant. Perhaps the most important development in this age was the institution of preaching as a regular expectation of weekly Christian worship, and this occurred both in the Catholic Church as well as in Protestant churches. The Council of Trent, which legislated Catholic reforms in the sixteenth century, mandated the development of diocesan seminaries so that candidates for the priesthood could be taught to preach homilies at weekly masses.[63] In the evolution of Protestant church culture, preaching assumed normative status as the regular expectation of weekly worship, whether or not eucharist was celebrated. The Catholic historian Jean Delumeau has argued that both catechesis and preaching were critical parallel activities in both Catholic and Protestant versions of reform in the age of the Reformation.[64]

The point of Protestant preaching was to deliver the gospel in a clear and articulate way based on the reading and interpretation of the Christian canon of scripture. Protestant doctrinal standards consistently define the preaching of the gospel as one of the essential elements of the church alongside faith and the right administration of the sacraments. In the words of the Augsburg Confession, the church is "the assembly of all believers among whom the gospel is preached in its purity and the holy sacraments are administered according to the gospel."[65] Lutheran churches continued to use the medieval genre of postils (*postillae*), commentaries on scripture organized according to the lectionary pattern for preaching. Postils were produced by Luther himself, by Philipp Melanchthon, and by the Lutheran spiritual writer Johann Arndt. The use of postils was important in the early Reformation period when clergy had not been trained to develop sermons and could utilize the pattern of the postils to develop sermons following the prescribed lectionary.

The Anglican Articles of Religion follow the definition of the church given in the Augsburg Confession very closely, including the proper preaching of "the Word of God" as an essential element defining the Christian church.[66] An example of a sermon proclaiming the gospel from the Reformation era is the Anglican homily "Of the Salvation of Mankind, by Only Christ our Saviour, from Sin and Death Everlasting,"[67] one of a series of homilies protected as doctrinal standards in the Church of England from the time of the Reformation and provided for preachers who had not been trained to compose their own sermons. The Second Helvetic Confession (1566), adopted at first by Swiss Reformed churches and then by other Reformed churches, asserts that "The Preaching of the Word of God is the Word of God," and in its explication of this assertion it applies sacramental language to the preaching of the gospel: just as a sacrament, rightly administered and rightly received, conveys the reality of Christ's grace, so this confession states that when "the Word of God" (scripture) is rightly preached by a duly called minister, then "the very Word of God" (Christ) is truly present, in spite of any failings of the preacher.[68]

As noted earlier, preaching became part of the regular weekly worship of Catholic and Protestant churches in the sixteenth century. This implied that preaching accompanied eucharist for Protestants (as well as Catholics) from this period and Protestants emphasized the role of eucharist as a way of proclaiming Christ through the reading of the scriptures, the preaching itself, and through the remembrance (anamnesis) of Christ's acts in the eucharist. Although the eucharist or holy communion might be celebrated only quarterly by some Protestant churches, Protestants had attempted by the implementation of quarterly eucharists to increase frequency of communion since in the late Middle Ages laypersons may have been accustomed to receiving the eucharist only once or twice in a year. Protestant churches differed within themselves on the manner of Christ's presence in the eucharist,[69] but all emphasized the role of eucharist as a remembrance of Christ's work. For the Reformed tradition this was often claimed to be the primary meaning of the supper. The Second Helvetic Confession (1566), for example, states that:

> By this sacred rite the Lord wishes to keep in fresh remembrance that greatest benefit which he showed to mortal men, namely, that by having given his body and shed his blood he has pardoned all our sins, and redeemed us from eternal death and the power of the devil, and now feeds us with his flesh, and give[s] us his blood to drink . . . For the Lord said: "Do this in remembrance of me."[70]

Similarly, the Westminster Confession (1646) asserts that a "real sacrifice" is not made in the eucharist, "but only a commemoration of that one offering up of himself, by himself, upon the cross, once for all . . ."[71] Whether or not this element of anamnesis or remembrance was understood to be the primary meaning of eucharist, all of the Protestant and related churches have a clear element of anamnesis in their celebration of eucharist. This can be seen in the words of the eucharistic prayer in the Anglican Book of Common Prayer (1662):

> Almighty God, our heavenly Father, who of thy tender mercy didst give thine only Son Jesus Christ to suffer death upon the Cross for our redemption; who made there (by his one oblation of himself once offered) a full, perfect, and sufficient sacrifice, oblation, and satisfaction, for the sins of the whole world; and

> did institute, and in his holy Gospel command us to continue, a perpetual memory of that his precious death and sacrifice, until his coming again . . .[72]

This passage illustrates the manner in which sacrificial language ("a full, perfect, and sufficient sacrifice, oblation, and satisfaction") inherited from the scriptures and the earlier Christian tradition had been incorporated into Christian worship in the Reformation age, although it also shows a trend on the part of Protestant church communities to focus very sharply on the issue of Christ's one sacrifice ("by his one oblation of himself once offered") in response to what they understood to be Catholic claims that Christ was sacrificed again in each celebration of the eucharist (similar claims were made in the Protestant doctrinal statements considered above). Combined with scripture lessons and consistent preaching, the eucharist thus served for Protestants to "proclaim the Lord's death until he comes" (I Corinthians 11:26).

An important development in Protestant worship was the use of hymns as an expression of the gospel. This came very early in the development of the Lutheran tradition: the Augsburg Confession noted that the celebration of the eucharist (it uses the term "mass") had not been significantly altered at that early point (1530) except for the addition of some German hymns in addition to the Latin responses of the mass.[73] Early Lutheran hymns often reflected the spirituality of the *Devotio Moderna*, a late medieval movement that had emphasized personal devotion to the humanity of Christ, especially the suffering and death of Christ. This could become a powerful means of communicating the central message of the gospel about Christ's work. So, for example, a medieval Latin hymn celebrating the wounds of Christ, including the wound of the thorns in Christ's brow, was refashioned in German by the Lutheran hymn writer Paul Gerhardt (ca. 1607–1676) and became,

> O sacred Head, now wounded,
> with grief and shame weighed down,
> now scornfully surrounded
> with thorns, thine only crown:
> how pale thou art with anguish,
> with sore abuse and scorn!
> How does that visage languish
> which once was bright as morn![74]

Churches of the Reformed and Anglican traditions did not use hymns in the sixteenth century, but developed a hymn tradition in the seventeenth and eighteenth centuries. The Congregationalist poet Isaac Watts (1674–1748) built on the work of earlier Puritan poets and authors and began to compose hymns for congregational use, going beyond the metrical psalms that had been used since the time of the Reformation in Reformed churches. Characteristic of Watts is the dramatic use of the first-person singular in addressing God.[75] This yields an intensely personal and affective appropriation of the gospel message about God's work of redemption in Jesus Christ:

> When I survey the wondrous cross
> on which the Prince of Glory died,
> my richest gain I count but loss,
> and pour contempt on all my pride.[76]

Watts's work of hymn composition was carried on by his younger contemporary Charles Wesley (1707–1788). Wesley could also employ dramatic language to express the profundity of God's work in Christ. In the following stanza, Charles Wesley invokes the image of "the first-born seraph," the chief of the heavenly host, attempting in vain to test the depths of divine love in the crucifixion:

> 'Tis mystery all: th' Immortal dies!
> Who can explore his strange design?
> In vain the first-born seraph tries
> to sound the depths of love divine.
> 'Tis mercy all! Let earth adore;
> let angel minds inquire no more.[77]

Known for his poems and hymns expressing the affective experience of Christian believers in their spiritual pilgrimage, Charles Wesley also composed poems that celebrated the cardinal events of the gospel narrative. In 1745 and 1746, he issued a series of books of hymns composed for specific celebrations in the Christian liturgical year, including *Hymns for the Nativity of Our Lord* (1745), *Hymns for Our Lord's Resurrection* (1746), *Hymns for Ascension-Day* (1746), and *Hymns of Petition and Thanksgiving for the Promise of the Father* subtitled *Hymns for Whitsunday* (1746).[78]

As Reformed and Anglican churches began to utilize hymns in their worship, they developed hymnals, the approval of which can be seen as acts of communal affirmation of the teachings embedded in the hymns. By the nineteenth century, a consistent pattern of Protestant hymnals involved a section of hymns following the calendar of the liturgical year, with hymns arranged according to the successive celebration of Advent,

Christmas, Epiphany, Lent, Easter, and Pentecost. In this way, hymnals themselves as well as the hymns contained in them served to reinforce the proclamation of the gospel in preaching and in the sacraments.

Protestant church cultures also saw the development of some expressions of the gospel message in contexts apart from that of traditional worship, at least, apart from the formal worship sponsored by Protestant churches. Moravian and Methodist churches would place a special emphasis on the singing of hymns and other Christian songs, and these churches developed special occasions for hymn singing, for instance, in association with Moravian and early Methodist "love feasts." Protestant churches took up the singing of carols derived from the medieval tradition of carol singing, especially from the nineteenth century when Protestants began to take a more congenial attitude toward medieval culture. Many carols would eventually become hymns sung in formal liturgical services, especially associated with the Christmas season and the celebration of Christ's birth. The eighteenth century saw the flourishing of the genre of musical oratorios, many on subjects related to Christ's life, and many of which were never intended to be performed in church services but were performed as musical concerts whether in churches or in other settings. The German composer Johann Heinrich Rolle, for example, composed an oratorio on the passion of Christ. But the best-known example of this genre is Handel's *Messiah* (1741), an elaborate retelling of the gospel narrative embracing the entire biblical story from Genesis through the Revelation. These Protestant instances of extraliturgical expressions of the gospel could be compared to the carols and passion plays of late medieval Catholicism and they serve as an important precedent for the development of extraliturgical musical genres in the culture of Evangelical churches, specifically, the genre of Gospel music in the late nineteenth century and then the genre of Contemporary Christian music in the late twentieth century.

The Meaning of the Gospel in the Traditions of Protestant and Related Churches

What is the meaning of the Christian gospel as it has been handed down in the Protestant and related churches considered in this chapter? The preceding discussion has called attention to the continuing use of ancient Christian creeds among Protestant churches, which shows the intention on the part of these churches to believe the same basic message about Jesus Christ that the earliest Christian communities had believed. This discussion has shown that Lutheran and Anglican churches included the Nicene Creed in their eucharistic worship from early on, and all of the Protestant and related churches considered in this chapter use the Apostles' Creed. Moreover, such Protestant groups as Reformed and Methodist churches have come to use the Nicene Creed in the last century. The simple narrative of Christ's saving acts that constitute the gospel is perhaps best known to Protestants in the words of these historic creeds, although these words are also embedded in the doctrinal statements of Protestant and related churches. Lutheran and Anglican churches followed the cycle of the Christian year from the time of the Reformation, and Reformed and Methodist churches have renewed this pattern which had been allowed for early in the history of their traditions, although not consistently practiced thereafter.[79] Here, again, the gospel narrative of Christ's life, death, and resurrection provides a basic framework for preaching and exposition of the faith in these communities.

The preceding discussion has shown at more than one point that the meaning of "gospel" in Protestant and related churches embraces both the narrative of Christ's work and the application of this in human salvation. The connection between Christ's works and human salvation was already present in the claim of the primitive kerygma that "Christ died for our sins" and in the eucharistic meanings of Christ's work given in the liturgical practice of the ancient Christian churches. The language of sacrifice used in Protestant doctrinal statements and in the liturgies of Protestant and related churches offers a way to understand how Christ's work could bring about human salvation, although the concept of Christ's sacrifice was nuanced in Protestant and related churches by Protestants' intense concern to assert the unique and complete nature of Christ's sacrifice in contention with their perception that Catholics taught that Christ's sacrifice was repeated or brought to completion in the mass. Moreover, although Protestant doctrinal statements associate Christ's sacrificial offering with Christ's whole life up to and including his crucifixion and burial, they do not consistently associate the resurrection with the sacrifice of Christ. As chapters 1 and 2 have shown, the complex of meanings associated with sacrifice in the ancient world allowed earlier Christians to understand the resurrection on the analogy of the smoke rising from a sacrificial offering, a sign of divine acceptance of the offering. Although this might seem like a fine point, the next chapter will show that in Evangelical Christian communities the redemptive meaning of Christ's work is very often pared down to the single element of Christ's death as a substitution for the death that humans owe for their complicity in sin. This may be a result of the unfamiliarity of modern people with the range of meanings associated with sacrifice in other cultures, but I am inclined to see the absence of the resurrection in Protestant descriptions of Christ's sacrifice as indicating a trend in this direction. This chapter has also observed that Protestant churches followed the medieval Latin tradition of interpreting Christ's death and resurrection as representing God's victory over the powers of death and evil, and in this respect Protestant churches continued to understand the resurrection as an important element of the saving work of Christ.

Protestant churches understood the gospel narrative as the center of the Christian scriptures, providing the key to understanding the meaning of the whole Bible. This is consistent with the fact that the gospel normed the writing and canonization of the Christian scriptures in the proto-orthodox Christian communities (chapter 1) and it is consistent with the liturgical reading of the scriptures in the ancient churches following the pattern of the Christian year and thus following the sequence of events in the gospel narrative (chapter 2). The development of this understanding of the meaning of the Bible came at a critical juncture, soon after the first publications of the whole Bible on movable type, bound in single volumes and available to laity. With a significant rise in literacy in northern Europe and with the increasingly available printed copies of the Bible, it was important to offer a sense of the whole biblical narrative normed by its internal narrative of the gospel.

Nevertheless, there were critical ambiguities surrounding the pattern of interpretation identified as "the analogy of faith": did it refer to the scriptures normed by the gospel message, or to the scriptures normed by whatever other passages of scripture might seem clearer? And there were similar ambiguities involved in the term "Word of God": beyond its use as a term for Christ (as in John 1:1–14), did "Word of God" mean the gospel message "contained in" the scriptures or did it denote the whole of the Bible (as it seems to have meant in the Reformed confessions)? There was a trend in some lines of Protestant culture to see the whole corpus of scripture as being equally inspired in all its parts, at least where its teachings were most clear. The next chapter will show that this trend was accelerated in Evangelical churches in response to modern scientific discoveries and could yield a view of the Bible as a book of oracles addressing all manner of scientific and historical facts even apart from its central meaning as preeminently conveying the gospel, or, as Luther put it, as the manger in which Christ is found.

The faith formally taught in the doctrinal statements affirmed by Protestant, Anglican, and related churches and celebrated in their historic as well as contemporary forms of worship has the gospel at its core. The introduction to this book raised the issue of divisions in old-line Protestant churches today, divisions in which issues of human sexuality are currently at the forefront. This chapter has tried to show that the gospel has served as the fundamental ground of unity for Protestant and related churches, indeed, the remainder of the book shows that the gospel serves as the fundamental ground for the unity of Christians more broadly. But in the current discussions over these issues, the gospel itself has not consistently appeared as a significant factor in discussion, and its absence can leave battle-weary combatants on all sides with the impression that their opponents are merely concerned with political or social agenda rather than being concerned with the gospel. I am not at all suggesting that the simple and ancient gospel message itself resolves issues about the inclusion of gay and lesbian persons in Protestant and related churches. It does not directly resolve this or any number of other issues that face the churches now and will face them in the future. I do meant to suggest, however, that a form of consensus or unity on these issues apart from the central meaning of the gospel would not be a unity worth striving for: it would be, in essence, unity won only at the price of throwing away the church's greatest treasure. The churches must hope to find unity or consensus on this and other issues only as they recognize in each other the gospel that lies at the heart of Christian unity and remains "the true treasure of the church."

4

The Gospel in Evangelical Communities

I love to tell the story,
'Twill be my theme in glory,
To tell the old, old story
Of Jesus and his love.
—Gospel Song by Katherine Hankey, ca. 1868

Evangelical Communities and Churches

This chapter considers the Christian gospel as it has been received and handed on by another group of Christian communities which can also be described as Protestant but which I will call Evangelical communities.[1] The word "Evangelical" itself refers to the content of the gospel (Greek *euaggelion*, Latin *evangelium*) and some interpreters have taken a focus on the gospel message to be a defining trait of these communities,[2] although from what has been said in the previous two chapters it should be apparent that the ancient Christian churches and the older Protestant churches also understand the gospel as lying at the center of the Christian faith.

I have used the term "Evangelical" in this chapter to describe a cluster of contemporary Christian communities characterized by emphases on the unmediated authority of the Christian scriptures, the need for a personal and affective experience of conversion to Christ, and highly voluntarist forms of organization.[3] Many Protestant churches claimed the title "Evangelical" (especially Lutheran churches), so "Evangelical" in this case has to denote a more specific group of Protestant churches. Even in this sense, "Evangelical" is a very broad category which admittedly overlaps with some of the Protestant and related church traditions described in chapter 3. In many ways and through most of their history Methodist churches have shared the general Evangelical ethos or culture described in this chapter, though their forms of organization are more traditionally structured than the Evangelical groups described here and Methodist churches also share the culture of older Protestant churches as well. Moreover, some Protestant and related churches have had movements within themselves (such as Anglican Evangelicalism) that share characteristics of Evangelical communities. It is for this reason that I have utilized the expression "Evangelical communities" in this chapter: the groups identified here include some groups that are formally organized as churches or congregations or even denominations, but they also include groups that exist within other church traditions and groups that cut across the boundaries of formal church or denominational organizations. So what is described in this chapter is a complex cluster of congregations, churches, and related organizations, generally identified by three common traits.[4]

First, Evangelical communities emphasize the unmediated authority of the Christian scriptures. The term "unmediated" indicates their claim that believers can interpret the scriptures without reference to other authorities such as church traditions or philosophical systems and without the need for scholarly apparatus for the interpretation of the scriptures. This presupposes the belief that the Holy Spirit inspires the reading and interpretation of the holy scriptures. Disciples of Christ theologian Michael Kinnamon states that the Stone-Campbell Restoration movement in the United States had attempted "to read the Bible unencumbered by clerical imposition or the accretions of theological tradition."[5] The same could be said of Evangelical movements more broadly. Evangelical communities often employ particular schemes for understanding the meaning of the whole Bible, such as a postmillennial or premillennial understanding of biblical history or the more complex Dispensationalist scheme favored by some conservative Evangelical communities. In some Evangelical communities, moreover, the doctrine of scriptural authority has been defined since the late nineteenth century as a teaching of biblical inerrancy or infallibility, including the inerrancy of the scriptures in teaching scientific and historical facts. This particular understanding of biblical inerrancy or infallibility set against modern scientific discoveries (like the theory of evolution) most clearly identifies particular churches and organizations as "Fundamentalist." George M. Marsden quotes the common saying that "A Fundamentalist is an Evangelical who is mad about something," but what they are consistently mad about is what they perceive to be the encroachment on biblical authority of modern scientific discoveries, threatening the foundations of Christian culture.[6] Not all Evangelicals are Fundamentalists, but Evangelical communities have consistently stressed the unmediated authority of the Bible.

A second general trait of Evangelical communities is that they emphasize the need for a personal experience of conversion. A Christian's justification is by faith, but faith cannot mean merely intellectual assent to propositions; it must involve affective trust in Christ, and in Evangelical culture the conversion experience is the point at which a person comes to this kind of faith.[7] Evangelical communities may emphasize other affective religious experiences such as "conviction" of sin (or "awakening"), "entire sanctification" (in Holiness churches) or the "Baptism of the Holy Spirit" accompanied by the initial evidence of speaking in unknown tongues (in Pentecostal churches), but the conversion experience is fundamental to all of them. Worship in Evangelical communities often concludes with an emotional appeal to participants to present themselves for prayers for conversion. The fact that many Methodist churches, from the middle of the twentieth century, began to place less emphasis on the conversion experience is one indication of their location in the interstices between more traditional Protestant denominations and the Evangelical communities described in this chapter.[8]

A third identifying trait of Evangelical communities is the fact that they are typically organized as highly voluntary societies that do not expect support from civil governments but do expect toleration from governments. This contrasts with the historic experience of Lutheran, Reformed, and Anglican churches considered in chapter 3, which were organized in the sixteenth century as state-supported churches. The mode of organization of Evangelical communities, even as they become more formally organized churches, presupposes the notion of religious toleration that has prevailed since the time of the European Enlightenment. In countries where there is an established church (such as the United Kingdom), Evangelical churches will often be categorized as "free" churches.[9] Organization as voluntary societies can make Evangelical communities a very fluid phenomenon, difficult to tie down to specific denominational structures that persist through time, and Evangelical congregations often operate independent of any denominational structures. In addition to formally organized denominations and independent congregations, Evangelical culture involves a complex web of other organizations, such as Evangelistic associations (like the Billy Graham Evangelistic Association), independent ministry organizations, Evangelical publishing and media outlets, and organizations dedicated to the evangelization of specific constituencies (such as Campus Crusade for Christ, which focuses on evangelization on college and university campuses).

A further trait of Evangelical communities, not a defining trait but a very distinctive mark, is that in their concern for evangelization they often utilize elements of contemporary performance or entertainment culture in presenting the gospel. These contemporary cultural elements often become part of their patterns of worship. This is not a new development. Some Evangelical preachers of the eighteenth century (such as George Whitefield) were trained in drama, some utilized printed tracts to advocate their doctrines and broadsheets to announce their preaching occasions.[10] Evangelicals in the late nineteenth century developed "Gospel" music from the popular music-hall entertainment of the Victorian age. Evangelicals played a leading role in the development of radio and television media for religious broadcasting in the middle of the twentieth century,[11] and the genre of "Contemporary Christian" music in the late twentieth century built on the performance culture of rock and roll and other forms of popular music. This trait may make the teachings of Evangelical communities more difficult to assess in comparison with more traditional formulas, but it also indicates that they have developed a deep well of artistic talent in expressing the gospel, and this chapter will consider some of the creative and contemporary expressions of the gospel message on the part of Evangelical communities.

Although Evangelical communities do not always conform to the pattern of denominational traditions, there are some identifiable denominational traditions considered in this chapter, including the following groups of churches:

Baptist churches, in a variety of denominations and independent congregations.

Holiness churches: denominations including the Church of the Nazarene, the Church of God (Anderson, Indiana), and the Salvation Army.

Pentecostal churches: denominations including the Church of God in Christ, the Church of God (Cleveland, Tennessee), the Assemblies of God, Elim Pentecostal churches, the United Pentecostal Church, and others.

Adventist churches, the largest of which is the Seventh-day Adventist Church.

Some contemporary megachurches and new Evangelical movements, including the Willow Creek Community Church (South Barrington, Illinois), Saddleback Church (Lake Forest, California), the Yoido Full Gospel Church (Seoul, Korea), the Potter's House (Dallas, Texas), Calvary Chapel (Costa Mesa, California), and the Vineyard Christian Fellowship (Anaheim, California). Many of these originated as single, large congregations but have now expanded to become global communities of churches.

The inclusion of Adventist churches in this list may surprise some readers because there has been a strong tendency among conservative Evangelical churches to regard Adventists as sectarian and outside of the main stream of Evangelical life. This impression was based on the fact that in the middle of the nineteenth century, early Adventists did not affirm the doctrine of the Trinity and some other historic Christian teachings. However, the doctrinal teachings of Adventist churches evolved significantly through the nineteenth and early twentieth centuries as a result of which they have come to acknowledge a version of of the doctrine of the Trinity and other historic Christian teachings. They do retain distinctive practices (such as worship on Saturday), but I will argue that the received and transmitted teachings of Adventist churches today identify them within the larger family of Evangelical communities.

Beyond the denominational diversity discussed in the previous paragraphs, Evangelical communities also embrace a wide range of ethnic and racial diversity. Historically black churches in the United States represent a distinctive expression of Evangelical culture that cuts across denominational boundaries.[12] These churches consist, for the most part, of Baptist, Methodist, and Pentecostal churches, with the latter group increasingly important through the twentieth century.[13] Black churches in the United States do show the traits of Evangelical communities described here with the exception that the historically black Methodist denominations (as other Methodist denominations in the United States) have an episcopal polity that gives them a strongly central organization as contrasted with the more voluntary and local organization typical of black Pentecostal and Baptist churches.[14] This exception reveals that black churches do follow in many ways the patterns of their denominational families and yet there are distinctive marks of black churches considered together as a community that crosses denominational boundaries. At the point in the late nineteenth century when white Evangelical churches turned to a premillennial eschatology and retreated from involvement with social and political issues, black churches retained a strong commitment to social transformation, giving these churches a distinctive combination of an Evangelical ethos and progressive social involvement. Some of the phenomena that have been described as being distinctive of black churches are shared much more broadly within the Evangelical communities.[15] W. E. B. Du Bois, for example, writing "Of the Faith of the Fathers" in his classic account of *The Souls of Black Folk* (1903) pointed to three phenomena that characterized slave religion and subsequent African American religious traditions: "the Preacher, the Music, and the Frenzy."[16] But each of these traits was also descriptive of the broader Evangelical ethos, even if white Evangelicals denied the importance of such phenomena as enthusiastic preaching interlaced with emotive congregational responses, the use of mournful spirituals, and the "frenzy" associated with Evangelical worship. This chapter will show some of the specific ways in which the culture of black churches in the United States reflect the Christian gospel as it has been handed down in Evangelical Christian communities.[17]

The churches and other communities identified in this chapter as Evangelical[18] represent a very large phenomenon in contemporary global Christianity. Estimates of the number of Pentecostals alone vary hugely, from two hundred million to five hundred million or even more, although the larger numbers undoubtedly include many persons in Central and South America who would also be included among the numbers of Catholics. Combined with other Evangelical groups, the overall category of Evangelical communities includes a number of Christians in the hundreds of millions, a significant percentage of the overall number of Christians in the world today.[19]

One factor that makes it difficult to describe the extent to which Evangelical communities teach the same gospel as other churches is a strong tendency, especially prominent in the first generations of leaders of such movements, to distinguish themselves from other church communities. I will refer to this as a "centrifugal" tendency, that is, a tendency that represents movement away from other church communities. In differentiating themselves from other churches, new movements emphasize the doctrines and practices that uniquely distinguish their churches rather than the common teachings shared with others. Thus, in the early decades of the Adventist movement, Seventh-day Adventists emphasized their distinctive (and evolving) understanding of the return of Christ, their rejection of traditional Trinitarian doctrine, and their practice of observing

Saturday as the Christian sabbath, which they understood to be a sign of the "remnant" community preparing for the second advent of Christ. Similarly, early Holiness leaders stressed the distinctive experience of entire sanctification and early Pentecostal leaders stressed the distinctive experience of baptism of the Holy Spirit accompanied by the initial evidence of speaking in unknown tongues.

By the third or fourth generations of leadership in these movements, however, a reaction typically appears in the form of a tendency to emphasize teachings and practices held in common with other churches. This could be described using the sociological language of "institutionalization" or "routinization of charisma,"[20] but I shall refer to it as a "centripetal" tendency on the part of Evangelical Christian movements because it represents movement toward the culture of the broader Christian community. So late in the nineteenth century and into the twentieth century, the Seventh-day Adventist Church, though continuing its distinctive eschatology and some of its distinctive practices (such as worship on Saturday), altered its doctrinal statements to express a more traditional christology and a doctrine of the divine Trinity much more consistent with that of traditional churches. Holiness leaders eventually began to emphasize their ties to other Evangelical churches, and many Pentecostal churches began to emphasize the gift of tongues as one among many spiritual gifts given to believers. A few generations into the life of a movement, these Evangelical communities begin to use doctrinal statements, traditional creeds, music, and elements of historic Christian liturgies to express their common understanding of the gospel and central Christian teachings (see the section below on "New Signs of Affirmation of the Gospel").

Popular views of Evangelical movements and churches tend to emphasize what I have called their centrifugal tendencies, and in reporting the scale and overall impact of contemporary Evangelical movements throughout the world it is sometimes presupposed that these movements will retain all of the centrifugal characteristics that distinguished them from other groups in the first generations of leadership. But centripetal tendencies are already at work in many of these movements that are resulting in more and more institutionalized and denomination-like structures that will evolve significantly and, I believe, will come to resemble more traditional Christian communities.[21]

The remainder of this chapter will examine the proclamation of the common Christian gospel on the part of Evangelical communities, considering first how the gospel has been stated in formal doctrinal statements on the part of Evangelical communities, then considering how patterns of worship and Christian formation in these churches express the common gospel. The chapter concludes by examining some new forms of expression of the gospel on the part of Evangelical communities that utilize more traditional ways of affirming of the gospel message and so illustrate what I have called the centripetal tendencies in Evangelical communities in recent decades.

The Gospel in Evangelical Doctrinal Statements

Most Evangelical church groups have developed doctrinal statements, although two important qualifications must be noted in considering these statements. First, the development of doctrinal statements is not always the first priority of Evangelical groups which tend to be focused intensely on their evangelistic mission especially in early generations of leadership. So the development of doctrinal statements is itself a sign of the centripetal tendencies described earlier. The second qualification I would note is that due to the highly voluntary nature of Evangelical groups, doctrinal statements are seldom understood as having binding authority over larger groups. They are more likely to be understood as consensus statements that reflect general trends and beliefs but which are not imposed on local congregations or on individual believers. So, for example, the statement of "Baptist Faith and Message," adopted by the Southern Baptist Convention in 1925 and revised in 2000 states that confessions of faith are always subject to revision and any Baptist group "large or small" can draw up its own confession. Moreover, the document states that confessions of faith "are statements of religious convictions, drawn from the Scriptures, and are not to be used to hamper freedom of thought or investigation in other realms of life."[22] Evangelical doctrinal statements can only state very generally the doctrinal tendencies of Evangelical communities, but after considering these more formal statements of doctrine on the part of Evangelical communities, this chapter will then turn to expressions of the gospel in Evangelical worship (including music) and training materials, and these modes of reception of doctrine will complement the more general and formal expressions of doctrine on the part of Evangelical communities.

Evangelical doctrinal statements do give consistent expression to the gospel message. The New Hampshire Confession was affirmed in 1833 by the New Hampshire Baptist Convention. Its statement "Of the Way of Salvation" asserts the most basic elements of the gospel narrative in affirming:

> That the salvation of sinners is wholly of grace; through the Mediatorial Offices of the Son of God, who took upon him our nature, yet without sin; honored the law by his personal obedience, and made atonement for our sins by his death; being risen from the dead he is now enthroned in heaven . . .[23]

This confession of faith affirms Christ's life (including his fulfillment of the divine law), death, and resurrection, identifying Christ's death as the key element in the work of atonement. This teaching of substitutionary atonement will be a consistent emphasis in doctrinal statements on the part of Evangelical communities. The same language is used in the statement of "Baptist Faith and Message" (1925 and 2000), which adds the phrase "who *by the Holy Spirit was born of the Virgin Mary and* took upon him our nature . . ."[24] and thus affirms the doctrine of the incarnation in words similar to those of the Apostles' Creed.

The Church of the Nazarene is the largest denomination representing the Holiness movement. Its Articles of Faith (1908) reflect the denomination's Methodist and Anglican heritage. The second Article of Faith affirms the gospel narrative in these words:

> We believe in Jesus Christ, the Second Person of the Triune Godhead; that He was eternally one with the Father; that he became incarnate by the Holy Spirit and was born of the Virgin Mary, so that two whole and perfect natures, that is to say the Godhead and manhood, are thus united in one Person very God and very man, the God-man.
>
> We believe that Jesus Christ died for our sins, and that He truly arose from the dead and took again His body, together with all things appertaining to the perfection of man's nature, wherewith He ascended into heaven and is there engaged in intercession for us . . .[25]

This utilizes terms reminiscent of the ancient creeds in speaking of the incarnation ("he became incarnate by the Holy Spirit and was born of the Virgin Mary"). The language of "two whole and perfect natures" in the one person of Christ reflects the language of the Council of Chalcedon (451) as transmitted in the Anglican and Methodist Articles of Religion. A further article on atonement states that "Jesus Christ, by His sufferings, by the shedding of His own blood, and by his meritorious death on the Cross, made a full atonement for all human sin . . ."[26] This is significant within the scope of Evangelical communities because it affirms that the atonement involves more than simply the death of Christ, as other Evangelical doctrinal statements are inclined to affirm.

One of the largest Pentecostal denominations is the Assemblies of God. In their "Statement of Fundamental Truths," they affirm the central events of the gospel narrative as follows:

> The Lord Jesus Christ is the eternal Son of God. The Scriptures declare:
>
> a. His virgin birth (Matthew 1:23; Luke 1:31,35).
> b. His sinless life (Hebrews 7:26; 1 Peter 2:22).
> c. His miracles (Acts 2:22; 10:38).
> d. His substitutionary work on the cross (1 Corinthians 15:3; 2 Corinthians 5:21).
> e. His bodily resurrection from the dead (Matthew 28:6; Luke 24:39; 1 Corinthians 15:4).
> f. His exaltation to the right hand of God (Acts 1:9,11; 2:33; Philippians 2:9–11; Hebrews 1:3).[27]

This does affirm Christ's "substitutionary work on the cross," but it is cast in a larger framework that attributes saving significance to each of the elements of Christ's life affirmed in the statement.

Contemporary Evangelical megachurches tend to follow the lead of traditional Evangelical doctrinal statements in their claims about the narrative of Christ's works that constitute the gospel. The statement of the Saddleback Church (Lake Forest, California) is representative:

> Jesus Christ is the Son of God. He is co-equal with the Father. Jesus lived a sinless human life and offered Himself as the perfect sacrifice for the sins of all men by dying on a cross. He arose from the dead after three days to demonstrate His power over sin and death. He ascended to Heaven's glory and will return again to earth to reign as King of kings, and Lord of lords.[28]

As is typical of Evangelical doctrinal statements, the death of Christ on the cross is seen as the central act that is significant for salvation, whereas the resurrection is a sign or demonstration of God's victory in Christ. Other Evangelical megachurches and new movements have similar brief statements.[29] The Vineyard USA has a more expansive "Statement of Faith" with an article on "Christ the Mediator and Eternal King" that incorporates much more traditional language, not only affirming Christ's substitutionary death, but also the doctrine of two natures in one person (echoing the language of Chalcedon), a statement that Christ was "Conceived by the Holy Spirit and born of the Virgin Mary" (using the words of the Apostles' Creed), and a consistent emphasis on Christ's fulfillment of Old Testament prophecies concerning the Messiah.[30]

The doctrinal statements examined in this section so far—from Baptist, Nazarene, Assemblies of God, and Evangelical megachurches—illustrate in some ways the centripetal tendencies mentioned earlier in the introduction to this chapter. The fact that Baptists added words reminiscent of the Apostles' Creed to the older text of the New Hampshire Confession in framing the 1925 statement of "Baptist Faith and Message" shows this trend, as do the doctrinal statements of the Church of the Nazarene and The Vineyard USA, utilizing the expression "conceived by the Holy Spirit [and] born of the Virgin Mary." The fact that the Nazarene and Vineyard doctrinal statements make reference to one person of Christ in "two natures," following the traditional language of the fourth Ecumenical Council (451 C.E.), may also show this trend, although in the case of the Church of the Nazarene this language was inherited from the Methodist Articles of Religion.

Doctrinal statements of the Seventh-day Adventist Church regarding the work of Christ display both the centrifugal and centripetal tendencies noted above as they have evolved over the last hundred years or more.[31] An early "Declaration of the Fundamental Principles Taught and Practiced by the Seventh-day Adventists" (1872) affirmed the following about the work of Christ:

> That there is one Lord Jesus Christ, the Son of the Eternal Father, the one by whom God created all things, and by whom they do consist; that he took on him the nature of the seed of Abraham for the redemption of our fallen race; that he dwelt among men full of grace and truth, lived our example, died our sacrifice, was raised for our justification, ascended on high to be our only Mediator in the sanctuary in Heaven, where, with his own blood, he makes atonement for our sins; which atonement, so far from being made on the cross, which was but the offering of the sacrifice, is the very last portion of his work as Priest, according to the example of the Levitical priesthood, which foreshadowed and prefigured the ministry of our Lord in heaven. See Lv 16; Heb 8.4, 5, 9:6, 7; etc.[32]

This doctrinal statement reflects the very distinctive theology that had developed in the early decades of the Adventist movement in the United

States in the middle of the nineteenth century. Having expected the second advent of Christ in 1844 by the interpretation of the Revelation and other biblical books, Adventists became convinced after the passing of this date that it marked the time when Christ entered the heavenly temple to make intercession for humans. The 1872 doctrinal statement does not identify Christ as a person of the divine Trinity—in fact, Seventh-day Adventists at this point were not committed to trinitarian theology. Most importantly, the doctrinal statement from 1872 understands that Christ's work of atonement consists preeminently in his work of heavenly intercession and it specifically denies that the crucifixion is to be identified as the most critical act of the atonement, as historic Evangelical doctrinal statements had claimed.

In the late nineteenth century and the early twentieth century, under the leadership of Ellen G. White (1827–1915) and others, the Seventh-day Adventist Church made a series of revisions to its doctrinal statement and came to affirm traditional Christian doctrines much more clearly, including an affirmation of trinitarian teaching, though cast entirely in scriptural terms and thus not utilizing words like "Trinity" or "substance" (and this is often the case in Evangelical doctrinal statements). In the most recent revision (2005), the Seventh-day Adventist statement of twenty-eight "Fundamental Beliefs" has the following in its statement on "The Son":

> God the eternal Son became incarnate in Jesus Christ. Through Him all things were created, the character of God is revealed, the salvation of humanity is accomplished, and the world is judged. Forever truly God, He became also truly man, Jesus the Christ. He was conceived of the Holy Spirit and born of the virgin Mary. He lived and experienced temptation as a human being, but perfectly exemplified the righteousness and love of God. By His miracles He manifested God's power and was attested as God's promised Messiah. He suffered and died voluntarily on the cross for our sins and in our place, was raised from the dead, and ascended to minister in the heavenly sanctuary in our behalf. He will come again in glory for the final deliverance of His people and the restoration of all things.[33]

The statement is cast as an item on Christ as the second person of the Godhead. Christ's work for human salvation is seen as embracing the fullness of his life, death, resurrection, and heavenly intercession. In fact, a subsequent item in this doctrinal statement reiterates the atoning nature of Christ's "life of perfect obedience to God's will, His suffering, death, and resurrection."[34] Moreover, the statement quoted here utilizes the words of the Apostles' Creed ("conceived of the Holy Spirit and born of the virgin Mary") to express belief in Christ's incarnation. The only possibly distinctive note is the statement that Christ "ascended to minister in the heavenly sanctuary in our behalf," but other Evangelical confessions also state that Christ is "now enthroned in heaven" (New Hampshire Confession) and that Christ "ever liveth to make intercession for his people" (Abstract of Principles of Southern Baptist Seminary, Louisville, 1859).[35]

The Gospel in Evangelical Worship

As indicated earlier, the status of formal doctrinal statements in Evangelical communities gives these doctrinal statements somewhat less than binding authority as a result of the highly voluntary and often strictly congregational nature of Evangelical organizations. For this reason, it is important to find some measures of doctrinal reception in Evangelical communities, that is, indicators of how these formal doctrines are received, taught, and practiced in churches. This section considers specific aspects of worship including preaching and music in Evangelical communities that illustrate how doctrines regarding the gospel are received and taught. The next section will consider the reception of the gospel reflected in Evangelical tracts and other literature that might be described as catechetical insofar as they seek to teach the content of the Christian faith and thereby to form believers in the faith.

Because of the wide range and the constantly evolving character of Evangelical communities, it is difficult to make general observations about worship in these church traditions, and it is especially difficult to make general observations that could be construed as having doctrinal weight in the sense in which I have understood doctrine in this study. However, there are some consistent features that characterize worship in most of the Evangelical church traditions considered here, and these features illustrate the reception of the more formal doctrinal commitments considered earlier in this chapter.

Although worship in Evangelical churches and communities is a highly varied phenomenon, the following typical marks should be noted as general context for considering how Evangelical worship expresses the gospel.

> Worship typically involves the singing of hymns or songs by the whole congregation and often additional Christian music per-

formed by a choir or praise ensemble (see the next part of this section for further reflections on music in Evangelical communities).
- Worship typically involves prayer on the part of the whole congregation.
- Worship typically comes to focus in the reading of the Bible and the interpretation of the Bible in a sermon delivered by an authorized or ordained minister.
- Worship typically concludes with a call (sometimes described as an "altar call" or "invitation") to participants to make public commitments, especially a first-time commitment to Christ but also commitments to renewal in faith, commitments to Christian vocations, and perhaps commitments to seek the blessings of entire sanctification (in Holiness churches) or the baptism of the Holy Spirit (in Pentecostal churches).

These features are not completely uniform across the range of churches considered here. In addition to these items, personal testimony to life-changing experiences of faith may be a significant part of the worship experience in many Evangelical churches. In some Evangelical communities, the sermon may take more the form of an extended lesson on the meaning of scripture passages.[36] The Lord's Supper is celebrated occasionally, typically monthly or quarterly in Evangelical communities, and it is sometimes celebrated at a time other than Sunday morning, for example, in a Sunday-evening or Wednesday-evening service.[37]

But speaking of Sunday worship raises another important issue for understanding worship and how it conveys the gospel in Evangelical communities. Part of the creative evangelistic work of these churches has been the development of a variety of forms of worship, including informal outdoor preaching, camp meetings, revival meetings, assemblies of various sorts (such as Sunday School assemblies), occasions for hymn singing or testimonies, and prayer meetings. In recent decades, praise services and "seeker" services have extended the range of these alternatives to traditional worship. It is often the case that Sunday morning worship in these churches will retain a somewhat more formal and traditional character, whereas Sunday evening worship or assemblies on other occasions will have a much more informal character and again, as noted earlier, contemporary performance culture is likely to influence worship in these less formal assemblies.

Evangelical preaching, at least in its earlier forms, involved an emotive appeal urging sinners to repent and be converted, and pressing converted believers towards Christian holiness and particular moral and vocational commitments. Preachers declaimed a sermon in relatively short oral "periods" in which the voice would rise to a strongly emphasized cadence consisting typically of one or two emphasized syllables, followed by a pause (caesura) during which the speaker would breathe.[38] In some Evangelical preaching traditions, including traditional black preaching in the United States, these caesurae mark the points at which congregational responses may be expected ("Amen!" "Yes!"). The sermon as a whole replicates the pattern set by the individual periods, rising to an emotional pitch, the "cadence" for the whole sermon in which the preacher calls on hearers to repent, believe, and perhaps make public commitments to a sense of vocation or to a particular moral program (like abstinence from alcoholic beverages).

This "invitation" or "altar call," the conclusion to the Evangelical sermon, almost always makes an appeal to "the gospel," and in Evangelical communities, "the gospel" means both the message about the work of Jesus Christ, focused on Christ's substitutionary death on the cross, and the application of the work of Christ which occurs by faith, that is, by personal and affective trust in Christ for salvation.[39] Churches that offer a strong Evangelical invitation will make repeated appeals simultaneous with hymns or songs calling for participants to respond to the gospel call to believe and be saved. In most Evangelical communities, the invitation is a moment of high drama: sinners might be converted by divine grace, believers might be renewed in faith, persons with a dependency might be delivered, Christians might claim a vocation to a particular form of ministry.[40] Holiness and Pentecostal churches call during the invitation for persons to receive the baptism of the Holy Spirit, either in the Holiness sense of the gift of entire sanctification or in the Pentecostal sense of an outpouring of the Spirit accompanied by tongues. In many Evangelical churches—especially Holiness and Pentecostal churches—the congregation will offer special prayers for persons to be physically healed during the invitation.

The hymns and songs characteristically sung by congregations in Evangelical communities are particularly revealing of their understanding of the gospel. As noted in chapter three, hymn texts by themselves cannot be taken as direct evidence of communal consensus in teaching, since they are the work of individual poets. However, as hymn texts come to be included in hymn collections and then used in congregations, they come to reflect the communities that use them. Evangelical communities evolved in English-speaking cultural contexts that used the hymns of Watts and Wesley and the broader English hymn tradition that had developed from their poetical works (see chapter 3). In the early nineteenth century on the American frontier Evangelical Christian communities sang folk songs that have come to be called spirituals, relatively simple songs that were often handed on in an oral tradition, that is, apart from written or printed music. An example of an American folk song or spiritual from the early nineteenth century reflecting the gospel message is "Wondrous Love":

> What wondrous love is this,
> O my soul, O my soul,
> What wondrous love is this,
> O my soul!
> What wondrous love is this
> that caused the Lord of bliss
> to bear the dreadful curse
> for my soul, for my soul,
> to bear the dreadful curse
> for my soul.[41]

The tune that accompanies this text, as it is traditionally sung, is in the so-called Dorian mode, which had been preserved in folk musical traditions.[42] This is to the modern ear a haunting sound, answering to mode I of Gregorian chant and conveying a sense of mystery and reverence. The text is quite simple, with most words repeated in subsequent verses, but changing "to bear the dreadful curse for my soul" to "to lay aside his crown for my soul," or substituting a new repetitive verse such as "To God and to the Lamb, I will sing, I will sing."

Spirituals were utilized both in Euro-American and African American congregations, and in camp meetings and other worship settings involving black and white worshipers. Indeed, many traditional songs (like "Wondrous Love") appear to have been sung across the cultural boundaries of black and white Americans, so that many songs labeled as "African American spirituals" (or "Negro spirituals") were used in British American congregations as well.[43] An example of a spiritual mourning the crucifixion of Christ that is traditionally sung in black churches in the United States is "Were You There?"

> Were you there when they crucified my Lord? (were you there?)
> Were you there when they crucified my Lord?
> Oh!—Sometimes it cases me to tremble,
> tremble, tremble.
> Were you there when they crucified my Lord?[44]

Like "Wondrous Love," the spiritual "Were You There?" involves a simple melody, with most words repeated in each verse, but changing the words "crucified my Lord" in subsequent verses to "nailed him to the tree," "pierced him in the side," "when the sun refused to shine," and finally "laid him in the grave." And like Watts's "When I Survey the Wondrous Cross," this spiritual evokes the believer's affection in contemplating the mystery of the cross: "sometimes it causes me to tremble . . ."

In the late nineteenth century in the United States, Evangelical communities were at the forefront of the development of a new and more complex musical style reflecting the musical performance culture of the Victorian age. This new Christian music has been historically identified as "Gospel" music, and in this case again the term "gospel" refers not only to the narrative of God's work in Jesus Christ but also to the experience of believers in appropriating this message. Produced and marketed by music companies in the United States and in the United Kingdom, Gospel music was distributed by way of small song books with titles such as *Songs of Redeeming Love* (1882), *Songs of the Soul No. 2* (1896), and *The Voice of Praise* (1904).[45] Subtitles of these collections reveal that the new songs were utilized in a variety of settings, such as revivals, Sunday school assemblies, "Sunday evening congregations," and "young peoples meetings."[46] Thus the new music made its appearance in the first place outside of the context of regular Sunday-morning worship, and in this respect it bears parallels to earlier forms of Christian music celebrating the gospel but not originally intended for the regular weekly worship of Christian congregations, for example, medieval carols or eighteenth-century sacred oratorios.

The following text of the widely used Gospel song "Revive Us Again" by William P. Mackay (1863) expresses the believer's joy in the work of God in Christ's death and resurrection:

> We praise thee, O God!
> for the Son of Thy love,
> For Jesus, who died,
> and is now gone above.
> Hallelujah! Thine the glory,
> Hallelujah! Amen.
> Hallelujah! Thine the glory,
> Revive us again.[47]

The focus on the saving effect of Christ's crucifixion in Gospel music was so strong that Gospel songs have been derided as "the blood hymns," but the blood imagery does invoke the sacrificial language that was part of the older Christian tradition in speaking of the work of Christ. The following Gospel song by Fanny J. Crosby, written sometime before 1882, is exemplary:

> Redeemed, how I love to proclaim it!
> Redeemed by the blood of the Lamb;
> Redeemed thro' His infinite mercy,
> His child and forever I am.
> Redeemed, redeemed,
> Redeemed by the blood of the Lamb;
> Redeemed, how I love to proclaim it!
> His child and forever I am.[48]

As was the case with spirituals, both black and white Evangelical communities in the United States utilized the genre of Gospel music, and both black and white musicians and poets contributed to the development of the genre.[49] Andraé Crouch's "The Blood Will Never Lose Its Power" (1966) offers a reflection on the work of Christ in the genre of the black Gospel music tradition:

> The blood that Jesus shed for me,
> Way back on Calvary,
> The blood that gives me strength from day to day,
> It will never lose its power.
> [Chorus:]
> It reaches to the highest mountain,
> It flows to the lowest valley.
> The blood that gives me strength from day to day,
> It will never lose its power.[50]

Crouch's song, like the one by Fanny Crosby, illustrates the tendency on the part of Gospel songs to emphasize the strength and comfort that comes from the divine grace offered in the gospel. But the gospel message itself—and here I mean very specifically the narrative of the life, death, and resurrection of Jesus Christ—is repeated with great consistency in the repertory of Gospel music. So the popular song by Katherine Hankey, the chorus of which is given at the beginning of this chapter, declares:

> I love to tell the story
> Of unseen things above,
> Of Jesus and his glory,
> Of Jesus and his love.[51]

Just as Gospel music developed as a Christian expression of the musical performance culture of the late nineteenth century, so the genre of "Contemporary Christian" music developed in the later twentieth century as a Christian expression of the musical performance culture associated with rock and roll, blues, punk, heavy metal, hip-hop, and other forms of popular music. However unorthodox it may sound, Contemporary Christian music has it its core the Evangelical message about God's love in Jesus Christ and the believer's experience of this love through faith in Christ. A good example is the popular Contemporary Christian song "Lord, I Lift Your Name on High" by Rick Founds, which has the chorus:

> You came from heaven to earth
>   to show the way.
> From the earth to the cross,
>   my debt to pay.
> From the cross to the grave,
>   from the grave to the sky;
> Lord, I lift Your name on high.[52]

Whether or not this song is based intentionally on I Corinthians 15:3–4, each of the elements of the primitive Christian kerygma is present in its chorus: it celebrates Christ's death "for our sins" (in the typical Evangelical formula of substitutionary atonement, "my debt to pay"), it celebrates Christ's burial and resurrection, then offers a concluding doxological ascription ("I lift your name on high").

Contemporary Christian music can also offer creative ways of retelling the narrative about Jesus. "Breath of Heaven (Mary's Song)" by Amy Grant and Chris Eaton (1992) is a performed song (that is, not designed for congregational singing) recorded in recent years by Amy Grant and Jessica Simpson, among others. It offers an insight into the birth of Jesus from the perspective of the Blessed Virgin, reminiscent of medieval carols celebrating the role of Mary in the Christmas narrative:

> I am waiting in a silent prayer.
> I am frightened by the load I bear.
> In a world as cold as stone,
> Must I walk this path alone?
> Be with me now.
> Be with me now.
> Breath of heaven,
> Hold me together,

> Be forever near me,
> Breath of heaven.
> Breath of heaven,
> Lighten my darkness,
> Pour over me Your holiness,
> For You are holy.[53]

It is sometimes objected that Contemporary Christian music lacks the depth of traditional hymnody, especially because of its highly repetitive nature. But spirituals were highly repetitive as are the contemporary Taizé songs utilized in many churches, and few would claim that they lack depth simply because of their repetitive nature. I would argue that the question of depth cannot be resolved immediately. I can imagine the same argument about lack of depth being inveighed against Gospel songs when they were first introduced in the late nineteenth century, but a process of reflection and elimination over a hundred years or more has enabled Christian communities to identify a corpus of Gospel music now utilized very broadly in Protestant and occasionally in Catholic worship. I suspect that a similar process will enable Christian communities in the future to identify a similar corpus of Contemporary Christian music, although by that time the distinction between Gospel and Contemporary Christian may be merely historical.

The Gospel in Evangelism and Training Media

Another indication of the Evangelical understanding of the gospel message comes by considering popularly utilized Evangelical tracts and other media designed for introducing persons to the Christian faith and for formation in Christian faith. These represent what in other Christian traditions might be described as catechetical materials. Evangelicals had utilized tracts since the eighteenth century. The British Evangelical leader Hannah More, for example, began producing a series of "Cheap Repository Tracts" from the 1790s after studying popular literature and learning how it caught the attention of common people.[54] The American Tract Society was organized in 1825 and since that time has made a variety of Evangelical literature available.

One of the most popular Evangelical tracts of recent decades is entitled "Have You Heard of the Four Spiritual Laws?" and was produced by Campus Crusade for Christ, Incorporated, from 1965. The organization's

Web site, which continues to make this tract available, indicates that more than a hundred million copies have been distributed.[55] The tract presents the Christian faith in four main points: (1) God's love for humankind, (2) human separation from God due to sin, (3) Christ as God's "provision" for human sin, and (4) the need to "receive" Jesus Christ by personal faith. It is the third point which states the gospel message most directly:

> Jesus Christ is God's only provision for man's sin. Through him
> you can know and experience God's love and plan for your life.[56]

Three subpoints are made following this thesis or "law": first, "He died in our place"; second, "He rose from the dead"; and third, "He is the only way."[57] On the second subpoint, the tract quotes I Corinthians 15:3–6. Consistent with other Evangelical literature, the emphasis here is on Christ's substitutionary death, and the resurrection is seen as the preeminent sign of God's victory in Christ.

A further and more contemporary instance of the reception of Evangelical teaching for Christian formation can be seen in the popular "Alpha" video teaching series developed by Nicky Gumbel at Holy Trinity (Anglican) Church, Brompton, London. Although this was developed in an Anglican parish and has been widely used in Catholic as well as Protestant churches, it reflects most clearly the Christian gospel as it has been understood in Evangelical Christian traditions. The Alpha Web site indicates that more than eight million persons have completed the Alpha course since its inception in the 1980s.[58] Nicky Gumbel's *Questions of Life: A Practical Introduction to the Christian Faith* (1993) summarizes the content of the Alpha course, and chapters 2 and 3 of *Questions of Life* deal directly with the gospel message about Jesus Christ. Chapter 2 is concerned primarily with the status of historical evidence for the veracity of the knowledge of Jesus given in the Christian scriptures.[59] Chapter 3 presents the meaning of the gospel message in response to the question, "Why did Jesus Die?" In this chapter Gumbel lays out "The Problem," which is human separation from God caused by sin and the death that humans owe because of their participation in sin. Then Gumbel describes "The Solution," which is God's "self-substitution" in Jesus Christ, God taking on the penalty of sin that humans universally owe. Gumbel proceeds to describe "The Result" of Christ's work using a number of metaphors, but in first place is the forensic metaphor of Christ who "paid the penalty of sin" for humankind on the cross. Other metaphors—those of the marketplace, the temple, and the home—give added depth for understanding the Christ event.[60]

New Signs of Affirmation of the Gospel

A visitor to the Sunday morning service at the Yoido Full Gospel Church in Seoul, Korea, might observe its ordained ministers in liturgical robes seated in the chancel behind a large communion table. The visitor recognizes a hymn tune played on the pipe organ as "Old 100th," a psalm tune derived from sixteenth-century Geneva, and the visitor hears the congregation singing to this tune in the Korean language a translation of a doxology composed by the seventeenth-century Anglican bishop Thomas Ken:

> Praise God, from whom all blessings flow;
> Praise him, all creatures here below;
> Praise him above, ye heavenly host;
> Praise Father, Son, and Holy Ghost.[61]

A few minutes later the visitor hears the congregation reciting something together. From the rhythm of their voices the visitor might realize that they are saying the Apostles' Creed, the baptismal creed that had been utilized in Western churches since ancient times.[62]

The Yoido Full Gospel Church is probably the largest Christian congregation in the world, numbering in excess of seven hundred thousand members. As the phrase "Full Gospel" in its name suggests, it is a Pentecostal church and Pentecostal churches traditionally have not had clergy wearing liturgical robes, choirs and congregations singing doxologies, or congregations reciting creeds. The Sunday morning worship of the Yoido Full Gospel Church is a clear sign of what I have called the centripetal tendency in the life of Evangelical movements.[63]

The worship of the Yoido Full Gospel Church is not at all an isolated phenomenon, though Korean Christian culture has been strongly influenced by Presbyterian and Methodist church cultures since the coming of missionaries from those denominations in the 1890s, and the Presbyterian and Methodist influence could account for the ease with which Pentecostal congregations in Korea can take on more traditional forms of worship. But the centripetal tendency in Evangelical worship can be seen much more broadly, for example, in Baptist congregations beginning to celebrate the season of Advent along with Christmas and Easter, and in Evangelical congregations utilizing doxologies, the *Gloria Patri,* responsive readings, and in some cases historic creeds. It can be seen in the practice of an Assemblies of God congregation in Texas that offers visitors a statement of the congregation's basic beliefs in a small sheet including only the

Apostles' Creed and the Nicene Creed (with the *filioque* clause).[64] It can be heard in the music of the choir of a Bible church in Maryland singing in the local shopping mall the fifth century (C.E.) text of Aurelius Clemens Prudentius's "Of the Father's Love Begotten," to the thirteenth-century chanted tune with which that text has come to be associated.[65]

A further indication of the centripetal tendencies of contemporary Evangelicalism can be seen in the so-called emergent church phenomenon mentioned in the introduction to this book. The emergent theologian Brian D. McLaren describes in the book how his congregation in Maryland began to use the Nicene Creed:

> Many years ago our church (nonliturgical in its origins) began using the Nicene Creed in our public worship. For the first year or two we edited one word in the Creed, changing "We believe in one holy catholic and apostolic church" to "We believe in one holy universal and apostolic church," embarrassed to use the word *catholic* for fear we would be accused (by angry ex-Catholics, for the most part) of latent papacy.[66]

The congregation eventually learned the meaning of "catholic" and so came to recite the creed in the received form without alteration. Other contemporary evangelical communities have developed what they call "ancient modern" worship, blending elements of ancient or medieval Christian traditions in a format of contemporary Christian worship.

The Meaning of the Gospel in Evangelical Communities

What then does the gospel mean in the Evangelical communities considered in this chapter? As in other church traditions, the basic narrative of Christ's life, death, and resurrection remains the center of the essential gospel message. In fact, "crucicentrism," a focus on the centrality of Christ's work of redemption on the cross, has been described as a distinctive mark of Evangelical culture,[67] although the material presented in chapters 2 and 3 show that the gospel message also characterizes ancient Christian churches and older Protestant churches as well. The gospel narrative is not typically conveyed in Evangelical communities by way of the historic creeds, though one of the trends noted in the last section is the fact that some Evangelical communities have begun to use the Apostles' Creed and the Nicene Creed. The narrative of Christ's work is affirmed in Evangelical doctrinal statements and in worship is conveyed through preaching and the use of the varied forms of Evangelical church music considered above.

In the context of Evangelical communities, the gospel came to denote both the saving narrative of Christ's work and the way in which believers appropriate this by affective, personal faith. There is no separating these matters in Evangelical culture, so in spirituals, Gospel songs, Contemporary Christian music, and the "Four Spiritual Laws" tract, the crux of Evangelical experience is the personal decision, prompted by divine grace, to "accept" or "receive" Jesus Christ, placing one's trust in Christ as one would trust one's dearest friend. Evangelical music celebrates the inspiration and strength, the power of divine grace derived from this experience.

Evangelical doctrinal statements place a very consistent and strong emphasis on the substitutionary death of Christ as the primary way of understanding the salvific meaning of the gospel. This is not inconsistent with earlier formulations: the most primitive strand of the gospel tradition examined in this book states that "Christ died for our sins . . ." and substitution was at least one of the meanings associated with sacrifice in ancient cultures. This does raise a problem, however: an emphasis on the substitutionary death of Christ can overshadow other meanings of the incarnation in Evangelical communities and can lead to the impression that Christ's miracles, Christ's teachings, Christ's suffering and even Christ's resurrection are simply signs of Christ's divinity but without saving significance. This is perhaps related to the Evangelical concern for the communicability or intelligibility of the gospel message in evangelizing modern persons, especially since the sacrificial contexts of ancient cultures are not easily comprehended by modern persons, and the notion of "substitution" of Christ's death in place of our own is a simpler concept to convey.

As Evangelical communities evolve, I expect in the future to see continuing instances of both the centrifugal and centripetal tendencies observed in this chapter, that is, the emergence of new Evangelical communities which appear to make a radical break with traditional Christian faith, and then over a period of generations begin to knit themselves back into the fabric of more historic Christian beliefs and practices. It is by now a long-standing pattern in the history of Evangelical communities, and this process represents one of the ways in which Christian faith grows in the contemporary world. But looking back more deeply in Christian history and experience, one can see similar patterns: the radical commitment of early Christian monks in the Egyptian desert of the fourth century and their eventual regularization in the structures of medieval monasticism, the radical challenge of mendicant orders in the thirteenth century and continuing struggles within these orders to maintain the primitive simplicity of their founders as the orders expanded in popular culture. Similar tendencies are already at work in Evangelical communities, as we have seen, and as these communities experience the centripetal force that drives them to identify themselves as part of the *magna ecclesia,* the "great congregation" of all the faithful, clarity about the central meaning of the gospel and the ability to perceive the gospel in older Christian communities become increasingly crucial matters.

5

The Gospel and the Ecumenical Movement

... we exist as Christians by the Tradition of the Gospel ...
testified in Scripture, transmitted in and by the Church
through the power of the Holy Spirit

—Fourth World Conference on Faith
and Order, Montreal, 1963

The Ecumenical Movement

The ecumenical movement is a movement of Christian churches that seeks to make visible their essential unity in Christ.[1] This definition presupposes that unity itself is a given and is in fact a gift of God; unity is not something that can itself be created by human beings. The concern of the ecumenical movement has been with the visible disunity of Christian churches, that is, whatever unity the churches may possess is not apparent in the manifold divisions of the churches. The ecumenical movement, then, seeks to make visible this essential unity of the church in a variety of ways: in worship, in teaching, and in practical forms of service and witness. As it is understood here, the ecumenical movement is not at all confined to activity on the part of the churches that have formally participated in the World Council of Churches (WCC), although the work of the WCC stands as a particularly concrete example of the accomplishments of the ecumenical movement in the twentieth century and beyond.

The Faith and Order movement is a particular expression of the ecumenical movement that has been concerned with church-dividing issues of doctrine (faith) and polity (order). Although Faith and Order work was incorporated into the WCC, the Faith and Order Commission of the WCC has a membership that is more inclusive than the membership of the WCC itself. Most notably, the Catholic Church is a full participant in the Faith and Order Commission of the WCC, although it is not a member of the plenary of the WCC. Similarly, some Pentecostal churches and other Evangelical churches participate (sometimes informally) in Faith and Order events even though they do not participate in other activities of the WCC or in other formal ecumenical bodies. This chapter considers some particular ways in which the ecumenical movement, especially in the twentieth century, came to recognize and celebrate the gospel as it is shared between Christians of visibly divided traditions.

One of the most important contributions of the Faith and Order movement to the ecumenical movement more broadly was its early recognition that the unity of Christian churches depends upon their common affirmation and transmission of the gospel. The first World Conference on Faith and Order was held in Lausanne, Switzerland, in August 1927. The final report of that conference included a section on "The Church's Message to the World—The Gospel." This section was adopted by the conference with no dissenting voices.[2] It includes a concise exposition of the basic Christian message, including the following:

> The message of the Church to the world is and must always remain the Gospel of Jesus Christ. The Gospel is the joyful message of redemption, both here and hereafter, the gift of God to sinful man in Jesus Christ. . . .
>
> Through His life and teaching, His call to repentance, His proclamation of the coming of the Kingdom of God and of judgment, His suffering and death, His resurrection and exaltation to the right hand of the Father, and by the mission of the Holy Spirit, He has brought us forgiveness of sins, and has revealed the fulness of the living God and His boundless love toward us.[3]

The identification of the gospel in this way became a standard feature of early Faith and Order documents. The final report of the third World Conference on Faith and Order, held in Lund, Sweden, in August 1952, has a similar though somewhat briefer account of the narrative of Christ's work in a section on "The Faith of the Church in the Father, the Son, and the Holy Spirit."[4]

This sense of the gospel as the core narrative of Christ's work came to influence the broader body of the ecumenical movement represented in the WCC after the Faith and Order movement became a constituent part of the WCC at the organizational assembly of the Council in Amsterdam in 1948. In some cases, the WCC simply expressed the desire for unity in the message proclaimed by the churches. A hymn written by Frederick B. Morley for the second Assembly of the World Council of Churches, which met in 1954 in Evanston, Illinois, expresses the desire that the churches together might proclaim "one message":

> O church of God, united to serve one common Lord,
> proclaim to all one message,
> with hearts in glad accord.[5]

This desire became much more explicit in the third plenary assembly of the WCC which met in 1961 in New Delhi and adopted a critical report on the unity of the church. In this report, unity is envisioned as a fellowship of churches "holding the one apostolic faith, preaching the one Gospel . . . "[6] A commentary following this statement explicates the meaning of "the one apostolic faith" as follows:

> The Holy Scriptures of the Old and New Testament witness to the apostolic faith. This is nothing else than those events which constitute God's call of a people to be his people. The heart of the Gospel (*Kerygma*) is Jesus Christ himself, his life and teaching, his death, resurrection, coming (*parousia*) and the justification and sanctification which he brings and offers to all men. There are important studies now being undertaken of the relationship between Scripture and Tradition (which is Christian Confession down the ages), and attention is drawn to the work of Faith and Order's Theological Commission on Tradition and Traditions.[7]

All of the critical elements that constitute the gospel message are present in this statement. It rehearses the events of Christ's "life and teaching, his death, resurrection, [and his second] coming (*parousia*)," it asserts that these events have brought about the possibility of human salvation ("the justification and sanctification which he brings and offers to all" human beings), and it asserts that this message is consistent with "The Holy Scriptures of the Old and New Testament," that is, the message is "in accordance with the scriptures." The last sentence of the quotation points to the work that was already underway examining the relationship between the Christian scriptures and Christian tradition, and the next section of this book considers this critical contribution to the understanding of the gospel in the ecumenical movement.

The Gospel as the Ground of Scripture and Tradition

From the early 1960s, the Faith and Order movement began to develop an ecumenical response to the crucially divisive issue of the authority of the Christian scriptures in relation to the authority of tradition in the churches. The Ecumenical movement at that point formally embraced older Protestant churches and Eastern Orthodox churches, but the Second Vatican Council (1962–1965) was underway and a critical meeting of the Faith and Order Commission in Montreal in 1963 included some Catholic participants who were participants in the Second Vatican Council and some Protestants serving as observers at the Vatican Council. These participants had to fly back and forth between Montreal and meetings in preparation for the late 1963 session of the Vatican Council in Rome.[8] With the participation of Catholics as well as Eastern Orthodox Christians in the work of Faith and Order, the issue of the relationship between the scriptures and the traditions of the churches that had been critically divisive at the time of the Protestant Reformation now faced the ecumenical movement.

In fact, differences over the authority of scripture and tradition had been divisive earlier in the history of the church: Irenaeus and Tertullian, mentioned in chapter 1, had to argue against the scriptures that had been used by Marcion, Valentinus, and other teachers in the second century.[9] Chapter 1 has shown how these controversies led to the definition of the Christian canon of scripture affirmed in the churches. In the Middle Ages, the authority of the bishops of Rome (popes) in relation to the authority of Ecumenical Councils became a critical issue dividing Latin and Greek Christianity.[10] It was the Reformation's sense of the unique authority of scripture, however, that set up the most problematic issues for the twentieth-century ecumenical movement. Protestants had sought a church reformed by fidelity to the scriptures and tended to see later traditions as evidence of corruption.[11] Catholic and Orthodox churches, by contrast, understood subsequent Christian traditions as the faithful development of the faith taught in the scriptures.

The fourth World Conference on Faith and Order, which met in Montreal in 1963, dealt with these historically divisive issues. Protestant, Eastern Orthodox, and Catholic theologians all participated in the dialogue. The report of this conference entitled "Scripture, Tradition, and traditions" is a landmark ecumenical document and has served as the basis for subsequent ecumenical development. The lowercase "t" in the title is significant, for the crucial breakthrough came in the nuanced way in which the document distinguished different senses of "tradition," especially the first sense given as follows:

- "Tradition" or "the Tradition," with an uppercase letter "T," is defined as "the Gospel itself, transmitted from generation to generation in and by the Church, Christ himself present in the life of the Church."
- The singular term "tradition," with a lowercase letter "t," is defined as "the traditionary process."
- The plural term "traditions" (also lowercase "t") is understood in three senses: (a) "the diversity of forms of expression"; (b) "what we call confessional traditions, for instance, the Lutheran tradition or the Reformed tradition"; and (c) "cultural traditions."[12]

It should be clear that what this document means by "Tradition" or "the Tradition" (the first definition given here) is what this book has consistently examined as the gospel as it was transmitted from the ancient church through the centuries. This is stated specifically in the document:

> Thus we can say that we exist as Christians by the Tradition of the Gospel (the paradosis of the kerygma) testified in Scripture, transmitted in and by the Church through the power of the Holy Spirit. Tradition taken in this sense is actualized in the preaching of the Word, in the administration of the Sacraments and worship, in Christian teaching and theology, and in mission and witness to Christ by the lives of the members of the Church. . . . We can speak of Tradition (with a capital T), whose content is God's revelation and self-giving in Christ, present in the life of the Church.[13]

The recognition of this particular sense of "Tradition" was a breakthrough in the dialogue over the relationship between scripture and tradition. Catholic, Orthodox, and Protestant participants all recognized a sense in which tradition precedes the Christian scriptures, that is, in the very particular sense in which I Corinthians 15:1–4 and other New Testament texts explicitly referred to the earlier transmission of the good news, the apostolic witness to Christ. In fact, this sense of tradition fit well with Protestant and Catholic New Testament scholarship, which had come to recognize the layers of tradition underlying New Testament texts and the importance of the pre-Pauline kerygma in the evolution of the New Testament literature.[14] This development allowed Protestants to value "tradition" in a new and much more positive way than in the past,[15] and it has served as a basis for subsequent ecumenical work, for example, the project of the World Council of Churches "Towards the Common Expression of the Apostolic Faith Today" (see the next section) and "The COCU Consensus" (1985), a basis for proposed church union in the United States.[16]

The Apostolic Faith in the Ancient Creeds

The Lausanne 1927 statement of the gospel as the churches' message to the world could stand on its own as an eloquent if terse summary of the Christian message at the beginning of the modern ecumenical movement. The 1963 explication of "Scripture, Tradition, and traditions" did not alter the basic sense of what the gospel, now identified as the heart of Christian "Tradition," meant on the part of the Faith and Order movement. This statement did clarify how utterly central the gospel message was in the formation of Christian scripture and in the complex relationships between Christian scripture and Christian tradition. In the 1980s and 1990s, the Faith and Order Commission undertook a new project that extended the Commission's work on the meaning of the Christian gospel by inviting churches to discern the apostolic faith in the historic creeds, preeminently in the Nicene Creed.

Behind this "Apostolic Faith" project lay the conviction in the broader ecumenical movement that unity between the churches would depend on three critical matters: common affirmation of the apostolic faith, mutual recognition of baptism and eucharist, and the development of structures that would allow for common decision making and common service on the part of the churches.[17] The project that led to the consensus document on *Baptism, Eucharist, and Ministry* (1982) addressed the second concern, and an on-going study of "The Nature and Mission of the Church" (still in draft form) deals with the third set of issues. The project on "The Common Expression of the Apostolic Faith Today" responded to the first of these three issues.

An early response was a proposal to develop a new statement of faith that would serve as a contemporary reaffirmation of the apostolic faith on the part of participating churches. A draft of "A Common Statement of Our Faith" was offered at a meeting of the Faith and Order Commission in Bangalore in 1978. This statement includes a somewhat awkward affirmation of the gospel in these terms:

> we confess the reality of the *Event of Jesus Christ*—his life, his death, his resurrection—and the reality of our answer of faith, given to that Event, that brings us, through the Spirit, to the [*sic*] incorporation into Christ, which means our salvation.[18]

But the project of developing a contemporary affirmation of the faith was quickly dropped in favor of an attempt to ask churches how they could discern the apostolic faith in historic creeds.

The Faith and Order movement had recognized from its very beginning in 1927 that because the Apostles' Creed was a Western creed and had not been used in Eastern churches, only the Nicene Creed could serve as a truly ecumenical statement of faith expressing the common faith of Eastern and Western Christians. It had also been recognized from 1927 that some ecclesial bodies were "noncredal," that is to say, did not utilize creeds as statements of faith.[19] In the light of these observations, the project on "The Common Expression of the Apostolic Faith Today" asked churches if they could discern the apostolic faith *expressed in* the Nicene Creed.[20] The focus of this study, then, was not to produce a consensus document but was, rather, to ask Christian communities how they discerned the common faith expressed in the Nicene Creed, meaning the received form of the Creed referred to consistently in the Faith and Order documents as the "Nicene-Constantinopolitan" Creed.[21]

The "Apostolic Faith" project undertaken by Faith and Order led to the publication in 1991 of *Confessing the One Faith: An Ecumenical Explication of the Apostolic Faith as it is Confessed in the Nicene-Constantinopolitan Creed* (381).[22] This document offers a commentary on the Nicene Creed, carefully noting differences between Christian communities and also points at which the Christian message stands in continuity with and differs with the claims of other religious traditions and the claims made by modern secular cultures. In commenting on the Creed's affirmation of Christ's suffering and death (¶¶ 127–161) and Christ's resurrection (¶¶ 162–192), *Confessing the One Faith* acknowledges the biblical images of Christ's death as accomplishing a vicarious sacrifice, but the contemporary commentary emphasizes the meaning of Christ's death and resurrection as overcoming the power of death.[23]

The Gospel in Ecumenical Liturgical Renewal

Chapters 2 through 4 have shown how the formal affirmation of the gospel in creeds and other doctrinal statements was "received" and confessed in practices of worship in the varied church traditions. There is a parallel to this phenomenon in the ways in which doctrinal claims on the part of ecumenical bodies came to expression in forms of Christian worship, especially in Catholic and Protestant churches, that had been transformed by the liturgical renewal movement of the twentieth century. Beginning early in the twentieth century Catholic scholars had worked on revising the inherited liturgies of the church with an emphasis on the active participation of the congregation in music and rituals. The Second Vatican Council's "Constitution on the Sacred Liturgy" (1963) validated the impetus toward liturgical reform and led to the adoption in 1970 of a revised Roman missal and a revised "Rite of Christian Initiation for Adults" including a new baptismal liturgy. Protestant and Anglican churches also engaged in liturgical study leading to liturgical reform and renewal. Reformed and Methodist churches renewed older forms of worship that had characterized their own traditions early on and came to celebrate the whole cycle of the Christian year by the middle of the twentieth century. From the 1960s forward, Catholic and Protestant liturgical renewal proceeded along very similar paths, incorporating ancient liturgical patterns and leading to revised Protestant and Anglican liturgies for baptism and eucharist that share many traits in common.

The rite of baptism was revised by Catholics and Protestants to include an explicit profession of faith using the Apostles' Creed set in an interrogatory format. Chapter one has shown how the creed was put in an interrogatory form in the Latin recension of *The Apostolic Tradition* and how the creed was recited aloud by candidates for baptism in Augustine's narrative of the conversion, profession of faith, and baptism of Marius Victorinus. In the ritual for adult baptism now utilized by Anglicans and Methodists and others, the celebrant examines the candidates by asking the following questions:

> Do you believe in God the Father?
> Do you believe in Jesus Christ, the Son of God?
> Do you believe in God the Holy Spirit?[24]

In this form, the candidates—and sometimes the whole congregation along with them—respond to each question by reciting the appropriate section (or "article") of the Apostles' Creed. In the Catholic Rite of Christian Initiation of Adults, the questions are themselves posed in the form of interrogations that involve the whole text of each article of the Apostles' Creed. The celebrant asks each candidate individually concerning each of the three articles. Concerning the first article, for example, the celebrant asks:

> [Name of the candidate], do you believe in God, the Father almighty, creator of heaven and earth?

And the candidate responds:

> I do.[25]

Although the interrogatory forms differ between the church traditions, in each case candidates are asked to make a full profession of the baptismal creed at the time of their baptism or confirmation. In doing so, they profess the ancient rule of faith that transmits the gospel narrative.

Liturgical revisions on the part of the Catholic Church and many Protestant churches in the twentieth century also made the proclamation of Christ in the eucharist more explicit by adopting memorial acclamations on the part of the congregation. The precedent for this was the custom of ancient African churches in which Christ's work was summarized in short acclamations stated by the whole congregation. The fact that these acclamations in the African churches were in Greek, though embedded in later Coptic liturgies, shows that they came from a very ancient practice of Christian churches in Africa and perhaps elsewhere.[26] Following this precedent, Protestant and Anglican churches as well as the Catholic Church added to the eucharistic prayer a set of memorial acclamations on the part of the congregation. In one form of the Catholic rite, the presiding minister says, "The mystery of faith," and the congregation replies,

> We announce your death, O Lord, and we confess your resurrection until you come again.[27]

In another form of these acclamations, the presiding minister says, "Let us proclaim the mystery of faith" and the congregation replies:

> Christ has died,
> Christ is risen,
> Christ will come again.[28]

The latter form of the acclamations was first used by Catholics in an English version of the 1970 ritual for the mass, but they were taken up by Protestant and Anglican churches as well in the 1970s and 1980s.[29] The use of the memorial acclamations in the eucharist makes explicit Paul's claim that "as often as you eat this bread and drink the cup, you proclaim the Lord's death until he comes" (I Corinthians 11:26) and it is significant that, following this scripture passage, the element of expectation of Christ's return is consistently a part of the memorial acclamations.

The Meaning of the Gospel in the Ecumenical Movement

The ecumenical movement in the twentieth century and beyond—especially the Faith and Order component of the ecumenical movement—has shown a central concern with the Christian gospel. When the content of the gospel is explicitly given, as it was in the final report of the 1927 Lausanne World Conference on Faith and Order or in the statement on unity accepted by the 1961 New Delhi assembly of the WCC, it includes the same elements identified in previous chapters as constituting the gospel, namely, the narrative of Christ's life, death and resurrection, the claim that God's salvation for humankind is effected through these events, and the claim that this faith is "in accordance with the scriptures," that is, that it affirms one God revealed in both the Old and New Testaments, the maker or creator of all things. A particular trend within Faith and Order work since 1982 has emphasized the discernment of the gospel in the Nicene Creed rather than the creation of a new creed or profession on the part of the ecumenical movement, and the study of *Confessing the One Faith* makes it clear how each of these elements of the gospel is affirmed in the Nicene Creed.

Even more importantly, the ecumenical movement has consistently represented the gospel as the heart of the Christian faith, the core of the "apostolic faith" the profession of which is essential for any expression of visible Christian unity. The use of an interrogatory affirmation of the baptismal creed (the Apostles' Creed) in the Catholic Church and in Protestant churches and the use of the memorial acclamations in the eucharist in these churches show how the ecumenical emphasis on the centrality of the gospel message expressed in the ancient creeds has been received in the converging liturgical practice of Christian communities.

Ecumenical statements on the Gospel make clear the connection between the gospel message and the salvation that God has effected through Christ's work that is proclaimed in the Gospel, but ecumenical statements, by their very nature, do not advocate one interpretation of the saving meaning of the gospel over others. *Confessing the One Faith* appropriately acknowledges sacrificial language in the scriptures and in Christian traditions and it emphasizes the theme of God's victory over death and evil in the resurrection of Christ, but this emphasis is in a section on the contemporary interpretation of the meaning of the Nicene Creed, and it is not surprising, given concerns (for example) for human liberation, that this theme would be emphasized in such a discussion.

6

The Mystery of the Gospel

Pray also for me, so that when I speak,
a message may be given to me
to make known with boldness
the mystery of the gospel.

—Ephesians 6:19

This book began with the question of whether there is a basic message or belief that is shared by most of the churches that count the world's two billion Christians as their constituents. It has focused on the professed and received beliefs of Christian communities, and it has focused on the "gospel" in the sense of the most basic narrative about the work of God in Jesus Christ and the claims that are most consistently made about this narrative. It has examined this gospel narrative as it was expressed in the most ancient proto-orthodox Christian communities, as it has been expressed in ancient Christian churches (Catholic, Eastern and Oriental Orthodox, and Assyrian churches), in a variety of older Protestant, Anglican, and related churches, and in a cluster of Christian communities that I have described as Evangelical churches and communities. It has, moreover, examined the gospel narrative and its meanings as expressed in the ecumenical movement of the twentieth century, with a particular focus on the Faith and Order movement that is a constituent part of the World Council of Churches (WCC).

Three Clusters of Meaning

All of this raises a critical question about the commensurability of what is taught as the gospel in these communities, that is to say, whether the gospel means the same thing through the deep "core sample" that has been examined in the previous chapters. I argue in the methodological afterword (chapter 7) that cultural systems are permeable in the sense that meanings can be shared across their boundaries, although meanings are inevitably transformed in the transition from one cultural system to another. An implication of this is that meanings can never be exactly or precisely the same between cultural and linguistic communities, but shared meanings can be discovered by careful analysis of language and contexts, by careful questions and careful dialogue. The question asked at the beginning of this paragraph might be reframed, then, to ask not whether the gospel means exactly "the same thing" between the widely varied communities considered here, but to ask what shared meanings have been discovered by applying these methods of study and dialogue in the previous chapters.

In what follows, then, I will discuss three sets or clusters of interrelated meanings associated with the gospel, based on words drawn from I Corinthians 3b–4. These are as follows: (1) "Christ died . . . he was buried . . . he was raised on the third day" (that is, the shared meaning of the basic narrative of God's acts in Jesus Christ); (2) "for our sins" (shared meanings of the connection between Christ's acts and human salvation); and (3) "in accordance with the scriptures" (the shared meaning that this narrative involves the same one God who acted on behalf of Israel and who is the creator of the material world). There are other meanings associated with the gospel that might be shared between these communities, but these three areas will provide a beginning point for considering the gospel as a message shared by many if not most of the world's Christian communities.

"Christ Died . . . He was Buried . . . He was Raised on the Third Day"

The first set of shared meanings of the gospel revolves around the simple story or narrative that is told by it, the narrative of Christ's life, death, and resurrection. Before asking what else this story may mean, one should note this very carefully: what it means is that Christ died and was raised from the dead. In the words of the New Delhi report on Christian unity received by the World Council of Churches in 1961, it is "nothing else than those events . . ." that constitute the gospel narrative.[1] In the Apostles' Creed and the Nicene Creed, in the celebration of eucharist with the anamnesis or remembrance of Christ's work, in the observance of the Christian year, in the doctrinal statements of Anglican, Protestant, and

Evangelical churches, in catechisms and liturgies and hymns, in spirituals and Gospel songs and Contemporary Christian music, in ecumenical consensus statements and in the memorial acclamations in the eucharist, the narrative of Christ's acts is consistently told and retold in Christian communities.

As the preceding chapters have shown, this narrative focuses on the life, death, and resurrection of Jesus Christ. Stripped to its bare minimum, it is the death and resurrection of Christ that is the consistent core of the message. In I Corinthians 15, the narrative includes reference to Christ's burial. Contemporary memorial acclamations include a reference to Christ's second advent ("Christ will come again"). The narrative of Christ's works might include Christ's incarnation, birth, life, teachings, miracles, suffering, crucifixion, death, burial, descent into the place of the dead ("hell"), resurrection, and second coming, but the death and resurrection of Jesus Christ are the two elements of this narrative that are consistently repeated.

The repeated use of this narrative by widely different Christian communities shows an intention to believe as other Christian communities have believed.[2] Some churches may accomplish this by retelling the story in their own words, or by using only the words of scripture as a way to tell the story on the part of their community. But the intention to tell the same story that other Christian communities have told is clearest when the words utilized are literally the words that other Christian communities have used, so the act of solemnly reciting the Apostles' Creed or the Nicene Creed is in itself a sign that a community wants to be identified with other communities that have recited the same words. The underlying importance of Evangelical communities deciding to use the Apostles' Creed or the Nicene Creed, then, is not simply to demonstrate doctrinal orthodoxy: in most cases the formal doctrinal statements of these churches affirmed the creeds' teachings. The underlying significance is that by using the very words of the historic creeds, even by the somewhat grudging use of the word "catholic," these churches signify their intention to believe as the broader Christian community has believed. And inherent in this is the intention to tell the same foundational story that other churches have told.

Although it might be objected that simply sharing a narrative does not amount to much in the way of shared meaning, the point should not be missed that a shared narrative has the power to give identity to the people who share it. The narrative contained within the Hebrew scriptures gave identity to the people of Israel. At the heart of the passover haggadah is a condensation of this narrative beginning with the words, "A wandering

Aramean was my ancestor . . ." (Deuteronomy 26:5), and this narrative continues to define the identity of Jewish people. Although the primitive gospel narrative did not go on explicitly to define a people (Luke's version of it, conjoined to the Acts of the Apostles, would do so), it nevertheless gave the nuclear story that would define the people to whom this message was preached, those who were marked by baptism into Christ and who would continue the memory (anamnesis) of Christ's work in the holy eucharist. It is a significant fact that, across the boundaries of languages and cultures and confessional traditions, Christian communities continue to define themselves by recourse to this single, foundational narrative.

"For Our Sins"

The gospel involves not only the constitutive narrative of the works of Jesus Christ; it also involves the claim that God has somehow brought about human salvation through the works of Jesus Christ recounted in this narrative: "Christ died *for our sins*." The Christian communities considered in the preceding chapters all make this claim in one way or another, although the range of meanings shared between these communities regarding this aspect of the gospel involves significantly varied accounts of how Christ's work accomplishes human salvation. The words given in I Corinthians 15 may suggest ways of understanding Christ's work, that is, they may evoke the servant songs of Isaiah or the notion of vicarious sacrifice or the sin offerings described in Leviticus, but the words "Christ died for our sins" by themselves are far too brief to make any of these meanings clear.

But when the narrative is embedded in the canonical gospels or simply juxtaposed beside the equally primitive narrative of the institution of the eucharist in I Corinthians 11:23–26, the gospel narrative becomes associated with passover, and this involves both the narrative meaning of the acts of God in delivering Israel from Egypt and the cluster of meanings associated with the passover sacrifice. Both of these clusters of meanings were transmitted through the ancient churches to modern Christian communities: the narrative meaning was transmitted in the narrative of the acts of Christ considered in the previous section, and the meanings associated with passover sacrifice were transmitted by way of the eucharistic liturgy as well as the celebration of the Christian year with its climax in the Easter triduum and the rich set of associations with passover in the churches' Easter celebrations.

Sacrificial meanings of the gospel were transmitted in ancient Christian churches, in the older Protestant and Anglican church traditions, and in some ways in the culture of Evangelical churches (for example, Gospel songs that invoked blood imagery). The preceding chapters have tracked some important changes in the meanings associated with sacrifice. In the ancient churches the sacrifice was understood to embrace Christ's whole life, his death, and his resurrection as his offering for humankind, although it is true that Christ's death could be claimed as the focal point of this complete offering, just as the death of a person can be thought of as the completion or consummation of their life. This is consistent with the rich set of meanings in ancient Christian communities that saw Christ as the recapitulation of true humanity, with each element of Christ's life sanctifying the corresponding aspect of human experience: Christ "became human so that we might become divine."[3] It means that the whole of Christ's life, including Christ's death and resurrection, was understood as having saving significance.

Doctrinal and liturgical texts from Protestant, Anglican, and related churches continued to transmit the sacrificial meanings associated with Christ's work, although these statements typically understand Christ's life and death as the essential offering ("oblation") or sacrifice, whereas the resurrection is seen as the sign of God's triumph over death and the powers of evil. I understand this in the light of the culture of the early modern period in Europe in which there was little if any direct experience of the practice of sacrifice and the meanings associated with sacrifice in ancient contexts, for in the ancient contexts the resurrection was understood as part of Christ's sacrifice. But then again, it is not a complete loss of meaning, for the sacrificial meaning associated with resurrection lay in its analogy to the rising smoke of a sacrificial offering which in turn was understood to denote the divine acceptance of the offering. So understanding the resurrection of Christ as the preeminent sign of God's victory over the evil powers is not far removed from understanding it as the sign of divine acceptance of the offering of Christ. It is just that the direct connection to sacrificial cultus and meaning is not drawn out so clearly in the Reformation period. Ecumenical statements on the saving meaning of Christ's work, similarly, point to a variety of meanings, including sacrificial meanings and the meaning of Christ's death and resurrection as a victory over death and evil, and in one case (*Confessing the One Faith*) the latter theme is emphasized in the contemporary ecumenical interpretation of the apostolic faith.

Evangelical communities reflect a strong tendency to see Christ's death as the preeminent event that has saving significance, especially as Christ's death is interpreted as a substitution for the death that humans owe for their complicity in sin. Insofar as substitution could be an element of sacrifice (that is, in a vicarious sacrifice), a part of the sacrificial meanings associated with the gospel is preserved in this way. Moreover, as chapter 4 shows, many of the formal doctrinal statements of Evangelical churches speak of the significance of the whole life of Christ and of Christ's resurrection, and these doctrinal statements sometimes ascribe saving significance to Christ's life and resurrection. What has been shown here, then, is not by any means a denial of the deeper sacrificial meanings of Christ's life and death and resurrection, nor a denial of the saving significance of Christ's whole life. It is simply a strong and consistent emphasis, especially in explaining the meaning of the Gospel, on the forensic aspect of Christ's death taking the place of the penalty that humans owe for sin. Evangelical literature that seeks to bring believers into greater theological depth acknowledges the sacrificial meanings associated with Christ's work and the theme of victory over Satan and the powers of evil.[4] In Evangelical communities, however, the wider range of meanings associated with Christ's life and death and resurrection has not as often been expressed, for example, in church music.

"In Accordance with the Scriptures"

A third cluster of meanings associated with the gospel has to do with the relationship between the gospel message and the Christian and Jewish scriptures. The gospel that Paul transmitted claimed that Christ's death and resurrection were both "in accordance with the scriptures." Since the New Testament did not exist when Paul wrote this, "the scriptures" in this passage refer to the Jewish scriptures that Christians would identify as the Old Testament. The repetition of the phrase with respect to the death and the resurrection of Jesus Christ shows how important this element of the gospel was: the primitive Christian message was understood as being in continuity with the Old Testament, and an implication was that "the God and Father of our Lord Jesus Christ" (Ephesians 1:3) was none other than the God of Abraham, Isaac, and Jacob, the same one who was the creator of the material world. This claim distinguished the proto-orthodox Christian communities of the second century from Marcionite, Valentinian, and other groups who did not accept the connection between Jesus Christ and the God of Israel praised as the creator of the material world. It is in this sense that the gospel "in accordance with the scriptures" itself served as a criterion in the discernment of the Christian canon of scripture in the earliest centuries.

A related cluster of meanings becomes associated with the gospel as the canon of Christian scripture was defined and used in ancient Christian communities. This has to do with the gospel's role in giving meaning to the whole of scripture—and by the early Christian centuries this had come to mean the Old and New Testaments. The ancient churches came to read the scriptures in the half-year period between Advent and Pentecost in a sequence following the events of the gospel message, so that the hearing and understanding of the scriptures was normed by the gospel pattern. After the development of printed and bound Bibles, from the fifteenth century, the Catholic Church made clear through the Council of Trent its understandings of the meaning of the scriptures,[5] and Protestant groups elaborated their understanding of the "analogy of faith" as the central meaning of scripture focusing on the gospel message. These definitions of the meaning of the canon, along with the continued reading of the scriptures in the sequence of the Christian year and combined with homilies or sermons following this pattern that Catholic churches and Protestant churches offered from the Reformation age reinforced the churches' understanding of the gospel as the central meaning of the Christian faith.

Some Protestant groups, as chapter 3 demonstrates, did not take the "analogy of faith" to mean coherence with the gospel narrative; some took this expression to denote the interpretation of scripture in the light of any other scriptures, the meaning of which is clearer to the interpreter. Moreover, as chapter 4 shows, there is little consciousness in Evangelical communities of a sense in which the gospel message can stand over or norm the scriptures themselves, although Evangelical churches celebrate the gospel message as the heart of the biblical message. The distinctive Fundamentalist claim that the scriptures are equally inspired in all their parts and infallibly inspired with respect to scientific and historical teachings can diminish the sense that the gospel is the core message that the Christian canon of scripture conveys. As Evangelical communities develop relationships with older Christian communities, the centrality of the gospel as a criterion for the interpretation of all of the Christian scriptures emerges as a central (and sometimes problematic) issue.

Some Responses to Issues

The three clusters of meaning associated with the gospel discussed earlier—the bare narrative of the events of Christ's life, death and resurrection, the association of these events with God's work of salvation, and the way in which the gospel gives meaning to the whole of the Christian scriptures—constitute grounds for the claim that the gospel is the central message whose meaning is shared in varying ways and to varying degrees by most of the communities that identify themselves as Christian. How are these conclusions relevant to the four sets of issues with which this study began?

Jesus in the Twenty-First Century

The material about the gospel in Christian traditions in the preceding chapters may make a small contribution to discussions about Jesus in contemporary culture and in contemporary scholarship. The discussion about Jesus in recent decades has centered on gospels, that is, both the literary criticism of the canonical gospels and the examination of other early Christian literature such as the Gospel of Thomas. The present work, and especially the material in chapter 1, calls attention to a critical historical fact that should be acknowledged in this contemporary discussion, and that is the claim on the part of churches that Christian faith—what could be described as "orthodox" or at least "proto-orthodox" Christian faith—existed before the writing and the canonization of the corpus of Christian scriptures.

It may be awkward for Protestants to consider Christian faith apart from the canon of Christian scriptures, except for the fact that the Christian scriptures themselves make claims about the gospel apart from (at least before) the writing and canonization of the Christian scriptures. According to the Acts of the Apostles, Peter preached the message about Jesus Christ on the day of Pentecost, three thousand persons were baptized, and these earliest believers "devoted themselves to the apostles' teaching and fellowship, to the breaking of bread and the prayers" (Acts 2:42). Thus, the Christian scriptures themselves make the claim that the earliest Christian community existed prior to the Christian scriptures. The earliest Christian communities did not have the Christian canon of scripture but they had "the apostles' teaching."[6]

A critical implication for contemporary discussions of Jesus is that these discussions need to involve the early Christian kerygma or teaching as well as the material in the canonical scriptures and in other early Christian literature. In my view, the importance of this has been too often minimized in discussions in the last few decades. The Theissen and Merz study of *The Historical Jesus* referred to in chapter one, to take one example, begins with a claim that there are two basic sources for knowledge about

Jesus: material from the canonical gospels and material that comes by way of Paul. They state that the latter (Pauline) material is historically earlier than the material from the canonical gospels, but they make the claim that the Pauline material is suspect because of "the pauline 'tendency' to see Jesus as a preexistent, mythical being."[7] This in itself indicates, of course, that the earliest historical material about Jesus is that which associates Jesus with divine status, contrary to the Enlightenment claim that the earliest material about Jesus must be that which portrays him simply as a human being.[8] But then, four hundred pages later in the book, Theissen and Merz describe a consensus of contemporary scholarship that the material embedded in I Corinthians 15:3b–4 derives from "the earliest period, close to the events themselves."[9] It would seem, then, that although the existence of the pre-pauline material is acknowledged, its significance for the contemporary discussion of Jesus is often missed, and Christian churches have a stake in this claim because the faith of historic Christian communities is grounded, in the first place, in the apostolic witness to Jesus Christ that preceded the composition and the canonization of the Christian scriptures.

The Presupposition of Christian Disunity

A further issue raised in the introduction has to do with the trend in some contemporary Christian theological reflection that presupposes that there is no basic agreement as to the meaning of the Christian faith. The material considered in this book clearly challenges such claims. If the gospel narrative itself, its association with salvation, and the claim that it constitutes the central meaning of the scriptures has been consistently affirmed by ancient Christian churches, Protestant and related churches, and Evangelical churches, with significant meanings shared between these widely varied traditions in their understandings of the gospel message, then I would regard it as a fair conclusion that there is at least one consistent teaching, perhaps even a doctrine or cluster of doctrines, that has constituted the center of Christian belief for most Christian communities.

Contemporary interpreters may not be convinced that the cluster of meanings associated with the gospel discussed above provides a sufficiently clear basis for the claim that there is a single message (gospel) shared by so many churches, but given the material studied in the chapters above, I would argue that a burden of proof must also rest on those who would make the counter claim. That is, the claim that there is no unity is a claim that must itself be demonstrated. It is an enormous factual and historical claim that needs to be documented by reference to historical and descriptive material, including serious consideration of the claims made on the part of Christian communities and ecumenical bodies. Otherwise it might be better to delimit historical and factual claims more carefully, for example, by clarifying that although there may indeed be consistent claims and interpretations of those claims shared very broadly by Christian communities, theologians and other interpreters do not agree on a central meaning of the Christian faith. That would be, in my view, a claim that could be demonstrated in a much more straightforward manner.

The Gospel and the Unity of Protestant and Related Churches

The third issue considered in the introduction has to do with the unity of Christian churches, and especially of the older Protestant and related denominations that in the United States and elsewhere are sometimes referred to in the present time as "old-line" churches. It might be worth recalling that the prototypical gospel passage in I Corinthians 15:1–4 was itself cited by Paul to address divisions in the Corinthian congregation, in this case, over the nature of the resurrection. Chapter 5 has shown how consistently the Faith and Order component of the ecumenical movement has insisted on the common affirmation of gospel as a fundamental element of Christian unity. These ecumenical formulations were enthusiastically embraced by old-line churches in their engagement with the ecumenical movement through the twentieth century, and their affirmation of the gospel as central to Christian unity was consistent with Reformation definitions of the church, according to which the preaching of the Word (the gospel) is a necessary element that constitutes a Christian church along with the gathering of believers and the appropriate administration of the sacraments.

Now these churches face the possibilities and present realities of internal divisions as a result of the critical contemporary issues mentioned in the introduction. An unfortunate concomitant of the dissension surrounding these issues is that the centrality of the gospel message and of other basic Christian commitments (as well as distinctive denominational teachings and practices) can be lost on all sides, and this in turn can allow persons (on all sides) to presume that their opponents lack commitment to essential or central Christian teachings and practices. So the profession of the gospel becomes a critical element in the internal unity of churches as well as their external unity with other Christian communities.

It does not help simply to point to multiple ironies that may be seen in the present predicament. But it might be helpful to recall that the same principle that has been claimed for the external unity of Christian communities must also apply to their internal unity. I do not at all mean that the gospel message considered in this book can be immediately applied to contemporary debates about homosexuality or other divisive issues in these churches. I do mean to suggest that these conversations need to be framed by a consistent profession by all parties of the message that has constituted the unity of Christian communities since the very beginning.

The Gospel and the Evolution of Evangelical Communities

In the preceding work, and especially in chapter four, I have laid out a particular argument about Evangelical communities in relationship to other (especially older) Christian communities. This is the claim that Evangelical communities often undergo an evolution from highly distinctive teachings and practices (what I have called the "centrifugal" tendencies of the early phases of their development) toward identification with the longer Christian tradition and the affirmation of teachings and practices characteristic of the broader Christian tradition (the corresponding "centripetal" tendency). I do not mean to suggest that this evolution is necessary or predetermined: it has happened in varying ways with Methodist, Adventist, Holiness, and Pentecostal churches. Whether a similar process will happen with Mormons or Jehovah's Witnesses remains to be seen and I do not take it as a given.

With those Evangelical groups that are responding to the centripetal tendency to enter into conversation with older Christian traditions, careful dialogue is needed, both for Evangelical communities to perceive the gospel in other Christian traditions and for other Christian traditions to understand the distinctive histories and gifts that particular Evangelical communities may bring. Participants on all sides must be willing to lay aside some inherited views of each other and experience afresh the reality of worship, teachings, and other practices in other Christian communities. The dialogues modeled in *Ancient Faith and American-Born Churches* (2006) may offer a starting point for methods helpful in such dialogues and for particular examples of carefully structured dialogue.[10]

The Gospel and Criteria for Christian Unity

Underlying many of the questions raised in this book is the issue of what is required for unity between and within Christian communities. Beyond "the apostles' teaching [*didache*] and fellowship . . . the breaking of bread and the prayers" (Acts 2:42), what should Christian communities expect of each other in order to recognize each other's communities as being fully Christian? What is necessary—as the ecumenical movement has often defined its own goal—for "full, visible unity" between and within the churches? The present study cannot resolve this issue, but it can point to the gospel as the message by which Christian traditions have most consistently defined their own core identity and thus as a central criterion in recognizing other communities as Christian.

I reveal now my own confessional prejudice and bias, but in contemplating the simplicity of the early Christian message and its expression through the range of Christian traditions considered here, one is struck with the way in which elaborate definitions of unity have sometimes obscured rather than clarified the gospel message. My own church affirms that in Jesus Christ "two whole and perfect natures—that is to say, the Godhead and manhood—were joined together in one person, never to be divided,"[11] reflecting the language used in the Definition of Faith of the Council of Chalcedon (451 C.E.). But how long did it take before Christian communities affirming this language could recognize the integrity of the faith of those who did not and do not accept this language—and here, I mean specifically the Assyrian Church of the East and the Oriental Orthodox churches? To put it more pointedly: how long did Christians have to curse other Christians before recognizing that their differences in definitional language were not in fact necessary differences of critical substance over the meaning of the Christian gospel itself? The answer, in this case, is approximately fifteen centuries.

The history of elaborate definitions of Christian unity is not a reassuring one. In the seventeenth century, in particular, Western churches—both Protestant and Catholic—developed detailed dogmatic definitions and their theologians cranked out volumes of scholastic defenses of these definitions while their nations engaged in open warfare against other Christian states. I would dare say that these particular definitions and the accompanying carnage did little to advance the gospel. By contrast, however, the experience of many of our churches through the twentieth century has shown the critical problems inherent when Christian communities lack a clear sense of definition about their own core identity, so there is no escaping the hard work of doctrinal definition and reception.

Related to this is a question of whether we have expected too much of what may be defined as "religion." One of the most influential definitions of "religion" is that given by anthropologist Clifford Geertz in a

1973 article on "Religion as Cultural System," where Geertz suggested that "religion" can denote an over-arching cultural system that frames a people's view of the world (a *Weltanschauung*) and their view of life (a *Lebensanschauung*).[12] I have come to question the extent to which such an understanding of "religion" can apply to Christianity, given what has been considered in this study of the gospel in Christian traditions. The gospel has always been embedded in larger cultural systems that function more as the over-arching views of life and reality that Geertz envisioned: the complex interweaving of Semitic and Hellenistic culture of Palestinian antiquity, the Byzantine culture that grew out of the Eastern Roman empire, medieval Latin culture influenced as it eventually was by Islamic and Jewish versions of Aristotelianism, and highly varied complexes of modern cultures. Geertz's definition would seem to demand that a "religion" should involve an elaborate set of cultural traditions defining views of the world and of life, but I find that very few of the elements of larger cultural systems involve centrally held religious beliefs and practices even if these religious beliefs and practices occupy the highest position in a community's sense of values. I am not convinced, to put this by way of example, that a community needs to embrace any form of Platonism or Aristotelianism to be recognized by other communities as Christian.

The gospel, I would say, is the central element in a fairly small cluster of interrelated beliefs and practices that have consistently characterized Christian communities and that have persisted through a sequence of larger host cultures. In a parallel way, one could make the case that there is a fairly small core of Jewish beliefs and practices that have persisted through many larger cultural systems,[13] and a small core of Islamic beliefs and practices that have been similarly embedded in broader cultural systems.[14] It is a strength of religious traditions that they have the ability to attach themselves to larger cultural systems while maintaining a nucleus or core of their own most central beliefs and practices; in this way they can survive the demise of larger cultural systems. But, I would say, this view of religious traditions seriously challenges the notion that Christianity, Judaism, or Islam can themselves be understood as "cultural systems" in the larger sense that Geertz envisioned.

What might be other concomitants of the gospel as defining the relatively small core of Christian beliefs and practices that has passed through a long series of larger cultural systems? One cannot begin to describe the gospel in Christian traditions, as the previous pages attest, without exploring some consistently related beliefs and practices, including the proclamation of the gospel itself, the profession of the Christian faith and identification with the Christian community through baptism and eucharist, the worship of the triune God, and the study and explication of the Christian scriptures normed by the gospel narrative. It is beyond the scope of this study to examine what beyond the gospel itself is strictly necessary for full, visible unity between Christian communities and of course it is only the prerogative of communities to make these determinations for themselves, but this study has consistently shown how the reception and profession of the gospel norms the criteria by which one Christian community can recognize others.

The Mystery of the Gospel

The previous chapters have revealed particular ways in which the gospel has become obscured. In contemporary discussions of Jesus, the gospel can actually be obscured by gospels, that is to say, the gospel message that preceded the writing of the New Testament can be obscured by analysis of New Testament texts and other early Christian literature abstracted from the earlier Christian traditions that the gospel literature transmitted. In the work of contemporary theologians, the gospel as the central message of Christian churches can be obscured by claims that there is not or cannot be such a central message and by focusing almost exclusively on the claims of theologians rather than the claims of churches. In the contemporary predicament of old-line Protestant churches, the unitive force of the gospel can be obscured by the emotional weight of divisive contemporary issues. In the evolution of Evangelical communities, the gospel can be obscured by the centrifugal and highly distinctive tenets and practices that often appear at the initiation of Evangelical movements.

It may be appropriate to consider, then, that in the Pauline and deuteropauline literature of the New Testament, the gospel is consistently connected with the term *mysterion,* a word that can have cosmic or metacosmic connotations but that can also mean simply a "secret."[15] As one interpreter explains it, the word can denote "a history which is outside the laws of cosmic occurrence and apprehension and which takes place according to God's secret counsel, but also the fact that this history is enacted in this world."[16] In the practice of Christian communities, the gospel is a sacred narrative solemnly recited whose full meaning is acknowledged to lie beyond the realm of human or angelic reason: "let angel minds inquire no more."[17] At the same time, the gospel is confessed by Christian communities to intersect with the coarse realities of human history:

"he was crucified under Pontius Pilate." The gospel is, in Luther's words, "the true treasure of the church." But it is sometimes a hidden treasure, a mystery or secret often overlooked, but from time to time rediscovered by Christians as the key that unlocks the meaning of the Christian scriptures and of the Christian faith itself.

7

A Methodological Afterword

> I too decided, after investigating
> everything carefully from the very first,
> to write an orderly account for you . . .
>
> —Luke 1:3

Historical and Ecumenical Study

The methods utilized in this book are principally historical and ecumenical and I hope that they will prove fruitful for a larger study of doctrines and practices commonly affirmed, received, and practiced in a wide variety of Christian churches. In a sense, the method utilized here was enunciated in the fifth century C.E. by the monk Vincent of Lérins, who asserted that ". . . in the catholic church itself great care must be taken that we hold that which has been believed everywhere, always, by all. For this is truly and properly 'catholic.'"[1] Writing from a seemingly isolated monastic retreat on an island off the Atlantic coast of France in 434 C.E., Vincent was aware of larger controversies in the church. His principle, to look for that which has been affirmed universally and consistently through the history of the Christian community, is essentially what I have attempted here, although from the perspective of the huge range of divided Christian communities in the early twenty-first century, Vincent's goal of universality ("everywhere, always, by all") of beliefs has to give way to a more modest assertion of what at least *most* historic and contemporary Christian communities have taught as the gospel.

The material referenced in the previous chapters can be divided roughly between that which is strictly historical, that which speaks on behalf of contemporary Christian communities, and that which attempts to enunciate agreements on the part of formally separated communities of Christians. The method adopted here is essentially historical and descriptive. It has not set up contemporary tests of theological truths and attempted to test the claims made here by these criteria; in this respect it is not "systematic" theology. But it is theology, that is, critical reflection on the Christian faith, and it intersects with the work of systematic theology to the extent that the latter reflects critically on the claims made by Christian communities. The historical work in the present study, then, has been principally to examine the claims that historic and contemporary Christian communities have made about the meaning of the gospel and to ask what meanings have been shared between these communities. It is objective historical study in the sense that an historian can make herself or himself vulnerable to evidence outside of oneself, outside the range of one's accustomed perceptions, and even outside the range of the communities of discourse or meaning of which one has been a part.[2]

This is also an ecumenical study. Ecumenical study is, in a sense, descriptive work since it is concerned with the claims made on behalf of networks of churches seeking to make visible their unity in Christ. A significant contribution of the Faith and Order movement is its consistent quest to understand what communities have actually taught and how their formally stated teachings or doctrines are actually lived out or "received" in the life of those communities. This study builds on a century of careful work between Christians of the various divided churches, trying to understand and then also to find ways forward for the sake of Christian unity.

Ecumenical conversations in the twentieth century showed that the existence of shared beliefs cannot be demonstrated abstractly; they must be demonstrated at the point of each belief and practice shared or alleged to be shared between Christian traditions. However, as George Lindbeck notes, there remains considerable suspicion as to whether in fact unity has been found on the basis of ecumenical dialogue:

> Over and over again in recent years, there have been reports from Roman Catholic, Orthodox, or Protestant theologians engaged in dialogues sponsored by their respective churches that they are in basic agreement on such topics as the Eucharist, ministry, justification, or even the papacy, and yet they continue—so

they claim—to adhere to their historic and once-divisive convictions. Those who hear these reports often find them difficult to believe. They are inclined to think that the very notion of doctrinal reconciliation without doctrinal change is self-contradictory, and they suspect that the dialogue participants are self-deceived victims of their own desire to combine ecumenical harmony with denominational loyalty.[3]

Given this level of suspicion, interpreters should be cautious not to prejudge the question of whether or not there can be shared beliefs and practices until particular claims have been examined in their own contexts and in the contexts of particular dialogues by which unity has been discerned. That is what I have attempted to do in this work.

Doctrine and Doctrinal Reception

This study has examined the gospel as it has been communally affirmed and communally received in Christian churches. That is to say, it focuses on what communities have formally agreed to teach ("doctrine") and the ways in which these teachings have been received in Christian communities. Cardinal Ratzinger explained in his *Introduction to Christianity* that doctrine and dogma emerge when the claim that "I believe" is stated in a communal context, that is, when "I believe" is stated as a response to a question that is posed, "Do you believe . . . ?"[4] Thus, even the first-person singular claim "I believe" in traditional Christian creeds and affirmations, understood in its context, makes a common or communal claim.

The expression "communally affirmed" means that a community has affirmed particular teachings and practices by its own processes for reaching and expressing consensus. This inevitably involves issues of church polity, because in historic Christian communities there exists a wide variety of modes by which communities come to consensus and affirm or express consensus. The most ancient Christian communities affirmed doctrines and practices through councils of bishops. Since the time of the Protestant Reformation other modes of consensus, such as representative church synods and congregational assemblies, have developed.

The expression "communally received" means that even when teachings are formally affirmed through a community's own processes (such as a council of bishops or a representative assembly), they must also be "received" by the community itself. That is, teachings must be actually taught and practices actually effected to constitute what I have called "communally affirmed and communally received teachings and practices." There are many cases in which teachings and practices have been formally affirmed but failed to be received in churches. Perhaps most notably, the union between Eastern and Western churches formally and solemnly affirmed by the Council of Florence, which insisted that Eastern churches use the *filioque* clause in the Nicene Creed, was not received in most of the Eastern churches and hence lacks in these churches the status of communally received teaching and practice despite the fact that Eastern church delegates at Florence formally approved these measures. The issue of communal reception implies a critical role played by all of the faithful, including the laity, in the process of affirming doctrines and practices on the part of a community.[5]

The understanding of "doctrine" as used in this study implies three overlapping but nevertheless distinguishable phenomena:

- In the first place is doctrine itself, which denotes *communally affirmed and communally received teachings,* the primary focus of this study, as discussed in the previous paragraphs.
- These communally affirmed and communally received teachings need to be distinguished from *theology* in a broader sense in which "theology" can denote any reflection on religious beliefs and practices.[6] There are undoubtedly sentinel theologians whose works carry great authority for specific Christian communities (Aquinas for Catholics, the Cappadocians for Eastern Orthodox churches, Luther for Lutherans, Calvin for Reformed churches, John and Charles Wesley for Methodist churches, etc.) but even in the case of these sentinel theologians and their communities one has to differentiate between the theologians' own thoughts, beliefs, and opinions, on the one hand, and those beliefs they advocated which were in fact communally affirmed and received, on the other.
- Communally affirmed and communally received teachings also need to be distinguished from *popular religious beliefs* which have not been formally affirmed by a community's own process for reaching consensus. Catholics in many places may think of themselves as "worshiping" saints (giving rise to traditional Protestant critique of these practices), even though formal Catholic teaching forbids "worship" of saints. Here the issue is not with "reception," because popular religious beliefs would imply a strong degree of reception had they been formally affirmed by communities, but

the lack of formal communal affirmation is the criterion that distinguishes popular religious beliefs from "doctrines."

Although the opposite of doctrine, as defined here, is "heresy," that is, beliefs that a community has rejected or anathematized, it is important to realize that there are many beliefs that are simply not defined as either doctrine or heresy by Christian communities. That is to say, definitions of doctrine and even of heresy allow for a wide ground of creative teachings that are defined as neither orthodoxy nor heresy.

Given the understanding of communally affirmed and communally received teachings described here, it is also important to ask how doctrines and authorized practices actually function to define communities as Christian. George Lindbeck lays out three possibilities for the manner in which doctrines function in Christian communities:

- In the first place is what Lindbeck calls a "propositionalist" understanding, namely, that "church doctrines function as informative propositions or truth claims about objective realities."[7] He associates this approach with traditional Catholic and Protestant understandings of doctrine, and questions whether there can ever be doctrinal reconciliation on the basis of this "static" understanding of what doctrines mean.
- In the second place is what Lindbeck calls an "experiential-expressivist" approach to doctrine in which doctrines are understood as "noninformative and nondiscursive symbols of inner feelings, attitudes, or existential orientations."[8] Lindbeck associates this approach with a trajectory of Protestant liberal theology beginning with Schleiermacher.
- In the third place is what Lindbeck himself advocates as a "cultural-linguistic" approach to the function of doctrine in which doctrines are understood as enunciating "rules" (*regulae*) that norm or regulate the ways in which Christians agree to speak about their most central teachings. Lindbeck argues that this approach allows for doctrinal reconciliation while not surrendering the claims about objective realities that these rules may describe.[9]

Given Lindbeck's taxonomy of functions of doctrine, I should indicate that I usually understand doctrine to function in the first manner listed, that is, as propositional claims about objective realities. The "experiential-expressivist" approach to doctrine as Lindbeck describes it seems to be an unregulated and un-normed evasion of what the communities have meant by their teachings, though one could question whether particular theologians such as Schleiermacher understood traditional doctrines as being exclusively expressive of religious experiences or feelings.[10] Lindbeck's description of the "regulative" function of some doctrinal language really is critical for historical and ecumenical understandings of Christian doctrine because in many cases doctrinal claims do in fact establish rules about how language is to be used, and one cannot understand historic teachings (such as the trinitarian and christological teachings of early Christian councils) or ecumenical consensus (such as the Lutheran-Catholic-Methodist "Joint Declaration on Justification") apart from the very specific uses of language embedded in them. However, Lindbeck wants to use the regulative model as an overarching framework in which one may understand Christian doctrinal claims (including their propositional claims about objective realities). I am inclined to understand most doctrinal statements (creeds, conciliar statements, Protestant confessions and articles of religion, ecumenical consensus statements) as making propositional claims that nevertheless cannot be understood apart from the distinct and sometimes novel uses of language embedded within them. I would note further that Lindbeck's concern with the way in which doctrine functions is related to a larger issue about the commensurability of claims and practices between Christian communities separated by wide ranges of history and culture.

Commensurability and Mutual Understanding

A crucial issue in this work is the question of the commensurability of religious claims between cultures, languages, and ecclesiastical contexts and through the vicissitudes of Christian history. Even if a substantial number of Christians, through the centuries and across confessional and cultural boundaries, were to agree on a set of words, for example, the Nicene Creed, or the Apostles' Creed, as expressing the gospel, how can interpreters know that what one community means by these words has at least enough in common with what other communities mean by the same words to claim a significant degree of commensurability between them? How can interpreters claim that Christian communities across the boundaries of time and cultures truly "share" the gospel in common with each other?

A suspicion of claims about what is shared in common between Christian traditions might be raised on the part of traditionalist advocates of one tradition against others. Catholic Bishop Christophe Bonjean of

Colombo, Ceylon (Sri Lanka), arguing on behalf of independent Catholic schools in 1861, lampooned pretensions to "common Christianity" on the part of Anglicans and others, writing that "common Christianity" or "general Christianity":

> is in sober truth, nothing more than a word without meaning; it may dazzle the ignorant, and throw dust into the eyes of the unreflecting; but it represents no fact, no reality, which an inquisitive mind could apprehend. It is a mere abstraction, a pure fiction, a bright phantom which becomes evanescent, the moment you stretch out your hand to catch it.[11]

Bonjean was correct in the sense that teachings common to Christian traditions had not in his time been demonstrated in the way in which the ecumenical movement would later try to show. He wrote in 1861, before the significant development of modern ecumenical dialogue or critical study of common Christian traditions. Since his time, common Christian teachings have not only been identified and critically examined through ecumenical dialogue, they have been affirmed and received both by ecumenical bodies and by participating ecclesial communities as well. Moreover, I argue that it is possible to discern common teachings across traditions, utilizing criteria laid out in the next paragraphs, even in some cases in which ecumenical dialogue has not yet formally declared such teachings or common practices.

Another objection to claims of common teachings and practices might come from contemporary philosophical perspectives that question whether there can be any significant commensurability between cultural systems or at least question the level of commensurability that is possible between cultural and linguistic systems. This book presupposes that cultural and linguistic systems are in some ways permeable, that is, cultural traditions and ways of speaking and understanding interpenetrate each other in complex ways that make possible not only occasional glimpses into the worlds of other cultural systems but also the sustained existence of subcultures and minority cultures within larger cultural systems. It implies, however, that there can never be a complete or perfect commensurability of meanings shared between cultural and linguistic communities; shared meanings are always imperfectly shared.

The permeability of cultural and linguistic systems allows for clusters of cultural traditions that exist through or alongside a sequence of other cultural systems. There are, for example, Jewish and Islamic cultural traditions that have coexisted with and persisted through a series of larger cultural traditions in which they have been embedded (see the reflections on this in chapter 6). I do not know of a good term for this that is analogous to "subculture" or "minority culture"—could one speak of Jewish or Islamic "para-cultures" or "juxta-cultures" or at least of trans-cultural phenomena? However it is named, a similar status must exist for Christian beliefs and practices that have persisted through ancient Semitic and Hellenistic cultures, medieval Latin and Byzantine cultures, and a host of modern cultures as well.

Commensurability is not easily demonstrated and, in the end, it may really be known only through prolonged study and careful dialogue. I note four aspects of commensurability here, each of which has been important for the methodology utilized in this book.

A first and critical issue has to do with the ways in which religious language and religious acts can express the intention to believe and practice as other Christians have believed and practiced, even when religious language and acts are not fully understood. One of the criteria of commensurability I have used, then, is to look for signs of the intention to believe and practice what other Christians have believed and practiced. Let me offer a few examples.

- When Methodists in the United States in the 1960s began to include the Nicene Creed in their hymnals and to use it in worship, they signaled their intention to believe and act as historic Christian communities had done (see chapter 3).
- When Seventh-day Adventists significantly revised their doctrinal statements in the early twentieth century to express a version of the doctrine of the Trinity (although not using that term), they signaled an intention to believe and to worship as other Christians believe and worship, even though the precise language that they utilized differed in significant ways from the trinitarian formulations of older churches (see chapter 4).
- The liturgical renewal movement of the twentieth century has affected Catholic as well as Protestant churches, and signals on the part of all of them an intention to worship in ways more consistent with the worship of the ancient church and of each other (see chapter 5).

These are examples of the intention to believe and practice as other churches believe and practice, and these signs are important in demonstrating a degree of commensurability between disparate Christian traditions. They simply show an intention for commensurability.

In the second place, linguistic and cultural study is crucial for demonstrating commensurability. The meanings of words change over the course of time, even within the scope of one linguistic system. Charles Wesley's eighteenth-century sentiment:

> To me, to all, thy bowels move—

was stated as a pious address to the Almighty, but contemporary connotations of the English-language expression "bowels move" do not befit Christian piety, especially when predicated of the divine, and thus contemporary Christian churches modify Charles Wesley's words and sing:

> To me, to all, thy mercies move—
> thy nature, and thy name is Love.[12]

In this case, one must grant the incommensurability of Charles Wesley's original words with contemporary ways of understanding the English language. How much more true this must be in moving from one language to another, and even more so in moving from an ancient and long unused tongue to a contemporary one. The melancholy truth is that there is only a very thin layer of commensurability available via translation when one remains locked within the bounds of one language, and careful linguistic as well as cultural and contextual study is necessary to unlock greater depths of understanding. Discerning commensurability in language is difficult work, but it is worth the effort. Spiritual depth and poetic insight are among its rewards.

In addition to linguistic and cultural study, a third tool for developing understanding and for testing commensurability is the use of careful dialogue that allows interpreters to probe the meanings of words (especially technical terms) and actions (especially distinctive actions) in differing Christian traditions. In the 1996–2000 quadrennium, a group within the Faith and Order Commission of the National Council of Churches of Christ in the USA developed a particular methodology for encouraging dialogue between widely disparate Christian traditions. This methodology was designated as the "Fordian method" after Dr. John Ford, CSC, of the Catholic University of America, who suggested the method and wrote a methodological essay explicating it.[13] Following this method, the group heard papers on specific theological topics between very widely separated Christian traditions. After the initial papers, participants on each side of the discussion were asked to identify three things following a musical metaphor:

- Points of *resonance*, that is, points on which the disparate traditions seem to teach or practice in common.

- Points of *dissonance,* that is, points where it seemed clear to one or the other participant that the disparate traditions were teaching or practicing very different things.
- Points of *nonsonance* (or sometimes the group just said "nonsense"), that is, points where one perspective was really not well understood or needed further clarification.

This method proved to be very helpful in uncovering issues separating traditions, sometimes issues lurking behind the technical terminologies used in different traditions. It also proved helpful in enabling participants to see some unexpected convergences between widely different traditions, even where very different words or practices were involved. The experience of being a part of this group lies in the background of this volume, and the methodology of careful inquiry is one of the tools utilized to build understanding and thus to deal with the problematic issues of commensurability between traditions.

Finally, I take note of a fourth rather melancholy truth about commensurability, which is to observe that commensurability of language and deeper mutual understanding is always a matter of degrees and not of absolutes. No human being fully understands the nuances of another; in this sense the philosophical-cultural critique must be on target. In the case of understanding between churches, simply comparing doctrinal sentences or liturgies does not significantly advance understanding. Can Pentecostals and Eastern Orthodox Christians really understand each other? To a degree, if they work at it. It takes long exposure, watching the gospel procession and hearing the gospel read in Greek in an Orthodox church, watching a Pentecostal congregation as someone is baptized in the Holy Spirit. A Methodist may understand them only to a degree, and only if he works really hard at it and only, I am sure, if some grace comes his way as well.

Notes

Introduction

1. These figures are based on the research of David B. Barrett and others at the Center for World Christianity at Gordon-Conwell Theological Seminary (http://www.worldchristianity.org). Barrett edited the *World Christian Encyclopedia: A Comparative Study of Churches and Religions in the Modern World, AD 1900–2000* (Nairobi: Oxford University Press, 1982) which offered statistics based on his research (cf. Global Table 27, p. 793), and his group annually updates a statistical table in the *International Bulletin of Missionary Research* (January issue) estimating numbers of Christians and adherents of other faiths in the world.

The epigraph gives the memorial acclamations uttered by congregations in the eucharistic prayer as it was revised in the twentieth century on the basis of ecumenical study by Catholics (in English-language contexts), Methodists, Anglicans, Lutherans, and others. They are cited here from *The Sacramentary: Approved for Use in the Dioceses of the United States of America by the National Conference of Catholic Bishops and Confirmed by the Apostolic See* (English translation prepared by the International Committee on English in the Liturgy; Collegeville, Minnesota: Liturgical Press, 1985), pp. 506, 511, 514, and 519–520 as the acclamations appear in eucharistic prayers I, II, III, and IV, respectively; cf. Rite II for the Holy Eucharist in *The Book of Common Prayer* of the Episcopal Church in the United States (New York: Oxford University Press, 1990), p. 363; and *The United Methodist Hymnal: Book of United Methodist Worship* (Nashville, TN: Abingdon Press, 1989), pp. 10, 14, 16, 18, 20, 22, 24, 25. See the extended note on these particular acclamations (and the controversy over their use in Catholic churches) in chapter 5 in the discussion of the gospel as it has been expressed in movements for liturgical renewal.

2. See the extended discussion of this critical passage at the beginning of chapter 1. References to the Greek text of the New Testament are to *The Greek New*

138 NOTES TO PAGES 2–5

Testament, ed. Kurt Aland, Matthew Black, Bruce M. Metzger, and Allen Wikgren (London: United Bible Societies, 1966).

3. Cf. II Corinthians 11:4, "For if someone comes and proclaims . . . a different gospel from the one you accepted . . ."

4. The term translated "entrusted" here (παραδοθείση) is the same term that denotes the "handing on" or transmission of an oral tradition; cf. chapter 1 and the discussion of the transmission of the gospel.

5. Bart D. Ehrman, *Lost Christianities: The Battles for Scripture and the Faiths We Never Knew* (New York: Oxford University Press, 2003), p. 13. See also chapter 1 of this book on the transmission and reception of the gospel in the earliest Christian communities.

6. See, for example, the work of Bart Ehrman on *Lost Christianities,* cited above.

7. Two examples from the 1960s and 1970s may be given as examples of the earlier trend toward an ecumenical reading of Christian history. George A. Hadjiantonious' 1961 study entitled *Protestant Patriarch: The Life of Cyril Lucaris, 1572–1638, Patriarch of Constantinople* (Richmond: John Knox, 1961) pointed out relations between Eastern Orthodox and Western Christians in the seventeenth century. Catholic Historian Jean Delumeau wrote in 1977 on aspects of the Reformation age common to Protestants and Catholics: *Catholicism Between Luther and Voltaire: A New View of the Counter-Reformation* (London: Burns and Oats, and Philadelphia: Westminster, 1977). Subsequently there has been an emphasis on distinctive traditions: for example, Eamon Duffy's study of Catholic spirituality in the Reformation (*The Stripping of the Altars: Traditional Religion in England, c. 1400–c. 1580;* New Haven, CT: Yale University Press, second edition revised, 2005), and in the same period there has been a huge expansion of literature on specific Protestant traditions since the 1970s, for example, studies in the Wesleyan tradition.

8. Cf. Steven Connor's account of "Postmodernism and the Academy" in his book on *Postmodernist Culture: An Introduction to Theories of the Contemporary* (Oxford: Basil Blackwell, 1989), pp. 3–23.

9. Dan Brown, *The Da Vinci Code* (New York: Doubleday Books, 2003), chapter 55, pp. 230–236. The criticism about the canonical gospels is given in the fictitious character of "Sir Leigh Teabing." An earlier instance of this, with a similar argument, is given in Kim Stanley Robinson, *Red Mars* (New York: Bantam Books, 1993), p. 52. Here the critique is offered in the fictitious character of "John Boone."

10. An early example would be Martin Dibelius, *From Tradition to Gospel* (London: Ivor Nicholson and Watson, 1934; translation of *Die Formgeschichte des Evangeliums,* 1933, tr. Bertram Lee Wolf).

11. See the account in chapter 5 of the Montreal World Conference of Faith and Order in 1963.

12. The last two volumes of the Cambridge History of Christianity series have the titles *World Christianities, c. 1815–c. 1914* (ed. Sheridan Gilley and Brian Stanley; Cambridge, UK: Cambridge University Press, 2006) and *World Christiani-*

ties, c. 1914–*c.* 2000 (ed. Hugh McLeod; Cambridge, UK: Cambridge University Press, 2006). The term "Christianities" also appears in the titles or subtitles of the following works from the 1990s and the present decade: Jonathan Z. Smith, *Divine Drudgery: On the Comparison of Early Christianities and the Religions of Late Antiquity* (Chicago: University of Chicago Press, 1990), Bart D. Ehrman, *Lost Christianities* (cited earlier), and Garry Wills, *Head and Heart: American Christianities* (New York: Penguin, 2007).

13. David H. Kelsey, *To Understand God Truly: What's Theological about a Theological School* (Louisville, KY: Westminster/John Knox, 1992), p. 33.

14. Kathryn Tanner's study *Jesus, Humanity and the Trinity: A Brief Systematic Theology* (Minneapolis, MN: Fortress Press, 2001) offers another instance of this trend. The introduction asks the question "what one thinks Christianity fundamentally stands for," and the response is as follows:

> There is no obvious, established answer to this question which simply being a Christian commits one to. Christianity over the course of its two-thousand-year history and throughout the extent of its global reach, exhibits a great variety of answers; Christians are simply not of one mind on this most fundamental of theological questions. (p. xiv)

Tanner may have intended this as a statement about agreement between individual Christians or perhaps about agreement between theologians, but her reflection here gives the impression that there is simply no substantial, historical agreement between Christians—as individuals or in the corporate sense. In this sense it contradicts claims to ecumenical consensus made through the twentieth century on the part of Christian communities.

15. Tanner's footnotes show consistent engagement with contemporary systematic theologians, and even when corporately affirmed documents (such as the Definition of Faith of the council of Chalcedon) are quoted, they are cited as they appear in the works of contemporary theologians; cf. her citations of the Chalcedonian Definition of Faith as it appears in Rahner (p. 5, n. 6), and Schleiermacher (p. 15, n. 26).

The broad trend to study systematic theology with reference to the works of other systematic theologians and philosophers, and without sustained and documented reference to communally affirmed and communally received doctrinal claims, can be documented by reference to John Macquarrie's *Principles of Christian Theology* (second edition; New York: Charles Scribner's Sons, 1977). An examination of Macquarrie's footnotes and other references in his central section on "Symbolic Theology" (in which one would expect to find just such a sustained and documented dialogue with doctrinal sources) reveals that there is indeed a dialogue going on but, for the most part, it is not a dialogue with doctrinal sources. This section refers to at least eight patristic or medieval theologians (Aquinas, Augustine, Anselm, Theophilus of Antioch, Athanasius, Justin Martyr, Origen, and Irenaeus), five modern philosophers, fourteen modern biblical scholars, and twenty-eight modern theologians ("modern" meaning from Schleiermacher to the present). It refers to the Book of Common Prayer on at least four occasions (Macquarrie is an Anglican theologian), it refers at least once to Calvin's *Institutes,* and there is a general undocumented reference to Luther. At one point Macquarrie discusses the trinitarian doctrine of the Nicene Creed in his text (pp. 193–195), and at another point he discusses Chalcedonian christological teachings in the text (p. 297), but both references are undocumented and have no support from critical textual or contextual studies. There is also a reference to the so-called Athanasian Creed (p. 190), but at this point Macquarrie's concern is to illustrate a point from Ian Ramsey's theory of religious language, which happened coincidentally to be discussing the Athanasian creed. At another point, Macquarrie generalizes about distinctions between Eastern and Western Christian understandings of the *filioque* clause appended to the Nicene Creed, but again the references are entirely undocumented (pp. 330–332). My point is that in his 195-page discussion of "Symbolic Theology," for all his references to other sources, Macquarrie offers very few references to corporately affirmed and corporately received doctrinal standards, and the most significant of these references to the Nicene Creed and the Chalcedonian Definition of Faith are undocumented. This drives home the truth of Macquarrie's claim that his work is not a "study of creed, confessions of faith, and the like" (p. 40), but in an extended account of "symbolical" or "symbolic theology," the lack of sustained reference to communally affirmed and received doctrinal material, including contemporary ecumenical material, is both remarkable and lamentable.

16. Barth's definitions of dogmatics both in his *Dogmatics in Outline* and in *Church Dogmatics* do not spell out the content of the gospel within the definitions themselves, but Barth went on to make it clear that in speaking of "the content of [the church's] proclamation," "the object and activity with which dogmatics is concerned" is "the proclamation of the Gospel" (*Dogmatics in Outline* [New York: Harper and Row, 1959], pp. 9 and 10; see *Church Dogmatics* 1:1 [G. W. Bromiley and T. F. Torrance, eds., and trans.; Edinburgh: T. & T. Clark, 1975], 1:3–11). Edmund Schlink's *Ökumenische Dogmatik: Grundzüge* (Göttingen: Vandenhoeck & Ruprecht, 1993) begins with "The Gospel as the Presupposition of the Church's Doctrine" (the introduction).

17. Joseph Ratzinger, *Introduction to Christianity* (*Einführung in das Christentum;* Kösel-Verlag, 1968; English translation by J. R Foster (New York: Seabury Press, 1970). I have also consulted the Spanish translation published under the title *Introducción al Cristianismo* (Salamanca: Ediciones Sígueme, eighth edition, 1996).

18. All of these theologians were associated at one point or another with Yale Divinity School or Perkins School of Theology at Southern Methodist University. Some representative works are as follows: Lindbeck, *The Nature of Doctrine: Religion and Theology in a Postliberal Age* (Philadelphia: Westminster, 1984). Ellen Charry, *By the Renewing of Your Minds: The Pastoral Function of Christian Doctrine* (New York: Oxford University Press, 1997); Bruce Marshall, *Trinity and Truth* (Cambridge, UK, and New York: Cambridge University Press, 2000); William Abraham, *Canon and Criterion in Christian Theology* (Oxford: Clarendon Press, 1998); *Waking from Doctrinal Amnesia* (Nashville, TN: Abingdon Press, 1995).

19. At the conclusion of my earlier study of *Christian Confessions* (Louisville, KY: Westminster/John Knox, 1996), I offered seven claims about teachings (and implied practices) nearly universally affirmed by Christian communities (pp. 261–289).

20. The term "old-line" in referring to Protestant and Anglican churches refers to denominations that prevailed in North America from colonial times and that have professed their fidelity to historic Christian teachings and practices. I use the term in preference to the expression "mainline" churches, which implied a level of cultural dominance that is no longer held by them in the United States. Within the scope of old-line churches I include Anglican (Episcopal), Presbyterian, Congregational (including United Church of Christ), Lutheran, and Methodist churches, although Methodist churches have come to their "mainline" or "old-line" status only in the last hundred years or so.

21. See C. C. Goen's study of *Broken Churches, Broken Nation: Denominational Schisms and the Coming of the American Civil War* (Macon, GA: Mercer University Press, 1985).

22. New relationships between ancient Christian communities are represented in the following ways: (a) The removal of mutual anathemas and growing ecumenical relationships between the Catholic Church and Eastern Orthodox churches: cf. the apostolic letter of Paul VI in *Acta Apostolicae Sedis* 58:1 (31 January 1966), p. 41, and the reports of Catholic-Eastern Orthodox dialogues in Jeffrey Gros, FSC, Harding Meyer, and William G. Rusch, eds., *Growth in Agreement II: Reports and Agreed Statements of Ecumenical Conversations on a World Level, 1982–1998* (Faith and Order Paper no. 187; Geneva: WCC Publications, and Grand Rapids, MI: William B. Eerdmans, 2000), pp. 647–687, reflecting dialogues held between 1980 and 1995; (b) Ecumenical agreements between Eastern Orthodox and Oriental Orthodox churches: First Agreed Statement of the Dialogue between the Eastern and Oriental Orthodox Churches (1989), in Gros, Meyer, and Rusch, *Growth in Agreement II*, pp. 191–193; and (c) The "Common Christological Declaration between the Catholic Church and the Assyrian Church of the East," in Gros, Meyer, and Rusch, *Growth in Agreement II*, pp. 711–712.

23. Cf. the papal encyclical *Ut Unum Sint* of Pope John Paul II, 30 May 1995; English translation published in *Origins: CNS Documentary Service* 25:4 (8 June 1995): 49–72.

24. On the definition of "Evangelical" in this context, see the beginning of chapter 4.

25. The "Chicago Call: An Appeal to Evangelicals" is given in Joseph A. Burgess and Jeffrey Gros, FSC, eds., *Growing Consensus: Church Dialogues in the United States, 1962–1991* (Ecumenical Documents V; New York: Paulist Press, 1995), pp. 575–579. The earlier Chicago "Declaration of Evangelical Social Concern" is given in the same collection, pp. 571–572.

26. The report is given in Harding Meyer and Lucas Vischer, eds., *Growth in Agreement: Reports and Agreed Statements of Ecumenical Conversations on a World Level* (Faith and Order Paper no. 108; New York: Paulist Press, and Geneva: World

Council of Churches, 1984), pp. 421–431. This report and subsequent reports of Catholic-Pentecostal dialogue are given in Gros, Meyer, and Rusch, *Growth in Agreement II,* pp. 713–779.

27. The text of the final report is given in Gros, Meyer, and Rusch, *Growth in Agreement II,* pp. 399–437.

28. Bradley Nassif, "Eastern Orthodoxy and Evangelicalism: The Status of an Emerging Global Dialogue" in Daniel B. Clendenin, ed., *Eastern Orthodox Theology: A Contemporary Reader* (Grand Rapids, MI: Baker Academic/Paternoster Press, second edition, 2003), pp. 211–248.

29. Published by the Institute on Religion and Public Life under the leadership of Richard John Neuhaus since the early 1990s.

30. *First Things* 43 (May 1994): 15–22.

31. Carl E. Braaten and Robert W. Jenson, eds., *In One Body through the Cross: the Princeton Proposal for Christian Unity* (Grand Rapids, MI: William B. Eerdmans Publishing Co., 2003).

32. The results of these dialogues are available in a volume entitled *Ancient Faith and American-Born Churches: Dialogues Between Christian Traditions,* ed. Ted A. Campbell, Ann K. Riggs, and Gilbert W. Stafford (New York: Paulist Press, 2005).

33. Brian D. McLaren, *A Generous Orthodoxy* (El Cajon, CA: Youth Specialties Books, an imprint of Zondervan Press, 2004) and the foreword to the book by John R. Franke.

34. Cf. articles by Scott Bader-Saye and Jason Byassee in *Christian Century* 121:24 (30 November 2004), pp. 20–27 and 28–31, respectively.

35. McLaren, op. cit.

36. See the introductions to chapters 2, 3, and 4 (respectively) on the meanings of "ancient Christian churches," "Protestant and related churches," and "Evangelical communities."

37. This is the definition of "doctrine" given in my earlier study of *Christian Confessions,* p. 2; cf. Jaroslav Pelikan, *The Christian Tradition: A History of the Development of Doctrine* (5 vols.; Chicago: University of Chicago Press, 1971–1989), 1:1, where doctrine is defined as "What the church of Jesus Christ believes, teaches, and confesses on the basis of the word of God"; and cf. Jaroslav Pelikan, *Credo: Historical and Theological Guide to Creeds and Confessions of Faith in the Christian Tradition* (New Haven, CT: Yale University Press, 2003), pp. 64–71.

CHAPTER 1

1. Gerhard Kittel, ed., *Theological Dictionary of the New Testament* (tr. and ed. Geoffrey W. Bromiley; Grand Rapids, MI: William B. Eerdmans Publishing Co., 1964), s.v. "εὐαγγέλιον," 2:721–736, and especially 729–735 on the use of the term in Paul's writings. The epigraph is from I Corinthians 15:3b–4, with connecting phrases ("that," "and that") removed; see the text following for further commentary on this passage.

2. Cf. Ehrman, *Lost Christianities,* pp. 176–179.

3. See the references to Dibelius, *From Tradition to Gospel* (earlier in this chapter) and to Dodd, *The Apostolic Preaching and Its Development* (later in this chapter). Robert Jewett's recently published Hermeneia commentary on Romans identifies a number of New Testament passages as including earlier formulae embedded in Acts and the Pauline and deuteropauline works, including Acts 3:15, 4:10, and 13:30, Romans 4:24, 5:6, 5:8, 8:10, and 14:15, I Corinthians 8:11 and 15:3, II Corinthians 5:14–15, Galatians 1:4, I Thessalonians 4:14 and 5:9–10. Cf. Jewett, *Romans: A Commentary* (Hermeneia Commentary Series; Minneapolis: Fortress Press, 2007), pp. 24, 340–341, and 361.

4. In this and subsequent passages that reflect the traditioning of the gospel, I have italicized what I identify as the words of the proclamation *per se,* to distinguish them from the surrounding framework. Similarly, I have also utilized my own indentation to show the form of these passages.

5. References to the New International Version of the Bible (NIV), copyright © 1973, 1978, and 1984 by the International Bible Society.

6. Kittel, *Theological Dictionary of the New Testament,* s.v. "δίδωμι," 2:171–172 (sections on "παραδοῦναι" and "παράδοσις").

7. Gerd Theissen and Annette Merz, *The Historical Jesus: A Comprehensive Guide* (London: SCM Press, 1998; translation by John Bowden from *Der historische Jesus: Ein Lehrbuch;* Göttingen: Vandenhoek & Ruprecht, 1996), p. 488; cf. the broader discussion of this passage, pp. 486–490. I note that when Theissen and Merz use the term "formula," they refer to the substance of what has been handed on, not to the introductory formulae (to which I have referred earlier). The recognition of the pre-Pauline materials as the earliest strand of Christian tradition has long been recognized in New Testament scholarship; cf. Hans Conzelmann, *An Outline of the Theology of the New Testament* (London: SCM Press, 1969; translation by John Bowden from *Grundriss der Theologie des Neuen Testaments;* Munich: Christian Kaiser Verlag, second edition, 1968), in which the first full section of the work discusses "The Kerygma of the Primitive Community and the Hellenistic Community," pp. 27–93, esp. "The Content of the Proclamation," pp. 62–71; cf. also Paul M. van Buren, *According to the Scriptures: The Origins of the Gospel and of the Church's Old Testament* (Grand Rapids, MI: William B. Eerdmans Publishing Company, 1998), pp. 10–12.

8. Theissen and Merz note that "The extent of the tradition cannot be defined with certainty; however, vv. 3b–5 are certainly tradition" (p. 487). I am surprised that they would consider verse 5 (resurrection appearances to Cephas and The Twelve) as part of the "tradition" handed on in this passage, because it seems to fit with the list of resurrection appearances that includes verses 6 through 10. In any case, there seems to be no doubt that the three phrases in verses 3b–4 are "traditioned" in the way Paul indicates.

9. In this passage, the definite article is not used with "Christ" as one might expect in the very earliest strata of tradition in which "the Christ" (ὁ χριστός) could simply be a noun denoting "the anointed [one]." Kittel makes the case, however, that in Paul's own usage, ὁ χριστός and χριστός are not distinguished at all: Kittel, *Theological Dictionary of the New Testament,* s.v. "χρίω" III:1:b, 9:541.

10. That the passage refers in some way to Old Testament scripture seems clear enough. However, there seems to be no consensus among scholars as to the precise reference of the expression "in accordance with the scriptures." Theissen and Merz offer suggestions that Christ's death "for our sins in accordance with the scriptures" has reference to Isaiah 53:5ff and Christ's resurrection "on the third day in accordance with the scriptures" may have reference to Hosea 6:2 (Theissen and Merz, p. 489).

11. Kerygma ("proclamation") is an appropriate term here in addition to εὐαγγέλιον ("gospel" or "good news"), because at the conclusion of the passage Paul writes, "so we proclaim" (οὕτως κηρύσσομεν) and κήρυγμα is the substantive meaning "proclamation" derived from this verb "proclaim."

12. Cf. Conzelmann, *Outline of the Theology of the New Testament,* pp. 63–64.

13. Ignatius of Antioch, letter to the Philadelphians 9:2; in Michael W. Holmes, ed. and tr., *The Apostolic Fathers: Greek Texts and English Translations* (Grand Rapids, MI: Baker Academic, third edition, 2007), pp. 244–245.

14. I Clement 25:1 (in Holmes, ed. and tr., *Apostolic Fathers,* pp. 78–79), 42:1–3 (pp. 100–101); letter of Ignatius of Antioch to the Ephesians 7:2 (pp. 188–189), 20:1 (pp. 198–199); letter of Ignatius of Antioch to the Magnesians, the salutation and 1:3 (pp. 202–203), 11 (pp. 210–211); letter of Ignatius of Antioch to the Trallians 9:1-2 (pp. 220–221); letter of Ignatius of Antioch to the Romans, the salutation (pp. 224–225), 6 (pp. 230–231); letter of Ignatius of Antioch to the Philadelphians, the salutation (pp. 236–237), 8:2 (pp. 242–243), and the passage from 9:2 cited in the text earlier (pp. 244–245); letter of Ignatius of Antioch to the Smyrnaeans 1:1-2 (pp. 248–249; this passage has a distinctly creedal form), 2 (pp. 250–251), 6:2 and 7:2 (pp. 254–255), 12:2 (pp. 260–261); letter of Polycarp to the Philippians 1:2 (pp. 280–281), 2:1-2 (pp. 282–283), 9:2 (pp. 290–291), 12:2 (pp. 294–295), and the Greek letter attributed to Barnabas, 16:9 (pp. 428–429). My own survey of the literature of the Apostolic Fathers has not found clear references to the gospel message in II Clement, the letter of Ignatius of Antioch to Polycarp (although there is a suggestive passage at 3:32, pp. 264–265), the *Didache,* or the *Shepherd of Hermas.* The Holmes edition (and translation) of the Apostolic Fathers includes the martyrdom or Polycarp and the letter to Diognetus, and some other second-century literature, but these pieces date from the middle of the second century or later and so I have not included them here.

15. Cf. Luke Timothy Johnson, *The Creed: What Christians Believe and Why It Matters* (New York: Doubleday Image Books, 2003), pp. 14–16.

16. Letter of Ignatius of Antioch to the Smyrnaeans 1:1-2 (in Holmes, ed. and tr., *Apostolic Fathers,* pp. 248–249).

17. Irenaeus, *Demonstration of the Apostolic Preaching,* par. 3; Latin text in Adelin Rousseau, ed., *Irénée de Lyon: Démonstration de la Prédication Apostolique* (Sources chrétiennes series, no. 406; Paris: Éditions du Cerf, 1995), p. 88; cf. John Behr, ed. and tr., *On the Apostolic Preaching* (Crestwood, NY: St. Vladimir's Seminary Press, 1996), p. 42. The translation given is my own though very close to Behr's. Cf. also the comment on Irenaeus's *Demonstration of the Apostolic Preaching* in Jaroslav

Pelikan and Valerie Hotchkiss, eds., *Creeds and Confessions of Faith in the Christian Tradition* (3 vols., with a collection of source material in original languages on CD ROM; New Haven, CT: Yale University Press, 2003; cited hereafter as Pelikan and Hotchkiss, *Creeds and Confessions*), 1:48.

18. Cf. I Timothy 6:13, "In the presence of God, who gives life to all things, and of Christ Jesus, who in his testimony before Pontius Pilate made the good confession . . ." Cf. also Conzelmann, pp. 87–88, on "binitarian" formulae in the New Testament and elsewhere. A similar binitarian formula appears in "The Martyrdom of Justin and His Companions," ¶ 2; in Herbert Musurillo, ed., *The Acts of the Christian Martyrs* (Oxford, Oxford University Press, 1972), pp. 42 and 48 (two recensions). One recension of the so-called *Epistola Apostolorum* (mid-second century) expresses the Christian faith beginning with a trinitarian pattern:

> In the Father, Ruler of the Universe,
> And in Jesus Christ, our Redeemer,
> In the Holy Spirit, the Paraclete,
> In the Holy Church,
> And in the Forgiveness of Sins.

The text is given in Carl Schmidt and Isaak Wajnberg, eds., *Gespräche Jesu mit seinen Jüngern nach der Auferstehung: Ein Katholisch-Apostolisches Sendschreiben des 2. Jahrhunderts (Texte und Untersuchungen* series, vol. 36; Leipzig and Berlin: Hinrichs Verlag, 1919), p. 32; cf. Hugo Duensing, ed., *Epistula Apostolorum nach dem Äthiopischen und Koptischen Texte* (Bonn: A. Marcus und E. Webers Verlag, 1925), p. 7. The translation here is that of John Leith, *Creeds of the Churches: A Reader in Christian Doctrine from the New Testament to the Present* (Atlanta, GA: John Knox, third edition, revised, 1982), p. 17. Pelikan and Hotchkiss, *Creeds and Confessions,* 1:53–54 cite another passage from the *Epistula Apostolorum* that has creedal claims. A primitive trinitarian version of the formula is given in the Dêr Balyzeh papyrus, which is itself dated to around 200 C.E., but the form of its trinitarian affirmation is probably earlier; cf. C. H. Roberts and Dom B. Capelle, *An Early Euchologium, the Dêr Balyzeh Papyrus* (Louvain, 1949); cf. Leith, *Creeds of the Churches,* p. 19.

19. "Binitarian" formulae appear in the literature of the Apostolic Fathers in II Clement 20:5 (in Holmes, ed. and tr., *Apostolic Fathers,* pp. 164–165); the letter of Ignatius of Antioch to the Ephesians, the salutation (pp. 182–183), 3:2 (pp. 184–185), 21:2 (pp. 200–201); the letter of Ignatius of Antioch to the Philadelphians, the salutation and 1:1 (pp. 236–237); the letter of Ignatius of Antioch to the Smyrnaeans, the salutation (pp. 248–249), and in the letter of Polycarp to the Philippians 12:2 (pp. 248–249). Trinitarian formulae and images appear in the literature of the Apostolic Fathers in I Clement 46:6 (in Holmes, ed. and tr., *Apostolic Fathers,* pp. 106–107), 58:2 (pp. 122–123); the letter of Ignatius of Antioch to the Ephesians 9:1 (pp. 190–191); the letter of Ignatius of Antioch to the Magnesians 13:1 (pp. 210–211); and the letter of Ignatius of Antioch to the Philadelphians, the salutation (pp. 236–237, in conjunction with a "binitarian" formula).

20. Irenaeus, *Adversus Haereses* I:10:1 (text in Brox, ed., 1:198–200); English translation in Pelikan and Hotchkiss, *Creeds and Confessions*, 1:49; cf. translation given by Leith in *Creeds of the Churches*, p. 21. I have indented the paragraphs to make clear the structure of the passage (see comments in the text following).

21. Irenaeus, *Adversus Haereses* I:10:2 (text in Brox, ed., 1:200); my own translation.

22. Cf. Pelikan, *The Christian Tradition*, 1:116–118.

23. Tertullian, *Adversus Praxean* 2:1–2; Latin text in Hermann-Josef Sieben, ed., *Tertullian: Adversus Praxean/Gegen Praxeas* (Fontes Christiani series, no. 34; Freiburg: Herder, 2001), pp. 102–104. The translation of the first portion of this passage is that of Pelikan and Hotchkiss, *Creeds and Confessions*, 1:56. The translation of the last paragraph, which includes the concluding formula of tradition, is that of Leith, *Creeds of the Churches*, pp. 21–22. As with the previously cited tradition from Irenaeus, I have blocked this into paragraphs and indented it to show the structure of the tradition as it is given by Tertullian. Tertullian gives similar instances of the "rule of faith" (this is the term he employs) in *De Praescriptione Haereticorum* 13:1–6 (in Pelikan and Hotchkiss, *Creeds and Confessions*, 1:56), *Adversus Praxean* 4:1 (in Pelikan and Hotchkiss, *Creeds and Confessions*, 1:57), and in *De Virginibus Velandis* (in Pelikan and Hotchkiss, *Creeds and Confessions*, 1:57).

24. Latin recension of the Apostolic Tradition; in Bernard Botte, ed., *Hippolyte de Rome: La Tradition Apostolique d'après les anciennes Versions* (Sources chrétiennes series, no. 11; Paris: Éditions du Cerf, 1968), pp. 84–86, which collates two Latin versions at this point; cf. Paul F. Bradshaw, Maxwell E. Johnson, and L. Edward Phillips, eds., *The Apostolic Tradition: A Commentary* (Hermeneia commentary series; Minneapolis: Fortress Press, 2002), pp. 116–118.

25. The translation given here is that of Pelikan and Hotchkiss, *Creeds and Confessions*, 1:61. I have removed the liturgical comments surrounding this text; cf. the translation of Leith, *Creeds of the Churches*, p. 23, which similarly removes the liturgical comments. In the Latin text given in Botte and in Bradshaw, Johnson, and Phillips, the initial article (on the Father) is missing. The translation in parallel columns given by Bradshaw, Johnson, and Phillips shows that the Bohairic, Arabic, and Ethiopic recensions of the text do have the initial article on the Father, though in these texts the article on the Son shows evidence of expansion over the simpler form given in the Latin recension. As with other versions of the tradition, I have added paragraphs and indentation to make clearer the structure of the tradition given in this document. Cf. Ratzinger, *Introduction to Christianity*, chapter 2, "The Ecclesiastical Form of Faith" and the first subtitle, "Introductory Remarks on the History and Structure of the Apostles' Creed," where Ratzinger supposes that all forms early Christian message were couched as questions (in the English translation, pp. 50–52; in the Spanish translation, pp. 59–61).

26. Origen, *De Principiis* preface, ¶ 4; text (Latin) in Henri Crouzel and Manlio Simonetti, eds. and trs., *Origène: Traité des Principes* (Sources chrétiennes series;

Paris: Éditions du Cerf, 1978), pp. 80–82. English translation in G. W. Butterworth, ed. and tr., *Origen: On First Principles* (London: SPCK, 1936), pp. 2–3.

27. Augustine, *Confessions*, book 8; here cited from the translation of R. S. Pine-Coffin, *Confessions* (London: Penguin, 1961), p. 160.

28. Augustine, *De Fide et Symbolo*, Latin text and French translation given in J. Rivière, ed. and tr., *Exposés généraux de la Foi* (Bibliothèque Augustinienne: Oeuvres de Saint Augustin series, no. 9; Paris: Desclée, de Brouwer, et Cie, 1947), pp. 18–75. Latin text and English translation given in E. P. Meijering, ed. and tr., *Augustine: De Fide et Symbolo* (Amsterdam: J. C. Gieben, 1987), pp. 15–159. Meijering gives a helpful summary of Augustine's understanding of the creed and the various forms of the creed that Augustine seems to have known, pp. 8–11. There is also a discussion of the creed as Augustine knew it and a translation (following the Latin text of Meijering) in Pelikan and Hotchkiss, *Creeds and Confessions*, 1:111–112.

29. This belief was reported by Rufinus of Aquileia (ca. C.E. 400) in his *Commentarius in Symbolum Apostolorum* ¶ 2; in J. N. D. Kelly, tr. and ed., *Rufinus: A Commentary on the Apostles' Creed* (Ancient Christian Writers series; Westminster, MD: the Newman Press, and London: Longmans, Green, and Co., 1955), pp. 29–31; cf. Pelikan, *Christian Tradition* 1:117.

30. Pelikan, *Christian Tradition* 1:117. Pelikan here refers to (and quotes) the passage in Origen, *De Principiis,* preface, ¶ 4 cited earlier.

31. A body of earlier scholarship on these and other groups utilized the term "Gnostic" as an over-arching category in which they could be placed. Despite some continuing work that utilizes this term (e.g., the work of Elaine Pagels), it is widely recognized now that the term "Gnostic" is so void of specific meaning as to be more harmful than helpful, so I have elected to refer to specific groups or movements rather than identifying them together as "Gnostic."

32. Although the expression "Hebrew Scriptures" is sometimes utilized as a term neutral to Christian and Jewish traditions, I will generally follow Christian tradition of naming these scriptures as the "Old Testament"; cf. Amy Jill Levine, "Jewish-Christian Relations from the 'Other Side': A Response to Webb, Lodahl, and White," *Quarterly Review* 20:3 (Fall 2000), pp. 297–300.

33. Pelikan, *The Christian Tradition,* 1:110–112.

34. Conzelmann, *Theology of the New Testament,* pp. 97–99. Dibelius, *From Tradition to Gospel* gives an overview of the process that led from primitive expressions of the gospel tradition such as I Corinthians 15:1–4 (pp. 18–20) to the composition of the four canonical gospels. In more recent scholarship, this development is taken up by Martin Hengel in *The Four Gospels and the One Gospel of Jesus Christ: An Investigation of the Collection and Origin of the Canonical Gospels* (tr. John Bowden; Harrisburg, PA: Trinity Press International, 2000), *passim.*

35. Muratorian fragment, in *Enchiridion Biblicum: Documenta Ecclesiastica Sacram Scripturam Spectantia* (fourth edition; Naples: M. D'Auria, and Rome: A. Arnoldo, 1961), nos. 1–7, pp. 1–3; cf. the English translation in Henry Bettenson, ed., *Documents of the Christian Church* (London: Oxford University Press, second edition, 1963), pp. 28–29.

36. Bart D. Ehrman, *The Orthodox Corruption of Scripture: The Effect of Early Christological Controversies on the Text of the New Testament* (New York: Oxford University Press, 1993).

37. Athanasius, Festal Letter 39, in *Enchiridion Biblicum,* nos. 14–15, pp. 7–9.

38. Frances Young, *Virtuoso Theology* (Pilgrim Press, 1993), pp. 60–61.

39. Pelikan, *Credo,* p. 147.

CHAPTER 2

1. The term "Oriental Orthodox," as contrasted with "Eastern Orthodox," is used only (so far as I know) in English, and it is admittedly an awkward construction since "Oriental" and "Eastern" have roughly the same meaning. In some languages (e.g., Spanish) "Eastern Orthodox" churches are referred to simply as "Orthodox," with Oriental Orthodox being distinguished as "Eastern" or "Oriental."

2. In referring to the "Assyrian Church," I mean the Assyrian Church of the East, the community that honors Mar Nestorius of Constantinople and has not affirmed Ecumenical Councils after the (first) Council of Constantinople. Additionally, I would note at this point that I have not included the Mar Thoma Church of India within the scope of ancient Christian communities considered in this chapter. The Mar Thoma Church existed from ancient times and counts its own origins to the missionary activity of the Apostle Thomas (hence "Mar Thoma"). It shares many traditions in common with other Eastern Christian churches. However, the Mar Thoma Church was also significantly influenced by Protestant churches (especially Anglicans) after the time of the Reformation and the incursion of Western peoples into India, and also shares in Christian traditions inherited from Anglicans and Protestants. For this reason I have considered the Mar Thoma Church within the scope of Protestant and related churches (chapter 3), noting that its great gift is directly related to the fact that it does not fit precisely in any of the wide categories of churches I have laid out here.

3. The section of the creed in the epigraph is from the translation by the International Consultation on English Texts, *Prayers we Have in Common* (Philadelphia: Fortress Press, second edition revised, 1975, p. 6).

4. J. N. D. Kelly, John Leith, and Pelikan and Hotchkiss accept the association of the Nicene-Constantinopolitan Creed with the assembly (or first Council) of Constantinople in 381 C.E.: Kelly, *Early Christian Creeds* (Burnt Mill, Harlow, UK: Longman Group Ltd., third edition, revised, 1972), pp. 296–331; Leith, *Creeds of the Churches,* p. 31; Pelikan and Hotchkiss, *Creeds and Confessions,* 1:160–161.

5. The translation given here is that of the International Consultation on English Texts as it is cited in the WCC Faith and Order study *Confessing the One Faith* (Faith and Order Paper no. 153; Geneva: WCC Press, 1991), pp. 11–12; c.f. the International Consultation on English Texts, *Prayers we Have in Common* (Philadelphia; Fortress Press, second edition revised, 1975, p. 6). Parenthetical words were supplied in the WCC publication to aid readability. The WCC document also gives a Greek text (pp. 10–11). Critical editions of the Greek and Latin

texts of this creed and an English translation are given in Pelikan and Hotchkiss, *Creeds and Confessions,* 1:162–163.

6. The claim anathematized in the form of the creed from the first Council of Nicaea, 325: cf. Pelikan and Hotchkiss, *Creeds and Confessions,* 1:158–159.

7. Robert C. Gregg and Dennis E. Groh, *Early Arianism: A View of Salvation* (Philadelphia: Fortress Press, 1981).

8. The New Testament scholar Larry W. Hurtado has examined what he calls the early Christians' "cult of Jesus," and finds the practice of devotion to Jesus to have roots in the very earliest years of the Christian movement: *Lord Jesus Christ: Devotion to Jesus in Earliest Christianity* (Grand Rapids, MI: William B. Eerdmans Publishing Co., 2003.

9. In describing the Christians of Asia Minor in the early second century, the Roman official Pliny the Younger wrote to the Emperor Trajan that it was the Christians' custom, *carmen . . . Christo quasi deo dicere,* "to sing a hymn to Christ, as to a god": Pliny the Younger, letter to the emperor Trajan; in R. A. B. Mynors, ed., *C. Plini Caecili: Epistularum Libri Decem* (Oxford: Clarendon Press, 1963), p. 339; my translation. Cf. Robert L. Wilken, "The Christians as the Romans (and Greeks) Saw Them," *Jewish and Christian Self-Definition,* ed. E. P. Sanders (3 vols.; Philadelphia: Fortress, 1980ff.) 1:111–113. Wilken points to Lucian's *Peregrinus* and to the *Martyrdom of Polycarp* as parallels to the passage in Pliny and as further instances of the practice of the worship of Christ as a central element in early Christian self-definition.

10. This is not to overlook a significant difference in interpretation between Eastern and Western churches on the particular meaning of the initial phrase, "We believe in one God . . ." Eastern interpreters have often taken this as a reference to the unity of the first person of the Trinity, that is, the Father, whereas Western interpreters from Augustine interpreted "one God" as a reference to the Trinity itself, and not specifically to the divine person of the Father. But in both cases the creed is understood as affirming the unity of God and the identity of God with the God described in Jewish scripture, "the God of Abraham, Isaac, and Jacob."

11. See the discussion of doctrine and doctrinal reception in chapter 7.

12. Homily 10, ¶ 23; in A. Mingana, ed. and tr., *Commentary of Theodore of Mopsuestia on the Nicene Creed,* (Woodbrooke Studies: Christian Documents in Syriac, Arabic, and Garshuni, vol. 5; Cambridge, UK: W. Heffer and Sons, 1932), p. 116; cf. the more recent German translation in Peter Bruns, ed., *Theodor von Mopsuestia: Katechetische Homilien* (Fontes Christiani series, vols. 17:1 and 17:2; Freiburg: Herder, 1994–1995), 1:238.

13. Decree of the emperor Basiliscus, given in Evagrius Scholasticus, *Ecclesiastical History* III:4 (in Michael Whitby, tr., *The Ecclesiastical History of Evagrius Scholasticus* [Translated Texts for Historians series, vol. 33; Liverpool: Liverpool University Press, 2000], p. 134). The decree refers to "the creed composed by the 318 holy Fathers who in company with the Holy Spirit were assembled in Nicaea long ago . . ." Although this could be construed as a reference to the original (325 C.E.) text of the Nicene Creed, Kelly argues that it was the "Constantinopolitan" version that is

referred to in the decree; cf. Kelly, pp. 344–345. Cf. also the claim that a Monophysite patriarch of Constantinople, Timothy, ordered that the (Nicene) creed should be recited at every ecclesial assembly, whereas in the past it had only been recited on Good Friday in association with catechesis and profession; in Theodore the Reader (also known as Theodore Lector or Theodore Anagnostes), *Ecclesiastical History*, epitome 501 (in Günther Christian Hansen, ed., *Theodoros Anagnostes: Kirchengeschichte* [Berlin: Akademie Verlag, 1995], p. 143).

14. Charlemagne himself alluded to this use of the Nicene Creed in a dialogue (ca. 809 or 810 C.E.) with Frankish clergy recorded by the monk Smaragdus, "Acta Collationis Romanae . . ."; in Jean-Paul Migne, ed., *Patrologiae Latinae Cursus Completus Omnium SS. Patrum, Doctorum Scriptorum Ecclesiasticorum* (217 vols.; Turnholti: Typographi Brepols Editores Pontificii, 1844–55; hereafter referred to as Migne, *Patrologia Latina*), 102:975. On the general acceptance of the Nicene-Constantinopolitan Creed in association with catechesis in the Western church, cf. Kelly, pp. 346–348.

15. As noted in the Introduction, the term "Monophysite" is today a disputed term, especially by those in Oriental Orthodox traditions who were traditionally described utilizing this term. In this case, then, the term is used according to the perception, on the part of those who did affirm the Chalcedonian teaching, that those who did not affirm the Chalcedonian teaching believed only in "one nature" of the incarnate Word.

16. Theodore the Reader, *Ecclesiastical History*, epitome 501 (in Hansen, ed., *Theodoros Anagnostes: Kirchengeschichte*, p. 143) and epitome 504 (in Hansen, p. 155).

17. Account of a gathering described very loosely as a "council" in Constantinople; in J. D. Mansi, ed., *Sacrorum Conciliorum Nova et Amplissima Collectio* (Florence: 1758; reprint edition of 1901), 8:1065–1066; translation of Kelly, p. 350.

18. Kelly, pp. 351–357.

19. Kelly, pp. 358–367; Pelikan, *Credo*, pp. 414–415.

20. Cf. *Catechism of the Catholic Church* (Catholic catechism approved by the apostolic constitution *Fidei Depositum* of John Paul II, 11 October 1992), ¶¶ 246–248; North American English translation: *Catechism of the Catholic Church* (Washington, DC: United States Catholic Conference, 1994) pp. 65–66; North American Spanish translation: *Catecismo de la Iglesia Católica* (Washington, DC: United States Catholic Conference, second edition, 2001), pp. 55–56.

21. Chalcedonian "Definition of Faith" (in Pelikan and Hotchkiss, *Creeds and Confessions*, 1:176–177).

22. "Exposition of Faith" of the third council of Constantinople (in Pelikan and Hotchkiss, *Creeds and Confessions*, 1:220–221); doctrinal statement of the second council of Nicaea (in Pelikan and Hotchkiss, *Creeds and Confessions*, 1:234–235).

23. Liturgy of St. John Chrysostom (in Pelikan and Hotchkiss, *Creeds and Confessions*, 1:285).

24. The creed is given in the liturgies of Ethiopian and West Syrian churches in Peter D. Day, *Eastern Christian Liturgies: The Armenian, Coptic, Ethiopian, and*

Syrian Rites: Eucharistic Rites with Introductory Notes and Rubrical Instructions (Shannon: Irish University Press, 1972), pp. 39–40.

25. The Armenian version of the Creed is given in Tiran Nersoyan, tr. and ed., *Divine Liturgy of the Armenian Apostolic Orthodox Church: With Variables, Complete Rubrics, and Commentary* (London: Saint Sarkis Church and Society for Promoting Christian Knowledge, fifth edition, revised, 1984), pp. 54–57. A note in this volume (presumably by Archbishop Nersoyan) states that this form of the creed has been used in the Armenian churches since early in the sixth century C.E. (p. 280).

26. *The Sacramentary: Approved for Use in the Dioceses of the United States of America by the National Conference of Catholic Bishops and Confirmed by the Apostolic See*, p. 413.

27. Based roughly on the assertion of Prosper of Aquitaine, *ut legem credendi lex statuat supplicandi*, "that the rule of prayer should establish the rule of faith" or belief; Prosper of Aquitaine, a treatise *Praeteritorum Sedis Apostolicae Episcoporum Auctoritas de Gratia Dei et Libero Voluntatis Arbitrio*, chapter 8 ("alias 11"); in Migne, *Patrologia Latina*, 51:209. There has been an accompanying debate as to whether Prosper was referring to the liturgy proper or simply to private prayer in this claim. Cf. the discussion of this statement in Pelikan, *Credo*, p. 166 and *The Christian Tradition*, 1:339.

28. Pelikan, *Credo*, pp. 405ff.

29. The term "eucharist" is from the word for "giving thanks," which appears in the passage cited earlier (I Corinthians 11:24) as "having given thanks" (εὐχαριστήσας). On the relationship between the tradition of the supper and the tradition of the kerygma, cf. Conzelmann, *Outline of the Theology of the New Testament*, pp. 51–52.

30. Joachim Jeremias, *The Eucharistic Words of Jesus* (Philadelphia: Fortress Press, 1966), esp. pp. 220–237.

31. Frances Young, *Sacrifice and the Death of Christ* (London: SPCK, 1975); although Young recognizes that sacrifices involved more than the destruction of a sacrificial victim, the title of this book carries the impression that it was Christ's death that was his essentially sacrificial work. Rowan Williams points out that for Irenaeus of Lyons (late second century), Christ's sacrifice is envisioned as a thank-offering rather than a sin-offering, and Christ's death is not held up as the primary meaning of the work of Christ: Rowan Williams, *Eucharistic Sacrifice—The Roots of a Metaphor* (Grove Liturgical Studies, no. 31; Bramcote, Nottinghamshire: Grove Books, 1982), pp. 10–12.

32. C. F. D. Moule makes the point that although some New Testament texts are "sharply focused on the death" of Christ, others emphasize the unity of Christ's death and resurrection, and others still emphasize "the whole incarnation rather than its culmination," *The Sacrifice of Christ* (London: Hodder and Stoughton, 1956), pp. 20–21.

33. One of the problems in ecumenical understanding at this point lies in the use of the term "prayers." For many Protestants, "prayer" implies worship, so the

application of the term to "prayers addressed to saints" implies worship of saints, and this is clearly ruled out in ancient Christian communities (most notably, for Eastern Orthodox and Catholics, in the distinction between worship [λατρεία] and "veneration" or "honor" [προσκύνησις] drawn at the second Council of Nicaea, 787 C.E. (cf. Pelikan and Hotchkiss, *Creeds and Confessions*, 1:232–241). I have placed the word in quotation marks to call attention to the contested and problematic meanings of the term "prayer" and to call for care in interpreting it.

34. In the ancient Syriac liturgy of the Assyrian Church of the East, the Liturgy of Addai and Mari, the institution narrative is not recounted directly from the scriptures, but as Assyrian church leaders and scholars who have studied the text point out, the entire service presupposes and refers to the institution narrative; cf. A. Gelston, *The Eucharistic Prayer of Addai and Mari* (Oxford: Clarendon Press, 1992), pp. 72–76 and 108–109.

35. Paul F. Bradshaw, *Early Christian Worship: A Basic Introduction to Ideas and Practice* (Collegeville, MN: Liturgical Press, 1996), p. 49; cf. Bradshaw, *The Search for the Origins of Christian Worship: Sources and Methods for the Study of Early Liturgy* (New York: Oxford University Press, 1992), pp. 89–92.

36. Cf. Gelston, *The Eucharistic Prayer of Addai and Mari*, pp. 72–76 and 108–109.

37. Bradshaw, pp. 89–92.

38. In Pelikan and Hotchkiss, *Creeds and Confessions of Faith in the Christian Tradition*, 1:286. The sentence as given is incomplete, but the priest then continues "Thine own of thine own we offer unto thee, on behalf of all and for all" (1:287).

39. In Bard Thompson, ed., *Liturgies of the Western Church* (Cleveland and New York: World Publishing Company, 1961), pp. 66 (Latin) and 67 (English). The direct address to the Holy Trinity that appears in this prayer is rare in Western liturgies.

40. Jaroslav Pelikan offers a detailed account of how the Liturgy of St. John Chrysostom reflects the Orthodox faith: *Credo*, pp. 405–413.

41. Concluding theotokion (prayer addressed to the Blessed Virgin) of Saturday evening vespers in Tone 4, found in the *Octoechos* (Book of Eight Tones).

42. As noted earlier, the narrative in I Corinthians 11:23–25 also presupposes the context of the Passover meal, although this is not explicitly stated in the text as it is in the canonical gospels.

43. The Paschal Homily of Melito of Sardis; in Alistair Stewart-Sykes, ed. and tr., *On Pascha: With the Fragments of Melito and Other Material related to the Quartodecimans* (Crestwood, NY: St. Vladimir's Theological Seminary Press, 2001), *passim*.

44. Tertullian, *De Baptismo* 19; in Dietrich Schleyer, tr. and ed., *Tertullian: De Baptismo: De Oratione* (Fontes Christiani series; Turnhout: Brepols Publishing, 2006), pp. 210–213.

45. Tertullian, *De Ieiunio adversus Psychicos* 14; in A. Reifferscheid and G. Wissowa, eds., in *Corpus Christianorum: Series Latina* (Turnhout: Brepols, 1954), 2:1272–1273. Cf. Tertullian, *De Corona Militis* 3:4; in Aem. Kroymann, ed. (in *Corpus Christianorum: Series Latina*, 2:1043).

46. Tertullian, *De Ieiunio adversus Psychicos*, 13 (in Reifferscheid and Wissowa, 2:1271).

47. Canons of the Council of Nicaea, nos. 5 and 20, and the letter of the synod of Nicaea to the Alexandrians; in Norman P. Tanner, SJ, ed., *Decrees of the Ecumenical Councils* (2 vols.; London: Sheed and Ward; and Washington, DC: Georgetown University Press, 1990), 1:8, 1:16, and 1:19. The forty-day period for Lent may not be immediately apparent in the English translation but the term translated "Lent" in the Latin text (and the equivalent of it in the Greek text) is *quadragesima*, which literally denotes a forty-day period (canon 5; in Tanner, 1:8). The Syriac text of the *Didascalia Apostolorum*, probably from the fourth century, also speaks of the forty-day period of fasting prior to Easter: *Didascalia Apostolorum* 3:8:7; in Arthur Vööbus, tr., *The Didascalia Apostolorum in Syriac* (Corpus Scriptorum Ecclesiasticorum Orentalium series; Louvain: Secrétariat du CorpusSCO, 1979), p. 38.

48. Clement of Alexandria (early third century) states that the Basilideans of Alexandria celebrated the baptism of Christ on one of two dates in the Egyptian calendar that answer to 6 and 10 January in the Julian calendar: *Stromateis* 1:21:146; in Marcel Caster, ed. and tr., *Clément d'Alexandrie: Les Stromates* (Sources chrétiennes series, no. 30; Paris; Éditions du Cerf, 1951), p. 150; John Ferguson, tr., *Clement of Alexandria: Stromateis, Books One through Three* (Fathers of the Church series; Washington, DC: Catholic University of America Press, 1991), p. 132. The Syriac text of the *Didascalia Apostolorum*, probably from the fourth century, states explicitly that Epiphany was observed on 6 January: *Didascalia Apostolorum* 3:8:6 (in Vööbus, tr., *The Didascalia Apostolorum*, p. 38). John Cassian indicated in the 350s C.E. that Egyptian Christians celebrated Christ's baptism and birth at the same time, but Western Christians maintained separate festivals for them: John Cassian, *Conferences* 10:2; in Michael Petscheinig, ed., *Cassiani Opera: Collationes XXIIII* (Corpus Scriptorum Ecclesiasticorum Latinorum series, vol. 13; Vienna: Verlag der Österreichischen Akademie der Wissenschaft, 2004), p. 286; cf. Colm Luibheid., tr. *John Cassian: Conferences* (Classics of Western Spirituality series; New York: Paulist Press, 1985), p. 125. Cf. also the "Canons of Athanasius," ¶ 16; in Wilhelm Riedl and W. E. Crum, eds. and tr., *The Canons of Athanasius of Alexandria: The Arabic and Coptic Versions Edited and Translated with Introductions, Notes, and Appendices* (London: Williams and Norgate, 1904; reprint edition of the American Theological Library Association in microfiche format), p. 27.

49. Ambrose of Milan speaks of the day of the Savior's birth (*Salvatoris natali*), although even this reference has been taken as referring to Epiphany, that is, 6 January; Ambrose, *De Virginibus* 3:1; in M. Salvati, ed. and tr., *Sant' Ambrogio: Scritti sulla Verginità* (Corona Patrum Salesiana series, vol. 6; Turin: Società Editrice Internazionale, 1955), pp. 120–121; cf. the footnote on this point. However, the passage from John Cassian's *Conferences* 10:2 cited above makes it clear that Christians in the Latin West by his time (the 350s C.E.) observed a separate day from Epiphany for the celebration of Christ's birth. An early instance of the date 25 December ("*viii kal. Ian.*") appears in a document entitled *Depositio Martirum* [sic] from the middle of the fourth century: in Theodor Mommsen, ed., *Chronica*

Minora Saec. IV. V. VI. VII. (Monumenta Germaniae Historica series, vol. 9; Berlin: Weidmann, 1892), p. 72.

50. Latin text in Clemens Blume, SJ, ed., *Sequentiae Ineditae: Liturgische Prosen des Mittelalters*, vol. 4 (Analecta Hymnica Medii Aevi series, vol. 34; Leipzig: O. R. Reisland, 1900), no. 23, *De Sancto Sepulcro*, pp. 27–28; my translation is based on the received text in the Western church, where the second line of the verse 1 is *immolent Christiani* and the second line of verse 2b (as it is identified in Blume) is *conflixere mirando*.

51. The original form of the Nicene Creed (325 C.E.) had included an anathema against specific Arian formulations, but the anathema did not become part of the received form of the Creed used in churches except for the Armenian Orthodox Church.

52. Irenaeus, *Adversus Haereses* 3.18.7; text in Brox, ed., 3:236; English translation in Alexander Roberts, James Donaldson, and Cleveland Coxe, eds., *The Ante-Nicene Fathers* (10 volumes; Buffalo: Christian Literature, 1885–1887), 1:448.

53. Cf. Pelikan, *The Christian Tradition*, 2:75–90.

54. Cf. Delumeau, *Catholicism Between Luther and Voltaire*, which argues that the stress on preaching and catechesis on the part of both Catholics and Protestants at the time of the Reformation marked the first large-scale catechesis of European Christians.

CHAPTER 3

1. Martin Luther, Ninety-Five Theses on Indulgences; in *D. Martin Luthers Werke: Kritische Gesamtausgabe* (Weimar: Hermann Böhlaus Nachfolger, 1926); hereafter cited as "Luther, *Werke* (*Weimarer Ausgabe*)," 1:236. English language translation in Helmut T. Lehman, general editor, *Luther's Works* (55 vols.; Philadelphia: Muhlenberg, 1960), 19:31.

2. Preface to the Augsburg Confession, in Pelikan and Hotchkiss, *Creeds and Confessions*, 2:54.

3. Cf. the Smalcald Articles (1537), which declare that the mass is "the greatest and most horrible abomination" (article 2:1; in Pelikan and Hotchkiss, *Creeds and Confessions*, 2:126) and declares that the pope is "the real Antichrist who has raised himself over and set himself against Christ" (article 4:10; in Pelikan and Hotchkiss 2:133). Papal and episcopal documents directed against Luther and other Reformers returned such language by way of anathemas and proclamations of excommunication.

4. Matthias of Janow, quoted in Jan Milič Lochman, *The Faith We Confess: An Ecumenical Dogmatics* (tr. David Lewis; Philadelphia: Fortress Press, 1984), p. x.

5. Pelikan, *The Christian Tradition*, 4:128. The term was also claimed by other Protestants and Anabaptists: Pelikan, *The Christian Tradition*, 4:314–315.

6. Martin Luther, Ninety-Five Theses on Indulgences; in Luther, *Werke* (*Weimarer Ausgabe*), 1:236; cf. *Luther's Works*, 19:31.

7. Martin Luther, Preface to the New Testament; in Luther, *Werke* (*Weimarer Ausgabe*), *Deutsche Bibel*, 6:7–8; cf. *Luther's Works*, 35:360. The English translation quoted here is that given in John Dillenberger, ed. and tr., *Martin Luther: Selections from His Writings* (Garden City, NY: Doubleday Anchor Books, 1961), pp. 16–17.

8. John Calvin, likewise, stated that the gospel is "the clear manifestation of the mystery of Christ," anticipated in the Old Testament and made clear in the New Testament, where the gospel is "the proclamation of the grace manifested in Christ": John Calvin, *Institutes of the Christian Religion* 2:9:2; in John T. McNeill, ed., *Calvin: Institutes of the Christian Religion* (2 vols.; Library of Christian Classics series; Philadelphia: Westminster, 1960), 1:424–425.

9. Martin Luther, preface to the Small Catechism, ¶ 3, "... now that the gospel has been restored."; in Pelikan and Hotchkiss, *Creeds and Confessions*, 2:31; in Leith, *Creeds of the Churches*, p. 108.

10. Pelikan, *The Christian Tradition*, 4:154. Pelikan also notes that in this broader sense, the term "gospel" "was not used in the same sense either in the New Testament or in the language of the church": 4:167.

11. The so-called Athanasian Creed, also referred to as the *Quicunque Vult* for its first words in Latin, is a Western creed, probably composed in Latin (that is, having no Greek original), and distinguished by its strong anathemas reminiscent of the anathemas attached to the earliest version of the Nicene Creed (325 C.E.). The provenance and date of the Athanasian Creed has been much disputed; some scholars argue that it was of Gallic provenance in the fourth or fifth centuries or even later. Many theologians and church bodies have objected to its anathemas, and as noted in the text following, many Anglican bodies have omitted the reference to the Athanasian Creed as they have adapted the Thirty Nine Articles of Religion.

12. Robert Kolb and Timothy J. Wengert, eds., Charles Arand, Eric Gritsch, Robert Kolb, William Russell, James Schaaf, Jane Strohl, and Timothy J. Wengert, trs., *The Book of Concord: The Confessions of the Evangelical Lutheran Church* (Minneapolis: Fortress Press, 2000), pp. 21–25. The German text of the Book of Concord did alter the texts of the Nicene and Apostles' creeds to affirm "the holy Christian church" and "one holy, Christian and apostolic Church," utilizing "Christian" in place of "catholic." The Kolb and Wengert edition of the *Book of Concord* notes that the term had been rendered in this way even before the Reformation. Other Protestant churches have sometimes substituted "universal" for "catholic."

13. Epitome, section I; in Pelikan and Hotchkiss, *Creeds and Confessions*, 2:168. On the Lutheran affirmation of the historic creeds, cf. Pelikan, *The Christian Tradition*, 4:177.

14. Leith, *Creeds of the Churches*, p. 269.

15. Second Helvetic Confession, 11:18; in Pelikan and Hotchkiss, *Creeds and Confessions*, 2:479.

16. 1995 edition of *The Ground of the Unity*, ¶ 4; in Pelikan and Hotchkiss, *Creeds and Confessions*, 3:858 and footnote on this point). An earlier version from 1981 had listed these doctrinal affirmations in the text of the document

itself, but as of the 1995 edition, they are referred to parenthetically: *The Ground of the Unity: A Doctrinal Statement Adopted by the Unity Synod of the Unitas Fratrum, or Moravian Church, Held at Herrnhut, German Democratic Republic, August 30 to September 12, 1981* (printed by the Moravian Church, n.p., [1981]), p. 2. On the creeds in Moravian liturgical usage, cf. Fred Linyard and Phillip Tovey, *Moravian Worship* (Grove Worship series, no. 129; Bramcote, Nottingham: Grove Books, 1994), pp. 8–9.

17. "L'ecumenismo e il dialogo interreligioso" (Consultative Commission on Ecumenical Relations of the Waldensian Church, 1998), ¶ 29, p. 8. A seventeenth-century Waldensian confession, the "Confession of Faith of 1655," affirms only the Apostles' Creed: *Confessione di Fede del 1655* (a publication available on the Web site of the Waldensian Church: http://www.chiesavaldese.org), article 33, p. 19. The material in this Web site was accessed December 2006.

18. Pelikan and Hotchkiss, *Creeds and Confessions*, 2:36–37; cf. Leith, *Creeds of the Churches*, pp. 115–117.

19. In Pelikan and Hotchkiss, *Creeds and Confessions*, 2:366.

20. In Pelikan and Hotchkiss, *Creeds and Confessions*, 2:44; cf. Leith, *Creeds of the Churches*, p. 124. On the Nicene creed in the eucharist, see Luther's *Formula Missae et Communionis* in Bard Thompson, ed., *Liturgies of the Western Church*, p. 132, "After the Gospel the whole congregation sings the Creed in German: Wir glauben all in einen Gott."

21. The version of the 1662 Prayer Book I have used is *The Book of Common Prayer: 1662 Version (Includes Appendices from the 1549 Version and Other Commemorations, with an Introduction by Diarmaid MacCulloch* (Everyman's Library edition, no. 241; London: David Campbell Publishers Ltd., 1999; cited hereafter as "*The Book of Common Prayer: 1662 Version*"), pp. 78 and 88. On the various versions and editions of the 1662 Prayer Book, cf. David N. Griffiths, *The Bibliography of the Book of Common Prayer, 1549–1999* (London: The British Library, and New Castle, DE: Oak Knoll Press, 2002), pp. 108–115.

22. *The Book of Common Prayer: 1662 Version*, p. 145.

23. *The Book of Common Prayer: 1662 Version*, pp. 92–94. Cf. the Articles of Religion, article 8, given in Pelikan and Hotchkiss, *Creeds and Confessions*, 2:530–531 and n. 1.

24. In Thompson, *Liturgies of the Western Church*, p. 153.

25. In Thompson, *Liturgies of the Western Church*, p. 172.

26. Calvin's Geneva liturgy of 1554; in John Calvin, *Opera Quae Supersunt* (59 vols.; Braunschweig: C. A. Schwetschke and Son, 1863–1900), 6:197 (and see footnote 1 on this page); cf. Bard Thompson, *Liturgies of the Western Church*, p. 204.; cf. Leith, *Introduction to the Reformed Tradition*, pp. 172–173.

27. This is the argument made by the Reformed interpreter Caspar Olevian in an *epitome* attached to an early edition of the *Institutes;* cf. Leith, *Introduction to the Reformed Tradition*, pp. 123 and 144.

28. The Savoy Liturgy (1661) associated with Richard Baxter; in Thompson, *Liturgies of the Western Church*, p. 386.

29. Article 1; in Pelikan and Hotchkiss, *Creeds and Confessions,* 2:58 (this is Tappert's translation from the German version of the Augsburg Confession); cf. Leith, *Creeds of the Churches,* p. 67.

30. Article 3; in Pelikan and Hotchkiss, *Creeds and Confessions,* 2:60; cf. Leith, *Creeds of the Churches,* p. 69.

31. Anglican Articles 1–2; in Pelikan and Hotchkiss, *Creeds and Confessions,* 2:528; cf. Leith, *Creeds of the Churches,* pp. 266–267.

32. Pelikan, *The Christian Tradition,* 4:212. Pelikan notes, however, that some Reformed theologians spoke of the authority of the historic creeds only "insofar as [*quatenus*] they agree with Scripture," 4:341.

33. Pelikan, *The Christian Tradition,* 4:321.

34. In Pelikan and Hotchkiss, *Creeds and Confessions,* 3:149–154. The Easter Liturgy is also given in the *Hymnal and Liturgies of the Moravian Church* (Moravian Church in America, Northern and Southern Provinces: 1969), pp. 54–61. On the Moravian Easter Litany and its use, cf. Linyard and Tovey, *Moravian Worship,* pp. 6, 10–11.

35. James F. White, ed., *John Wesley's Sunday Service of the Methodists in North America* (Nashville, TN: United Methodist Publishing House, 1984; currently available in reprinted form from Order of St. Luke Publications; this is a reprint edition of the 1784 *Sunday Service of the Methodists in North America* with an introduction by James F. White). The Apostles' Creed is given in the services for morning and evening prayer, pp. 12 and 18. This version actually has the clause about the descent into hell, but it was removed from subsequent printings of the *Sunday Service.* Cf. Ted A. Campbell, *Methodist Doctrine: The Essentials* (Nashville, TN: Abingdon Press, 1999), pp. 43–44.

36. A formal statement of the African Methodist Episcopal Church entitled "Special Declaration on Apostolic Succession and Ritualism" (1884) asserts that "we grant that the orderly repetition of the . . . Apostles' Creed . . . may conduce to the attainment" of spiritual worship; in the *Doctrine and Discipline of the African Methodist Episcopal Church, 2004–2008* (Nashville, TN: African Methodist Episcopal Church, 2005), p. 22.

37. The Nicene Creed was first formally included in the *Methodist Hymnal* of 1964 (subsequently renamed *The Book of Hymns;* Nashville, TN: Methodist Publishing House, 1964 and 1966), number 739. In the *United Methodist Hymnal* of 1989, the Nicene Creed is placed in first position among the creedal statement, no. 880.

38. *The United Methodist Hymnal* (1989), no. 882 and in the form in which the Apostles' Creed is used for the profession of faith within the baptismal covenant, p. 35.

39. Augsburg Confession, article 3; in Pelikan and Hotchkiss, *Creeds and Confessions,* 2:60; cf. Leith, *Creeds of the Churches,* pp. 68–69.

40. Anglican Articles 2–4; in Pelikan and Hotchkiss, *Creeds and Confessions,* 2:528; cf. Leith, *Creeds of the Churches,* p. 267.

41. Westminster Confession of Faith 8:3–4; in Pelikan and Hotchkiss, *Creeds and Confessions,* 2:616–617; cf. Leith, *Creeds of the Churches,* pp. 202–204.

42. Methodist Articles of Religion 2 and 3; in Pelikan and Hotchkiss, *Creeds and Confessions*, 3:202; in Leith, *Creeds of the Churches*, p. 354.

43. Augsburg Confession, article 3; in Pelikan and Hotchkiss, *Creeds and Confessions*, 2:60.

44. Anglican Articles of Religion, articles 2 and 31; in Pelikan and Hotchkiss, *Creeds and Confessions*, 2:528 and 536.

45. Westminster Confession of Faith 8:5; in Pelikan and Hotchkiss, *Creeds and Confessions*, 2:617.

46. Cf. David N. Power, *The Sacrifice We Offer: The Tridentine Dogma and Its Reinterpretation* (New York: Crossroad, 1987) discusses Protestant and ecumenical attitudes toward the Tridentine understanding of eucharistic sacrifice in the introduction, pp. xiii–xv, and in the first chapter, pp. 1–20.

47. Luther, Small Catechism, section on the Apostles' Creed, ¶ 3; in Pelikan and Hotchkiss, *Creeds and Confessions*, 2:37; cf. Leith, *Creeds of the Churches*, p. 116.

48. Heidelberg Catechism, Lord's Day 13, response to question 34; in Pelikan and Hotchkiss, *Creeds and Confessions*, 2:435.

49. Luther, Small Catechism, section on the Sacrament of Holy Baptism, ¶ 6; in Pelikan and Hotchkiss, *Creeds and Confessions*, 2:40; cf. Leith, *Creeds of the Churches*, p. 120.

50. Luther, Preface to the New Testament; in Luther, *Werke* (*Weimarer Ausgabe*), *Deutsche Bibel*, 6:7–8; cf. *Luther's Works*, 35:360. English translation from Dillenberger, ed. and tr., *Martin Luther*, pp. 16–17.

51. First Helvetic Confession, item 11; in Pelikan and Hotchkiss, *Creeds and Confessions*, 2:284.

52. Campbell, *Christian Confessions*, pp. 134–144.

53. Luther, "Preface to the Old Testament" (1523–1545); in Luther, *Werke* (*Weimarer Ausgabe*), *Deutsche Bibel*, 8:12; cf. *Luther's Works*, 35:236.

54. Martin Luther, a thesis prepared for a disputation with Hieronymus Weller and Nikolaus Medler, September 11, 1535, thesis "On Faith," no. 41; in Luther, *Werke* (*Weimarer Ausgabe*) 39:1:47; the English translation is that given in Gerhardt Ebeling, *Word and Faith* (London: SCM, 1963), p. 82.

55. Cited by Leith, *The Reformed Tradition*, p. 32; Leith in turn cites R. Newton Flew and Rupert E. Davies, eds., *The Catholicity of Protestantism: Being a Report Presented to His Grace the Archbishop of Canterbury by a Group of Free Churchmen* (London: Lutterworth Press, 1950), pp. 13–14; who in turn cite J. G. Walch, *Luther: Sämtliche Schriften* (1745), vol. xvi, col. 399.

56. This is not consistently the case with Protestant statements about scripture: doctrinal statements from the Reformed tradition often do equate the whole of scripture with "the Word of God" (Second Helvetic Confession 1; in Pelikan and Hotchkiss 2:460–461; cf. Leith, *Creeds of the Churches*, p. 132) or with "the Word of God written" (Westminster Confession of Faith 1:2; in Pelikan and Hotchkiss 2:604; cf. Leith, *Creeds of the Churches*, pp. 193–194).

57. Anglican Article 7; in Pelikan and Hotchkiss, *Creeds and Confessions*, 2:530; cf. Leith, *Creeds of the Churches*, p. 268.

58. Westminster Confession 7:5–6; in Pelikan and Hotchkiss, *Creeds and Confessions*, 2:615–616; cf. Leith, *Creeds of the Churches*, pp. 202–204.

59. The Greek text is κατὰ τὴν ἀναλογίαν τῆς πίστεως.

60. So the Westminster Confession 1:9 states that "The infallible rule of interpretation of Scripture is the Scripture itself; and therefore, when there is a question about the true and full sense of any Scripture (which is not manifold but one), it must be searched and known by other places [passages] that speak more clearly"; in Pelikan and Hotchkiss, *Creeds and Confessions*, 2:608; cf. Leith, *Creeds of the Churches*, p. 196.

61. Guillaume du Buc (Bucanus), *Institutiones Theologicae seu Locorum Communium Christianae Religionis ex Dei Verbo et Praestantissimorum Theologorum Orthodoxo Consensu Expositorum Analysis* (Geneva, 1609), 4:21–24; the definition given is *constans et perpetua sententia Scripturae in apertis Scripturae locis exposita et symbolo apostolico, decalogo et oratione dominica;* cited in Heinrich Heppe, *Reformierte Dogmatik* (Kreis Moers: Buchhandlung des Erziehungsvereins, 1935), p. 30 (in footnote); English translation as given in Ernst Bizer, ed., and G. T. Thompson, tr., *Reformed Dogmatics: Set Out and Illustrated from the Sources* (London: Allen and Unwin, 1950), p. 35; I note that in the English translation the material from du Buc has been moved to the main text. On the matter of the "analogy of faith," see Scott J. Jones, *John Wesley's Conception and Use of Scripture* (Nashville, TN: Kingswood Books, 1995), pp. 45–46.

62. Flew and Davies, eds., *The Catholicity of Protestantism*, p. 14.

63. The Council of Trent had called for the establishment of diocesan seminaries to train priests for their work, including the preparation of homilies: session 23, *Decretum de Reformatione*, ch. 18 (15 July 1563); in Mansi, 33:146–149.

64. Delumeau, *Catholicism between Luther and Voltaire*, pp. 175–202.

65. Augsburg Confession 7; in Pelikan and Hotchkiss, *Creeds and Confessions*, 2:62; cf. Leith, *Creeds of the Churches*, p. 70.

66. Anglican Articles of Religion 19; in Pelikan and Hotchkiss, *Creeds and Confessions*, 2:533; cf. Leith, *Creeds of the Churches*, p. 273. As indicated earlier, the term "Word of God" was capable of a variety of meanings, and sometimes did denote precisely the gospel. In other cases it can denote Christ as the incarnate Word, and in Reformed doctrinal statements it can refer to the canon of scripture. The definition of the church in the Westminster Confession does not explicitly include the preaching of the word, though it notes that particular churches may be "more or less pure, according as the doctrine of the gospel is taught and embraced, ordinances administered, and public worship performed more or less purely in them": Westminster Confession of Faith 25:4; in Pelikan and Hotchkiss, *Creeds and Confessions*, 2:639; cf. Leith, *Creeds of the Churches*, p. 222.

67. Anglican homily "Of the Salvation of Mankind, by Only Christ our Saviour, from Sin and Death Everlasting"; in Leith, *Creeds of the Churches*, pp. 239–251.

68. Second Helvetic Confession, chapter 1; in Pelikan and Hotchkiss, *Creeds and Confessions*, 2:460; cf. Leith, *Creeds of the Churches*, p. 133. The precise statement

is "Wherefore when this Word of God is now preached in the church by preachers lawfully called, we believe that the very Word of God is preached, and received of the faithful..." This replicates the Augustinian claim, subsequently affirmed in Catholic and Protestant doctrine, that the sacraments are effective in virtue of God's work in them (*ex opere operato*), and not in virtue of the minister of the sacrament (*ex opere operantis*).

69. Campbell, *Christian Confessions*, pp. 179–183.

70. Second Helvetic Confession, chapter 21; in Pelikan and Hotchkiss, *Creeds and Confessions*, 2:510–511; in Leith, *Creeds of the Churches*, p. 170.

71. Westminster Confession 29:2; in Pelikan and Hotchkiss 2:642; cf. Leith, *Creeds of the Churches*, p. 225.

72. *Book of Common Prayer: 1662 Version*, p. 156.

73. Augsburg Confession 24; in Pelikan and Hotchkiss, *Creeds and Confessions*, 2:83; cf. Leith, *Creeds of the Churches*, p. 84.

74. The Latin original was part of a longer medieval poem celebrating the wounds of Christ sometimes attributed to Bernard of Clairvaux or Bonaventure, *Salve Mundi Salutare*. Gerhardt's poem is based on a verse of this longer poem that celebrated the wound of the thorn in Christ's head: *Salve caput cruentatum;* text in Ioannes [John] M. Neale, ed., *Hymni Ecclesiae: E Breviariis Quibusdam et Missalibus Gallicanis, Germanis, Hispanis, Lusitanis Desumpti* (London and Oxford: John Henry Parker, 1851), p. 123. A German text of Gerhardt's translation, "O Haupt voll Blut und Wunden" is given in *Evangelisches Gesangbuch: Ausgabe für die Evangelisch-Lutherischen Kirchen in Niedersachsen und für die Bremische Evangelische Kirche* (Bremen: Verlagsgemeinschaft für das Evangelische Gesangbuch Niedersachsen, 1994), no. 85. The version cited here is the English translation of James W. Alexander (1830) as given in *The United Methodist Hymnal* (1989), no. 286.

75. J. R. Watson, *The English Hymn: A Critical and Historical Study* (Oxford: Oxford University Press, 1997), pp. 110–170.

76. Isaac Watts, hymn "Crucifixion to the World by the Cross of Christ," in *Hymns and Spiritual Songs* (1707); the version I have consulted is the twenty-sixth edition (London: T. Hawes and Co., T. Longman, C. and R. Ware, H. Woodfall, J. Buckland, J. Waugh, T. Field, E. and C. Dilly, W. Strahan, J. Fuller, and G. Leith, 1766), 3:289; contemporary orthography and spelling as in *The United Methodist Hymnal* (1989), no. 298. Cf. Watson's comments on Watts's use of the first-person singular in *The English Hymn*, pp. 160–170.

77. Charles Wesley, hymn on "Free Grace," first published in *Hymns and Sacred Poems* (London: William Strahan, 1739), p. 118; contemporary orthography as in *The United Methodist Hymnal* (1989), no. 363.

78. *Hymns for the Nativity of Our Lord* (no publisher indicated; 1745), *Hymns for Our Lord's Resurrection* (London: W. Strahan, 1746), *Hymns for Ascension-Day* (Bristol: Felix Farley, 1746; I have consulted the second edition of 1747), and *Hymns of Petition and Thanksgiving for the Promise of the Father: Hymns for Whitsunday* (Bristol: Felix Farley, 1746).

79. Reformed confessions typically allowed for (but did not mandate) the celebration of Christmas, Good Friday, Easter, and other festivals associated with the Christian year, although other patterns of annual preaching were also used, such as preaching through the articles of one of the Reformed confessions themselves. The Heidelberg Catechism, for example, is arranged in fifty-two consecutive sections to be used in preaching each Sunday of the year: Pelikan and Hotchkiss, *Creeds and Confessions*, 2:429–457. John Wesley's edition of the Anglican Prayer Book, *The Sunday Service of the Methodists in North America* (1784) included a lectionary arranged according to the Christian year (in White, ed., *John Wesley's Sunday Service*, pages labeled "A2" through "A4"), although there is little evidence that the lectionary and the pattern of the Christian year was followed by Methodists until the liturgical renewal movement of the twentieth century began to affect Methodist churches.

CHAPTER 4

1. The epigraph is the chorus of a Gospel song by Katherine ("Kate") Hankey, ca. 1868, cited from *The Revivalist: A Collection of Choice Revival Hymns and Tunes* (Troy, New York: Joseph Hillman, revised and enlarged edition, 1872), no. 509, although this publication does not credit Ms. Hankey, it notes that the song was "written for Chaplain C. C. McCabe"; cf. *The United Methodist Hymnal* (1989), no. 156. Other publications in Gospel song books are listed below.

2. D. W. Bebbington, *Evangelicalism in Modern Britain: A History from the 1730s to the 1980s* (London: Unwin Hyman, 1989), pp. 2–4. In addition to a commitment to biblical authority and personal conversion, Bebbington also stresses crucicentrism, that is, a focus on the cross of Christ as a central trait of Evangelicalism, and this theme will also be considered in the conclusion of this chapter. Cf. also George M. Marsden, *Understanding Fundamentalism and Evangelicalism* (Grand Rapids, MI: William B. Eerdmans, 1991), pp. 1–2. Marsden also stresses the Evangelical emphasis on the cross as an integral part of the Evangelical proclamation of the gospel.

3. Cf. the discussion of "Evangelical" and "Free" churches in Ted A. Campbell, *Christian Confessions*, p. 186 and n. 191, and Ted A. Campbell, "The Complete Evangelical" (*Circuit Rider* 9:5 [May 1985]: 3–5).

4. On the traits of Evangelicalism, see the works referred to earlier by Bebbington (*Evangelicalism in Modern Britain*) and Marsden (*Understanding Fundamentalism and Evangelicalism*).

5. Michael Kinnamon, "The Place of an Authoritative Teaching Office in the Christian Church (Disciples of Christ)," in Ted A. Campbell, Ann K. Riggs, and Gilbert W. Stafford, eds., *Ancient Faith and American-Born Churches: Dialogues Between Christian Traditions* (New York: Paulist Press, 2005), p. 215.

6. Marsden, *Understanding Evangelicalism and Fundamentalism*, pp. 1–2.

7. This emphasis on personal conversion grew out of European and British religious movements (including Pietism among Lutheran and Reformed

churches) in the seventeenth and eighteenth centuries that stressed the nature of true Christianity as lying in the heart and the affections; cf. Ted A. Campbell, *The Religion of the Heart: A Study of European Religious Life in the Seventeenth and Eighteenth Centuries* (Columbia: University of South Carolina Press, 1991), *passim.*

8. In my earlier study of *Christian Confessions,* I included Methodist churches solely in the category of "Free and Evangelical Churches" (part IV of that book; pp. 185–256). Subsequent reflection has led me to identify Methodist churches as sharing the cultures of traditional Protestant (and related) churches and of Evangelical communities but these are admittedly analytical definitions and the reality is that Methodist churches share traits in common with older Protestant churches and with Evangelical communities.

9. Although the term "free church" has a somewhat larger denotation, and includes all denominations not established by the state so, for example, in the U.K. Quaker groups are thought of as "free churches" although they don't fit the patterns of Evangelical churches described here. Similarly, the United Reformed Church in the United Kingdom is a "free church" that fits the pattern of older Protestant denominations more than the culture of Evangelical churches.

10. Harry S. Stout, *Divine Dramatist: George Whitefield and the Rise of Modern Evangelicalism* (Grand Rapids, MI: William B. Eerdmans, 1991), pp. xvii–xxiv as a summary of Stout's thesis about Whitefield's use of the media of a consumer culture (including theater and various forms of publication) in the service of the Evangelical cause.

11. George M. Marsden, *Reforming Fundamentalism: Fuller Seminary and the New Evangelicalism* (Grand Rapids, MI: William B. Eerdmans, 1987), pp. 14, 50. Marsden points out that old-line Protestant churches acted through the Federal Council of Churches in the United States to control access to radio and television for religious broadcasting. This forced Evangelical preachers (such as Charles Fuller) and organizations to develop their own radio and eventually television outlets.

12. I will use the expression "black" in this chapter to indicate Christian communities historically made up of African American and Afro-Caribbean people and some first-generation Africans as well.

13. See David T. Shannon and Gayraud S. Wilmore, eds., *Black Witness to the Apostolic Faith* (Grand Rapids, MI: William B. Eerdmans Publishing Company, for the Commission on Faith and Order of the National Council of the Churches of Christ in the USA, 1985), which includes essays by J. Deotis Roberts (Baptist), Thomas Hoyt (Christian Methodist Episcopal Church), and Leonard Lovett (Church of God in Christ, one of the leading African American Pentecostal denominations and arguably the oldest of all Pentecostal denominations). See also item no. 1 in the "Conclusion and Recommendations" of the conference statement, "Toward a Common Expression of Faith: A Black North American Perspective," p. 69: "The Afro-American Christian tradition, embodied particularly in Black Baptist, Methodist, and Pentecostal denominations, but continuing also in other Black-led Protestant and Roman Catholic congregations, has been and continues to be an indigenous expression of the faith of the apostles in North America."

14. The historically black Methodist denominations referred to in this paragraph include the African Methodist Episcopal Church, the African Methodist Episcopal Zion Church, and the Christian Methodist Episcopal Church, and the term "episcopal" in the names of these denominations indicates the episcopal polity that characterizes these denominations.

15. For a critical discussion of this issue, see Milton G. Sernett, "Black Religion and the Question of Evangelical Identity" in Donald W. Dayton and Robert K. Johnson, eds., *The Variety of American Evangelicalism* (Downers Grove, IL: InterVarsity Press, 1991), pp. 135–147.

16. W. E. B. Du Bois, *The Souls of Black Folk* (New York and Toronto: The New American Library, and London: The New English Library, Limited, 1963), pp. 210–212; the quotation is from p. 210.

17. The volume edited by Shannon and Wilmore (referenced earlier) contains a series of essays on the transmission of the apostolic faith, including the gospel message, in the African American church tradition.

18. I have not included here two important groups that should probably be included within the range of Evangelical communities, but because of their historic rejection of doctrinal statements, it is very difficult to characterize their doctrinal views. These groups are (1) Bible-teaching churches (a variety of denominations including Plymouth Brethren and other churches typically identified as "Bible Churches," often emphasizing a Dispensationalist understanding of the Christian scriptures) and (2) Restorationist churches (that is, churches of the Stone-Campbell Restoration tradition that originated in the United States in the early nineteenth century, including churches identified as "Disciples of Christ" and "Churches of Christ."). I will have reference to these groups at some points in the discussion following.

19. Philip Jenkins, *The Next Christendom: The Coming of Global Christianity* (Oxford: Oxford University Press, 2002) discusses the explosive growth of Christianity in the southern hemisphere, and discusses specifically how Evangelical and Pentecostal groups account for much of this growth, cf. pp. 60–66.

20. J. Milton Yinger, *The Scientific Study of Religion* (London: Macmillan, 1970), pp. 518–519. Cf. also Campbell, *Religion of the Heart*, pp. 159–169.

21. These reflections on "centrifugal" and "centripetal" tendencies in Evangelical movements grew out of ecumenical dialogues between 1996 and 2000 in the Faith and Order Commission of the National Council of Churches in the United States in which the group paired newer traditions (traditions that typically originated in North America) with older Christian traditions in dialogue, although the terms "centrifugal" and "centripetal" are my own. Representatives of the "newer" traditions in these dialogues often pointed out what I have called "centripetal" tendencies that heightened their similarities to other Christian communities. The results of these dialogues are presented in Campbell, Riggs, and Stafford, *Ancient Faith and American Born Churches*.

22. "The Baptist Faith and Message" (2000), preamble; on the Web site of the Southern Baptist Convention: http://www.sbc.net/bfm/bfmpreamble.asp;

this material was accessed December 2006; similar wording is used in the 1925 version: cf. Pelikan and Hotchkiss, *Creeds and Confessions*, 3:438; and Leith, *Creeds of the Churches*, p. 345.

23. New Hampshire Confession, item 4; in Leith, *Creeds of the Churches*, p. 335.

24. Baptist Faith and Message (1925), item "The Way of Salvation"; in Leith, *Creeds of the Churches*, p. 346 (I have removed subsequently added words and phrases indicated by square brackets in Leith's edition); cf. Pelikan and Hotchkiss, *Creeds and Confessions*, 3:439 (this gives the text as subsequently revised in the 1950s); in the 2000 version, available in a PDF document available on the Web site of the Southern Baptist Convention: http://www.sbc.net/filedownload.asp?file=/bfm/pdf/The%20Baptist%20Faith%20and%20Message.pdf, [p. 4]; italics indicate the added words. On the christology of the statement of "Baptist Faith and Message," see Warren McWilliams, "'Rooted and Grounded in Jesus Christ': Christology and Soteriology in *The Baptist Faith and Message* (1963)" in Jeff B. Pool, ed., *Sacred Mandates of Conscience: Interpretations of* The Baptist Faith and Message (Macon, GA: Smith and Helwys, 1997), pp. 133–135.

25. Articles of Faith of the Church of the Nazarene, article 2; in *Manual/1989* (Kansas City, MO: Nazarene Publishing House, 1989), pp. 29–30; cf. Pelikan and Hotchkiss, *Creeds and Confessions*, 3:410. The original text of this article, as given in the 1908 *Manual of the Pentecostal Church of the Nazarene* (Los Angeles: Nazarene Publishing Co., 1908), p. 25, was not as clear about the narrative of the saving work of Jesus Christ: "The eternal existent Son, the second Personality of the Adorable Trinity, is essentially divine. As the divine Son, He became incarnate by the Holy Spirit, being born of the Virgin Mary, thus joining to Himself inseparably the divinely begotten Son of Man, called Jesus. So that two whole and perfect natures, that is to say, the God-head and man-hood, are thus joined in one person, very God and very man."

26. Articles of Faith of the Church of the Nazarene, article 6; in *Manual/1989*, p. 31; cf. Pelikan and Hotchkiss, *Creeds and Confessions*, 3:411. This article does not appear in the original (1908) *Manual of the Pentecostal Church of the Nazarene*.

27. General Council of the Assemblies of God, "Statement of Fundamental Truths," under "The Deity of the Lord Jesus Christ"; available in a PDF document with the title "The General Council of the Assemblies of God Statement of Fundamental Truths" available at the denomination's Web site (http://www.ag.org/top/Beliefs/Statement_of_Fundamental_Truths/sft_full.cfm), pp. 2–3. An earlier version of the "Statement of Fundamental Truths" (given in Pelikan and Hotchkiss, *Creeds and Confessions*, 3:426–431) does not have the statement quoted above and does not specifically affirm Christ's death and resurrection except under the articles on the Lord's Supper and Baptism, although they are implied in the claim that Christ, "having purged our sins . . ." etc. (3:430).

28. Saddleback Church (Lake Forest, California), statement on "What We Believe" (there are two statements with this title on the church's Web site; this

quotation is taken from the longer of the two: http://www.saddleback.com/flash/ believe2.html). The material on this Web site was accessed December 2006.

29. The Potter's House, "Belief Statement," article on "Jesus Christ" (on the church's Web site: http://www.thepottershouse.org/PH_beliefs.html). Calvary Chapel (Costa Mesa, California), statement on "The Gospel" (on the church's Web site: http://www.calvarychapel.com/?show = thegospel), the statement beginning, "Jesus, the one and only Son of God . . ." Willow Creek Community Church, statement of "What We Believe" (on the church's Web site: http://www.willowcreek.org/what_we_believe.asp), the statement beginning "Jesus Christ, second Person of the Trinity . . ." Yoido Full Gospel Church, statement on "Understanding the 'Full Gospel' Theology" (on the church's Web site: http://english.fgtv.com/Gospel/main.asp), section 2:1 on "Faith in the Cross on Calvary." The material on these Web sites was accessed December 2006.

30. The Vineyard USA, "Statement of Faith" (available in an untitled PDF document on the church's Web site: http://www.vineyardusa.org/about/beliefs.aspx), article 6 on "Christ the Mediator and Eternal King." This material on this Web site was accessed December 2006.

31. Cf. Denis Fortin, "Nineteenth-Century Evangelicalism and Early Adventist Statements of Belief" (*Andrews University Seminary Studies* 36:1 [Spring 1998]), points out general similarities between early Adventists and the broader Evangelical movements in the United States in the nineteenth century, including commitment to the experience of the new birth (conversion, p. 55), commitment to scriptural authority (pp. 55–56), and commitment to mission and evangelization (p. 57). Fortin explains that in the view of early Adventists after the time of the Millerite "disappointment," the principal issue contested between Seventh-day Adventists and other Evangelical groups was not the date of Christ's second advent, but was rather the issue of Christ's intercession in the heavenly temple (see the text following).

32. Seventh-day Adventist Church, "Declaration of the Fundamental Principles Taught and Practiced by the Seventh-day Adventists" (1872), item 2; in Pelikan and Hotchkiss, *Creeds and Confessions,* 3:360–361. Unfortunately, this is the only Seventh-day Adventist doctrinal statement given in the Pelikan and Hotchkiss collection, which leads to the impression that the Seventh-day Adventist Church is still committed to the very distinctive views enshrined in this document. Moreover, the 1872 statement itself was not formally approved by Adventist church bodies, although a revision of it in 1875 was included in the *Manual* of the Seventh-day Adventist Church; cf. Fortin, pp. 63–66.

33. Seventh-day Adventist Church, statement of 28 "Fundamental Beliefs" (revision of 2005), item 4; in a PDF document available on the denomination's Web site: http://www.adventist.org/beliefs/fundamental/index.html; the document was accessed December 2006).

34. Ibid., item 9.

35. New Hampshire Confession, item 4; in Leith, *Creeds of the Churches,* p. 335; Abstract of Principles of Southern Baptist Theological Seminary, Louisville

(1859), item 7; in Pelikan and Hotchkiss, *Creeds and Confessions,* 3:318; cf. Leith, *Creeds of the Churches,* p. 341. Cf. also the statement in the Articles of Faith (article 2) of the Church of the Nazarene that Christ "ascended into heaven and is there engaged in intercession for us": in *Manual/*1989, pp. 29–30; cf. Pelikan and Hotchkiss, *Creeds and Confessions,* 3:410.

36. This is especially true in Bible-teaching churches that have a strong commitment to a doctrine of election similar to that held in Reformed churches. In congregations committed to the doctrine of election, the Evangelical invitation may not be an emotional appeal as it is in other Evangelical communities. Also, one of the strands of the Stone-Campbell movement, that associated with Barton W. Stone, was revivalistic in character, but the strand of the movement associated with Thomas and Alexander Campbell insisted only on simple belief in Christ, not necessarily an affective experience of conversion, so the Evangelical invitation is not consistently a part of worship in these churches.

37. Churches of the Stone-Campbell Restoration tradition (Disciples of Christ, Churches of Christ, and independent Christian churches) celebrate the Lord's Supper every Sunday.

38. John Wesley referred to the use of such oral periods in his "Treatise concerning Pronunciation and Gesture": "you should take care not to begin your periods either too high or too low for that would necessarily lead you to an unnatural and improper variation of the voice" (I:3, item 6; in Thomas Jackson ed., *The Works of the Reverend John Wesley,* A.M. [14 vols.; London: Wesleyan Conference Office, 1873], 13:520), and "You may make a short pause after every period; and begin the next generally a little lower than you concluded the last" (III:17; in Jackson, ed., 13:524).

39. Cf. O. C. Edwards, Jr., *A History of Preaching* (Nashville: Abingdon Press, 2004), pp. 506–507 and 509–520 (on the pattern of Evangelical preaching set by Charles G. Finney).

40. David Bennett offers a historical account of the development of *The Altar Call: Its Origins and Present Usage* (Lanham, MD: University Press of America, 2000).

41. Early American spiritual; cited from *The United Methodist Hymnal* (1989), no. 292.

42. I say "as it is traditionally sung," because musicologists have pointed out that the tune was often printed as if it were in a different mode (Aeolian), but traditional singers recorded from the 1930s sing it in Dorian mode despite the way in which it was printed: Buell E. Cobb, Jr., *The Sacred Harp: A Tradition and Its Music* (Athens, GA: University of Georgia Press; Brown Thrasher Books, second edition, 2001), p. 33. Cobb here cites the earlier research of the musicologist George Pullen Jackson (see later). The tune as given in *The United Methodist Hymnal* (1989, no. 292) reflects the tune as sung in the Dorian mode.

43. Cf. the conclusion of George Pullen Jackson, *White and Negro Spirituals: Their Life Span and Kinship: Tracing 200 Years of Untrammeled Song Making and Singing among Our Country Folk* (Locust Valley, NY: J. J. Augustin, 1943; reprint edition of 1970) stated explicitly in his concluding section, "Farewell to

Africa," pp. 291–292. Jackson's argument was that although there are variations between white and black spirituals, these songs themselves were essentially the same between black and white communities in the south. His highly combative conclusion does not completely rule out the possibility of African influences or even of African songs, but he argues that direct connections with African music had not been demonstrated in the way in which he had demonstrated connections between black and white spirituals in the southern United States. It might be noted that in his particular context Jackson was arguing against Southern cultural segregationists who did not want to admit the connection between black and white church music. A different perspective, from much later in the twentieth century when scholars had become concerned to demonstrate African elements in traditional African American church music, is offered by J. Jefferson Cleveland in an article written in collaboration with William B. McClain: "A Historical Account of the Negro Spiritual" in J. Jefferson Cleveland, ed., *Songs of Zion* (Supplemental Worship Resources, no. 12; Nashville, TN: Abingdon Press, 1981), no. 73. Cleveland and McClain make the case for African rhythms and other elements of African music in black spirituals, and they also emphasize the distinct ways in which spirituals expressed the concerns of enslaved African Americans, for instance, in songs with "double meanings," that is, songs that have a Christian and spiritual meaning and could also carry encoded messages between African American communities.

44. African American spiritual; cited from *Songs of Zion*, no. 126.

45. John O. Sweney, C. C. McCabe, T. C. O. Kane, and William J. Kirkpatrick, *Songs of Redeeming Love* (Philadelphia: Perkinpine and Higgins, 1882). *Songs of the Soul, No. 2: For Use in Sunday Evening Congregations, Revivals, Camp Meetings, Social Services, and Young Peoples Meetings* (ed. James M. Black; Cincinnati: Curts and Jennings, and New York, Boston, Pittsburgh, and San Francisco: Eaton and Mains, 1896). *The Voice of Praise: A Compilation of the Very Best Sacred Songs for Use in Sunday Schools and Praise Services* (Philadelphia: Hall-Mack Company), 1904.

46. See the subtitles of *Songs of the Soul, No. 2* and *The Voice of Praise* cited earlier. Later collections (from the early twentieth century) reveal that these songs were beginning to be used in regular worship: *Praise Evangel: For Sunday-Schools, Revivals, Singing Schools, Conventions, and General Use in Christian Work and Worship* (Lawrenceburg, TN: James D. Vaughn, 1919).

47. Song by William P. Mackay, 1863; in *The Revivalist* (1872), no. 577. Also in *Chorus of Praise: For Use in Sunday Schools, Young People's Meetings, Revivals, Prayer Meetings, and All the Social Services of the Church* (ed. James M. Black; New York, Boston, Pittsburgh, Detroit and San Francisco: Eaton and Mains, and Cincinnati, Chicago, and St. Louis: Curts and Jennings, 1898), no. 154; *Assembly Songs* (ed. J. Ernest Thacker, George A. Fisher, and R. E. Magill; Richmond, VA: Presbyterian Committee for Publication, 1910), no. 224; *Praise Evangel* (1919), no. 49.

48. Gospel song by Fanny J. Crosby; in Walter Hines Sims, ed., *Baptist Hymnal* (Nashville, TN: Convention Press, 1956), no. 203. Cf. a similar hymn of Fanny Crosby celebrating redemption in the blood of Christ, quoted in Edith L. Blumhofer,

Her Heart Can See: The Life and Hymns of Fanny J. Crosby (Grand Rapids, MI: William B. Eerdmans, 2005), p. 265.

49. J. Jefferson Cleveland, "A Historical Account of the Black Gospel Song," in *Sings of Zion,* no. 172.

50. Musical score by Andraé Crouch, 1966; cf. *Songs of Zion,* no. 184. (The year 1947 is given in this publication as the date of the song, but Crouch was born in 1942 and the song bears the copyright date 1966. The original publication date of 1966 has been confirmed by Manna Music, Inc.) Copyright © 1966, renewed 1994 by Manna Music, Inc., and ASCAP.

51. Hymn by Katherine ("Kate") Hankey, ca. 1868, cited from *The Revivalist* (1872), no. 509. Also in *Chorus of Praise* (1898), no. 104; *Assembly Songs* (1910), no. 114; cf. *The United Methodist Hymnal* (1989), no. 156.

52. Musical score by Rick Founds. 1989, Maranatha Praise, Inc./ASCAP.

53. Musical score by Amy Grant and Chris Eaton, "Breath of Heaven (Mary's Song)." 1992, Age to Age Music, Inc./Riverstone Music/SGO Music Ltd.

54. Mary Alden Hopkins, *Hannah More and Her Circle* (New York and Toronto: Longmans, Green, and Co., 1947), p. 212. These early tracts often took the form of narratives illustrating Christian truths and also calling for persons to remain in their appropriate "stations" (this was in the aftermath of the French Revolution). The first and best known of Hannah More's Cheap Repository Tracts was published anonymously in the 1790s and was entitled "Village Politics, addressed to all the Mechanics, Journeymen, and Laborers, in Great Britain, by Will Chip, a Country Carpenter": *The Works of Hannah More* (New York: Harper and Brothers, 1868), 1:358ff.

55. The printed copy to which I have reference is the well-known mustard-colored tract design, ca. 1972, bearing the title "Have You Heard of the Four Spiritual Laws?" with a copyright statement dated 1965 in the inside of the front cover. The same text is available on the Campus Crusade Web site: http://www.campuscrusade.com/Tracts_and_Booklets/41awseng.htm and a Macromedia Flash (tm) version is available online at http://www.campuscrusade.com/fourlawsflash.htm. Information on these Web sites was accessed December 2006.

56. "Have You Heard of the Four Spiritual Laws?" in the printed edition referred to above, p. 6. The text of the contemporary Macromedia Flash version online (see the URL given earlier) agrees with the printed text.

57. "Have You Heard of the Four Spiritual Laws?" in the printed edition referred to earlier, pp. 6-7.

58. See the main Alpha Web site: http://alpha.org/. This Web site information was accessed December 2006.

59. Nicky Gumbel, *Questions of Life: A Practical Introduction to the Christian Faith* (Colorado Springs: Cook Ministry Resources, second edition, 1996), pp. 23-41.

60. Gumbel, *Questions of Life,* pp. 43-55. For another explanation of the Christ event as understood by Evangelical theologians, see Gilbert Bilezikian, *Christianity 101: Your Guide to Eight Basic Christian Beliefs* (Grand Rapids, MI: Zondervan,

1993). pp. 51–84 and 143–147. Bilezikian is a professor emeritus of Wheaton College and is a founding member and elder of the Willow Creek Community Church. The book carries a foreword by Bill Hybels, founder of the Willow Creek Church. Bilezikian's explanation of the Christ event is more theologically sophisticated and deals with a variety of meanings of the work of Christ, though the teaching of substitutionary atonement is prominent (pp. 144–145).

61. Thomas Ken, *A Manual of Prayers for the Use of the Scholars of Winchester College and All Other Devout Christians, to Which are Added Three Hymns: for Morning, Evening, and Midnight* (originally published in 1695; London: J. Hazard, 1735), p. 138, at the conclusion of the morning hymn (pp. 136–138). The version given above with contemporary orthography and punctuation is from *The United Methodist Hymnal* (1989), no. 95.

62. My own experience of visiting the Yoido Full Gospel Church on Sunday morning 29 May 2005. Subsequent e-mail correspondence with congregational leaders confirmed the use of the Thomas Ken doxology and the Apostles' Creed.

63. The process of affirming the faith in more traditional ways has been accelerated among Evangelical communities in Korea due to the strong influence of American Presbyterians and Methodists on Korean Protestantism, because these were the first Protestant communities established in Korea. The period in which this occurred, the 1890s, was a period in which American Methodist and Presbyterian churches were themselves experiencing the renewal of traditional liturgical forms of worship.

64. This has been the practice of Cathedral Christian Center in Beaumont, Texas (an Assemblies of God congregation, formerly "Cathedral in the Pines Christian Center") since the 1970s.

65. On Saturday, 20 December 1997, I heard the choir of the Derwood Bible Church (Derwood, Maryland) singing this piece at Lake Forest shopping mall in Gaithersburg, Maryland. I subsequently wrote a letter (in my computer files) expressing my appreciation.

66. Ibid., pp. 221–222. See the notes in chapter 3 about the alteration of this word in the Nicene Creed in the German text of the *Book of Concord,* which has "Christian" in place of "catholic."

67. Bebbington, *Evangelicalism in Modern Britain,* pp. 2–4; Marsden, *Understanding Fundamentalism and Evangelicalism,* pp. 1–2.

CHAPTER 5

1. The epigraph is from the Fourth World Conference on Faith and Order (Montreal 1963), report on "Scripture, Tradition, and traditions," ¶ 39; in Günther Gassmann, ed., *Documentary History of Faith and Order, 1963–1993* (Faith and Order paper no. 159; Geneva: World Council of Churches, 1993), p. 10.

2. Some sections of the report are labeled as having been adopted "unanimously"; this one is labeled as having been adopted *nemine contradicente,* which indicates that there were abstentions but no negative votes.

3. Final report of the first World Conference on Faith and Order, Lausanne, 3–21 August 1927, ¶¶ 9 and 11; in Lukas Vischer, ed., *A Documentary History of the Faith and Order Movement, 1927–1963* (St. Louis, MO: Bethany Press, 1963), p. 29.

4. Final report of the third World Conference on Faith and Order, Lund, 15–28 August 1952, ¶ 13; in Vischer, *Documentary History of the Faith and Order Movement, 1927–1963*, pp. 88–89.

5. Musical score (hymn) by Frederick B. Morley, written for the 1954 plenary assembly of the World Council of Churches in Evanston, Illinois, in a competition sponsored by the Hymn Society of America; cited from *The United Methodist Hymnal* (1989), number 547. Copyright © 1954, renewed 1982 by the Hymn Society.

6. New Delhi assembly of the World Council of Churches, 1961, section III on unity; in Gassmann, ed., *Documentary History of Faith and Order, 1963–1993*, p. 3; cf. Vischer, *Documentary History of the Faith and Order Movement, 1927–1963*, p. 144.

7. Ibid., ¶ 12; in Vischer, *Documentary History of the Faith and Order Movement, 1927–1963*, p. 148.

8. Catholics were not yet full participants in the work of the Faith and Order Commission, as they would soon become, but Catholic observers participated actively in the Montreal conference just as Protestant observers were at that time involved in the Second Vatican Council.

9. Pelikan, *Christian Tradition*, 1:112–116.

10. Campbell, *Christian Confessions*, pp. 36–38, 79–80.

11. Ibid., pp. 134–136.

12. Fourth World Conference on Faith and Order (Montreal 1963), report on "Scripture, Tradition, and traditions," ¶ 39; in Gassmann, ed., *Documentary History of Faith and Order, 1963–1993*, p. 10.

13. "Scripture, Tradition, and traditions," ¶¶ 45 and 46 (in Gassmann, ed., *Documentary History of Faith and Order, 1963–1993*, p. 11). Cf. John Leith's explication of this sense of the gospel as the core of Christian tradition in his *Introduction to the Reformed Tradition* (Atlanta, GA: John Knox, 1977), pp. 17–24.

14. See the reference earlier to Conzelmann, who summarized earlier German scholarship on the pre-pauline materials. In English-language New Testament scholarship, C. H. Dodd's *The Apostolic Preaching and Its Developments* (1956) developed the notion of a primitive kerygma into a broader attempt to see a particular pattern of early Christian preaching in a wide variety of New Testament texts. However, the conclusions of ecumenical scholarship in regard to the kerygma or gospel proclamation preceding and underlying the New Testament texts do not rely on the broader scheme that Dodd developed.

15. Albert C. Outler, "History as an Ecumenical Resource: The Protestant Discovery of 'Tradition,' 1952–1963," presidential Address, American Catholic Historical Association, 28 December 1972; in *Catholic Historical Review* 59:1 (1973): 1–15.

16. *Confessing the One Faith: An Ecumenical Explication of the Apostolic Faith as it is Confessed in the Nicene-Constantinopolitan Creed (381)* (Faith and Order paper no. 153; Geneva: WCC Publications, 1991), ¶ 7, pp. 2–3. Although the reference to

Montreal 1963 is not explicit at this point, the language of this paragraph closely follows that of the Montreal document on "Scripture, Tradition, and traditions." Cf. also "The COCU Consensus" V:6; in Burgess and Gros, eds., *Growing Consensus*, pp. 41–42. This paragraph follows the Montreal document in close detail.

17. Summarized in *Confessing the One Faith*, ¶ 1, p. 1.

18. In Gassmann, ed., *Documentary History of Faith and Order, 1963–1993*, pp. 169–170.

19. Final report of the first World Conference on Faith and Order, Lausanne, 3–21 August, 1927, ¶ 31; in Vischer, ed., *Documentary History of the Faith and Order Movement, 1927–1963*, p. 33–34.

20. *Confessing the One Faith*, ¶¶ 12–13, p. 4.

21. See the 1982 report "Towards the Common Expression of the Apostolic Faith Today" in Gassmann, ed., *Documentary History of Faith and Order, 1963–1993*, pp. 191–200. In particular, ¶ 10, item b, "... we consider that designing a new creed, intended to replace the Nicene Creed as the Ecumenical Symbol of the apostolic faith, is not appropriate" (p. 193).

22. *Confessing the One Faith, passim.*

23. The sections on Christ's suffering and death (¶¶ 127–161) and Christ's resurrection (¶¶ 162–192) are given in *Confessing the One Faith*, pp. 54–64 and 64–72, respectively. The language about vicarious sacrifice is explored in ¶¶ 133–134 (p. 56), and the emphasis on the victory over the powers of death is given in ¶ 143 (pp. 58–59) and ¶ 176 (p. 67).

24. Cited here from *The Book of Common Prayer* of the Episcopal Church in the USA (Prayer Book approved by the Episcopal General Convention of 1976; New York: Oxford University Press, 1990), p. 304. Cf. *The United Methodist Hymnal* (1989), pp. 35–36; the *AMEC Bicentennial Hymnal* (Nashville: African Methodist Episcopal Church, 1984), no. 802, where the celebrant asks the candidate(s) "Do you believe in God, the Father..." and the entire text of the Apostles' Creed follows, to which the candidate is expected to respond, "All this I steadfastly believe."

25. Rite of Christian Initiation of Adults, ¶ 219; in *The Rites of the Catholic Church: As Revised by Decree of the Second Vatican Ecumenical Council and Published by the Authority of Pope Paul VI* (English translation prepared by The International Commission on English in the Liturgy; New York: Pueblo, 1983), pp. 99–100.

26. Josef Jungmann, SJ, *The Mass: An Historical, Theological and Pastoral Survey* (Collegeville, MN: Liturgical Press, 1976; English translation by Julian Fernandes, SJ, ed. Mary Ellen Evans), p. 195 and n. 180. Jungmann's source for the acclamations in the Coptic liturgy is F. E. Brightman, *Liturgies Eastern and Western*, vol. 1, *Eastern Liturgies* (Oxford: Oxford University Press, 1896), 1:177. See also the anamnesis of Christ's work in the Liturgy of Addai and Mari, "... celebrating this great and awesome mystery of the passion and death [and burial] and resurrection of our Lord Jesus Christ" (in A. Gelston, *The Eucharistic Prayer of Addai and Mari* [Oxford: Clarendon Press, 1992], p. 55; the expression "and burial" appears in some manuscripts of the liturgy).

The acclamations reflect such New Testament passages as I Corinthians 11:26, "For as often as you eat this bread and drink the cup, you proclaim the Lord's death until he comes"; I Thessalonians 4:14, "For since we believe that Jesus died and rose again, even so, through Jesus Christ, God will bring with him those who have died"; I Corinthians 15:3-4, "For I handed on to you as of first importance what I also received, that Christ died for our sins in accordance with the scriptures, and that he was buried, and that he was raised on the third day in accordance with the scriptures . . ."

27. In the Latin text of the mass approved in 1970, the priest says, *Mysterium fidei*, "The mystery of faith," and the congregation replies, *Mortem tuam annuntiamus, Domine, et tuam resurrectionem confitemur, donec venias*, "We announce your death, O Lord, and we confess your resurrection until you come again." The Latin text is cited from the revised *Ordo* of 1970 as given in *Missale Parvum ad Usum Sacerdotis Itinerantis* (Vatican City: Typis Polyglottis Vaticana, 1970), pp. 50, 56, 60, and 66.

28. These acclamations in English, which are not a direct translation from the Latin given above, are cited here from *The Sacramentary: Approved for Use in the Dioceses of the United States of America by the National Conference of Catholic Bishops and Confirmed by the Apostolic See* (Collegeville, MN: Liturgical Press, 1974), pp. 507, 512, 515, 520–521; cf. *The Sacramentary* (1985), pp. 506, 511, 514, and 519–520. This particular form of the memorial acclamations has been contested by conservative Catholics who maintain that the expression "Christ has died" is inappropriate in eucharistic contexts where Christ is present. The issue is now being examined by the United States Council of Catholic Bishops, but Catholics of course do not dispute the claim that Christ truly died.

29. Cf. Rite II for the Holy Eucharist in *The Book of Common Prayer* of the Episcopal Church in the United States, p. 363; and *The United Methodist Hymnal* (1989), pp. 10, 14, 16, 18, 20, 22, 24, 25.

CHAPTER 6

1. Report on Unity adopted by the third assembly of the World Council of Churches in New Delhi, 1961, ¶ 12; in Vischer, *Documentary History of the Faith and Order Movement, 1927–1963*, p. 148.

2. On signs of the "intention" to believe on the part of a community, see chapter 7 in the section on "Commensurability and Mutual Understanding."

3. Athanasius, "On the Incarnation of the Word," 54; text in E. P. Meijering, ed. and tr., *Athanasius: De Incarnatione Verbi: Einleitung, Übersetzung, Kommentar* (Amsterdam: Verlag J. C. Gieben, 1989), p. 357; my translation.

4. See, for example, Bilezikian, *Christianity 101*, pp. 71–72 (sacrificial meanings), 72–73 (victory over evil).

5. Council of Trent, decrees 1–2; in Pelikan and Hotchkiss, *Creeds and Confessions*, 2:822–824.

6. The Greek text is: τῇ διδαχῇ τῶν ἀποστόλων.

7. Theissen and Merz, *The Historical Jesus*, p. 17.

8. A point emphasized by Martin Hengel, *The Four Gospels and the One Gospel of Jesus Christ*, pp. 151–152.

9. Theissen and Merz, *The Historical Jesus*, p. 488.

10. The work referred to earlier, edited by Ted A. Campbell, Ann K. Riggs, and Gilbert W. Stafford, offering dialogues conducted under the auspices of the Faith and Order Commission of the National Council of the Churches of Christ in the USA in the quadrennium 1996–2000. See also the methodological considerations at the end of chapter 7 of this book on "Commensurability and Mutual Understanding."

11. Article of Religion 2 of the Twenty-Five Articles of Religion used by the United Methodist Church, the African Methodist Episcopal Church, the African Methodist Episcopal Zion Church, and the Christian Methodist Episcopal Church, derived from the Thirty-Nine Articles of Religion of the Church of England; in Pelikan and Hotchkiss, *Creeds and Confession of Faith in the Christian Tradition*, 3:202.

12. Clifford Geertz, "Religion as a Cultural System," *The Interpretation of Cultures* (New York: Basic Books, 1973), pp. 87–125.

13. Michael L. Satlow, for example, argues for a "polythetic" definition of "Judaism," a definition that identifies a cluster of elements (including beliefs and practices) that typically characterize Jewish communities, but not uniformly, that is to say, some particular elements do not appear in every community that identifies itself as being Jewish: *Creating Judaism: History, Tradition, Practice* (New York: Columbia University Press, 2006), pp. 1–18 and through the book more broadly.

14. For example, the beliefs and practices epitomized in the so-called Pillars of Islam: cf. Mahmoud M. Ayoub, *Islam: Faith and History* (Oxford: Oneworld Publications, 2004), pp. 55–69.

15. Kittel, *Theological Dictionary of the New Testament*, s.v. "μυστήριον," 4:819. The meaning of the term denoting a "secret" is discussed earlier in the article in the section on μυστήριον as it is used in the canonical gospels.

16. Ibid., 4:820.

17. Charles Wesley, hymn on "Free Grace," in *Hymns and Sacred Poems* (1739), p. 118; contemporary orthography as in *The United Methodist Hymnal* (1989), no. 363. Cf. the evening prayer in the Orthodox *Octoechos*, which holds the mystery of Christ to be "unknown even by the angels."

CHAPTER 7

1. Vincent of Lérins, *Commonitorium* 2:[3]. Latin text in Reginald Stewart Moxon, ed., *The Commonitorium of Vincentius of Lerins* (Cambridge: Cambridge Patristic Texts, 1915), p. 10. The English translation is my own.

2. Allan Megill identifies four distinct (though related) senses of the term "objectivity" as used in historical studies and other fields of study. In the first place, he says, is "absolute objectivity," the notion or perhaps simply the goal of representing things "as they really are," apart from subjective interpretations. It is this

sense of the term that predominates when historians and others disavow the possibility of objectivity. Second, he distinguishes "disciplinary objectivity," that is, the objectivity that arises when an individual follows procedures or standards accepted by a community. So, for instance, medical and legal communities adopt certain procedures and standards and an individual may be said to operate "objectively" when she follows the group's agreed-upon standards, even though this does not make a claim to objectivity in the absolute sense. In the third place is "dialectic" objectivity, really a cluster of notions, all of which suggest in one way or another that knowledge of the world arises from the interaction of our own subjective interest and our willingness to consider that which presents itself as an object external to ourselves. In the fourth place is "procedural" objectivity, "which aims at the practice of an impersonal method of investigation or administration": Allan Megill, "Introduction: Four Senses of Objectivity," in Allan Megill, ed., *Rethinking Objectivity* (Durham, NC: Duke University Press, 1994), pp. 1–20. Disavowing the first of these four senses of objectivity, I would strive for the positive implications of what he identifies as senses 2, 3, and 4.

3. Lindbeck, *The Nature of Doctrine*, p. 15.

4. Ratzinger, *Introduction to Christianity*, pp. 50–52, 54–56 (in the English translation), pp. 59–61, 63–65 (in the Spanish translation). Although this particular claim—that all forms of the primitive Christian profession were cast as questions and responses—does not seem defensible to me, it is nevertheless clear that the profession of faith in the early Christian community was an essentially communal act and not an act of individual profession. Cf. Augustine's narrative of the conversion of Marius Victorinus. Victorinus comes to believe as a Christian and confides this to his friend Simplicianus, who replies that he will not believe that Victorinus is a Christian until he sees him in church. To this Victorinus initially offers the clever but evasive response, "Is it then the walls of the church that make the Christian?" But eventually Victorinus make his public profession; Augustine, *Confessions* 8; in the translation of R. S. Pine-Coffin, *Confessions* (London: Penguin, 1961), p. 160. On the communal context of the baptismal creed, cf. also Lochman, *The Faith We Confess*, pp. 10–11.

5. William G. Rusch, *Reception: An Ecumenical Problem* (Philadelphia: Fortress Press in cooperation with the Lutheran World Federation, 1988) discusses historical and contemporary issues surrounding ecumenical reception. He stresses that although ecumenical work on reception in the 1960s focused on the reception of conciliar teachings (at the time of and following the Second Vatican Council), ecumenical reception must be considered in a broader sense as the dynamic work of the Holy Spirit enabling Christian communities to discern the gospel in, and thus "receive," ecumenical teachings and actions. See also Jaroslav Pelikan's chapter on "The Orthodoxy of the Body of the Faithful" (chapter 12 in Pelikan, *Credo*, pp. 336–364 and especially pp. 336–352).

6. Lindbeck, *The Nature of Doctrine*, p. 76. Pelikan also stresses the corporate nature of doctrine (*The Christian Tradition* 1:1–4) but notes that it is sometimes difficult "to draw the line of demarcation between the teachings of the church and the theories of its teachers" (1:3).

7. Lindbeck, *The Nature of Doctrine*, p. 16.

8. Ibid.

9. Ibid., briefly on pp. 17–19 and then at greater length on pp. 72–90 and throughout the book.

10. That is to say, Schleiermacher seems to have believed in the objective realities described in traditional doctrines as well as understanding a range of religious and aesthetic experiences as grounds for the explication and understanding (and even the defense) of traditional teachings. I question the allegation that Schleiermacher himself "reduced" Christian claims to experiential or aesthetic claims.

11. Christophe Bonjean, *Denominational vs. Common Mixed Schools* (Colombo: Examiner Press, 1861; cited on the Internet in the newsletter of the Asian district of the Society of St. Pius X for July–September 2001 at http://www.sspxasia.com/Newsletters/2001/July-Sep/The_Second_Apostle_of_Sri_Lanka_Archbishop_Bonjean.htm).

12. Charles Wesley's hymn "Wrestling Jacob," in John and Charles Wesley, *Hymns and Sacred Poems* (Bristol: Felix Farley, 1742), stanza 9; cf. the contemporary version with the word "bowels" changed to "mercies" in *The United Methodist Hymnal*, no. 387.

13. The dialogues carried on in this group are available in the volume *Ancient Faith and American-Born Churches;* Dr. Ford's methodological essay entitled "Theological Language and Ecumenical Methodology" is given on pp. 15–23.

Bibliography

Abraham, William. *Canon and Criterion in Christian Theology*. Oxford: Clarendon Press, 1998.
———. *Waking from Doctrinal Amnesia: The Healing of Doctrine in The United Methodist Church*. Nashville, TN: Abingdon Press, 1995.
African Methodist Episcopal Church. "Special Declaration on Apostolic Succession and Ritualism" (1884). In *The Doctrine and Discipline of the African Methodist Episcopal Church, 2004–2008*. Nashville, TN: African Methodist Episcopal Church, 2005, pp. 20–23.
Aland, Kurt. See entry under *The Greek New Testament*.
Ambrose, *De Virginibus*. See entry under M. Salvati.
Ante-Nicene Fathers. See entry under Alexander Roberts.
Apostolic Fathers. See entry under Michael W. Holmes.
The Apostolic Tradition. See entries under Bradshaw and Botte.
Assemblies of God. See entry under General Council of the Assemblies of God.
Athanasius, *De Incarnatione*. See entry under Meijering.
———, "Canons of Athanasius." See entry under Wilhelm Riedl.
Augustine. *Confessions*. R. S. Pine-Coffin, tr. London: Penguin, 1961.
———, *De Fide et Symbolo*. See entries under Meijering and Rivière.
Ayoub, Mahmoud M. *Islam: Faith and History*. Oxford: Oneworld, 2004.
"Baptist Faith and Message." See entry under Southern Baptist Convention.
Baptist Hymnal. See entry under Sims.
Barrett, David B., ed. *World Christian Encyclopedia: A Comparative Study of Churches and Religions in the Modern World, AD 1900–2000*. Nairobi: Oxford University Press, 1982.
Barth, Karl. *Church Dogmatics*. G. W. Bromiley and T. F. Torrance, eds., and trs. Edinburgh: T. & T. Clark, 1975.
———. *Dogmatics in Outline*. New York: Harper and Row, 1959.

Bebbington, D. W. *Evangelicalism in Modern Britain: A History from the 1730s to the 1980s*. London: Unwin Hyman, 1989.

Behr, John, ed. and tr. [Irenaeus of Lyons] *On the Apostolic Preaching*. Crestwood, NY: St. Vladimir's Seminary Press, 1996.

Benedict XVI, Pope. See entry under Ratzinger.

Bennett, David. *The Altar Call: Its Origins and Present Usage*. Lanham, MD: University Press of America, 2000.

Bettenson, Henry, ed. *Documents of the Christian Church*. London: Oxford University Press, second edition, 1963.

Bible. See entries under *The Greek New Testament* and under specific versions of the Bible consulted here: the New Revised Standard Version and the New International Version.

Bilezikian, Gilbert. *Christianity 101: Your Guide to Eight Basic Christian Beliefs*. Grand Rapids, MI: Zondervan, 1993.

Black, James M., ed. *Chorus of Praise: For Use in Sunday Schools, Young People's Meetings, Revivals, Prayer Meetings, and All the Social Services of the Church*. New York: Eaton and Mains, 1898.

——, ed. *Songs of the Soul, No. 2: For Use in Sunday Evening Congregations, Revivals, Camp Meetings, Social Services, and Young Peoples Meetings*. Cincinnati: Curts and Jennings, 1896; New York: Eaton and Mains, 1896.

Black, Matthew. See entry under *The Greek New Testament*.

Blume, Clemens, SJ, ed. *Sequentiae Ineditae: Liturgische Prosen des Mittelalters*, vol. 4. Analecta Hymnica Medii Aevi series, vol. 34. Leipzig: O. R. Reisland, 1900.

Blumhofer, Edith L. *Her Heart Can See: The Life and Hymns of Fanny J. Crosby*. Grand Rapids, MI: William B. Eerdmans, 2005.

Bonjean, Christophe (Bishop). *Denominational vs. Common Mixed Schools*. Colombo: Examiner Press, 1861. Cited on the Internet in the newsletter of the Asian district of the Society of St. Pius X for July–September 2001: http://www.sspxasia.com/Newsletters/2001/July-Sep/The_Second_Apostle_of_Sri_Lanka_Archbishop_Bonjean.htm.

The Book of Common Prayer: 1662 Version (Includes Appendices from the 1549 Version and Other Commemorations, with an Introduction by Diarmaid MacCulloch). Everyman's Library edition, no. 241. London: David Campbell Publishers Ltd., 1999.

The Book of Common Prayer of the Episcopal Church in the United States. New York: Oxford University Press, 1990.

Book of Concord. See entry under Kolb.

Botte, Bernard, ed. *Hippolyte de Rome: La Tradition Apostolique d'après les anciennes Versions*. Sources chrétiennes series, no. 11. Paris: Éditions du Cerf, 1968.

Braaten, Carl E., and Robert W. Jenson, eds. *In One Body through the Cross: The Princeton Proposal for Christian Unity*. Grand Rapids, MI: William B. Eerdmans, 2003.

Bradshaw, Paul F. *Early Christian Worship: A Basic Introduction to Ideas and Practice*. Collegeville, MN: Liturgical Press, 1996.

———. *The Search for the Origins of Christian Worship: Sources and Methods for the Study of Early Liturgy.* New York: Oxford University Press, 1992.

Bradshaw, Paul F., Maxwell E. Johnson, and L. Edward Phillips, eds. *The Apostolic Tradition: A Commentary.* Hermeneia commentary series. Minneapolis, MN: Fortress Press, 2002.

Briggs, Charles Augustus, *Theological Symbolics.* New York: Charles Scribner's Sons, 1914.

Brightman, F. E., ed. *Liturgies Eastern and Western*, vol. 1, *Eastern Liturgies.* Oxford: Oxford University Press, 1896.

Brown, Dan. *The Da Vinci Code.* New York: Doubleday Books, 2003.

Brox, Norbert, ed. *Irenäus von Lyon: Adversus Haereses/Gegen Häresien.* Fontes Christiani series. 5 vols. Freiburg: Herder, 1993–2001.

Bucanus. See entry under du Buc.

Burgess, Joseph A., and Jeffrey Gros, FSC, eds. *Growing Consensus: Church Dialogues in the United States, 1962–1991.* Ecumenical Documents V; New York: Paulist Press, 1995.

G. W. Butterworth, ed. and tr. *Origen: On First Principles.* London: SPCK, 1936.

Calvary Chapel (Costa Mesa, California) Statement on "The Gospel." Available at http://www.calvarychapel.com/?show=thegospel. Material on this Web site was accessed December 2006.

Calvin, John, *Institutes of the Christian Religion.* See entry under McNeill.

———. *Opera Quae Supersunt.* 59 vols. Braunschweig: C. A. Schwetschke and Son, 1863–1900.

Campbell, Ted A. *Christian Confessions.* Louisville, KY: Westminster/John Knox, 1996.

———. "The Complete Evangelical." *Circuit Rider* 9:5 (May 1985): 3–5.

———. *Methodist Doctrine: The Essentials.* Nashville, TN: Abingdon Press, 1999.

———. *The Religion of the Heart: A Study of European Religious Life in the Seventeenth and Eighteenth Centuries.* Columbia: University of South Carolina Press, 1991.

Campbell, Ted A., Ann K. Riggs, and Gilbert W. Stafford, eds. *Ancient Faith and American-Born Churches: Dialogues between Christian Traditions.* New York: Paulist Press, 2005.

Campus Crusade for Christ, Incorporated. "Have You Heard of the Four Spiritual Laws?" Campus Crusade for Christ, 1965.

Canons of Athanasius. See entry under Riedl.

Capelle, Dom B. See entry under C. H. Roberts.

Cassian, *Conferences.* See entries under Luibheid and Petscheinig.

Caster, Marcel, ed. and tr. *Clément d'Alexandrie: Les Stromates.* Sources chrétiennes series, no. 30; Paris: Éditions du Cerf, 1951.

Catechism of the Catholic Church. Catholic catechism approved by the apostolic constitution *Fidei Depositum* of John Paul II, 11 October 1992. North American English translation: *Catechism of the Catholic Church.* Washington, DC: United States Catholic Conference, 1994. North American Spanish translation: *Catecismo de la Iglesia Católica.* Washington, DC: United States Catholic Conference, second edition, 2001.

Catholic Church. See entries under *Catechism of the Catholic Church,* International Consultation on English Texts in the Liturgy, *Missale Parvum ad Usum Sacerdotis Itinerantis, Sacramentary* (two entries).

Charry, Ellen. *By the Renewing of Your Minds: The Pastoral Function of Christian Doctrine.* New York: Oxford University Press, 1997.

Church of the Nazarene. *Manual/1989.* Kansas City, MO: Nazarene Publishing House, 1989.

———. See entry under Pentecostal Church of the Nazarene.

Clement of Alexandria, *Stromateis* (or *Stromata*). See entry under Caster.

Cleveland, J. Jefferson, ed. *Songs of Zion.* Supplemental Worship Resources, no. 12: Nashville, TN: Abingdon Press, 1981.

Cobb, Buell E., Jr. *The Sacred Harp: A Tradition and Its Music.* Athens: University of Georgia Press, Brown Thrasher Books, second edition, 2001.

Connor, Steven. *Postmodernist Culture: An Introduction to Theories of the Contemporary.* Oxford: Basil Blackwell, 1989.

Conzelmann, Hans. *An Outline of the Theology of the New Testament.* London: SCM Press, 1969. Translation by John Bowden from *Grundriss der Theologie des Neuen Testaments.* Munich: Christian Kaiser Verlag, second edition, 1968.

Crouzel, Henri, and Manlio Simonetti, eds. and trs. *Origène: Traité des Principes.* Sources chrétiennes series, vol. 252. Paris: Éditions du Cerf, 1978.

Crum, W. E. See entry under Wilhelm Riedl.

Davies, Rupert E. See entry under R. Newton Flew.

Day, Peter D. *Eastern Christian Liturgies: The Armenian, Coptic, Ethiopian, and Syrian Rites: Eucharistic Rites with Introductory Notes and Rubrical Instructions.* Shannon: Irish University Press, 1972.

Delumeau, Jean. *Catholicism between Luther and Voltaire: A New View of the Counter-Reformation.* London: Burns and Oats, and Philadelphia: Westminster, 1977.

Depositio Martirum [sic]. See entry under Mommsen.

Dibelius, Martin. *From Tradition to Gospel.* London: Ivor Nicholson and Watson, 1934. Translation of *Die Formgeschichte des Evangeliums,* 1933, Bertram Lee Wolf, tr.

Didascalia Apostolorum. See entry under Vööbus.

Dillenberger, John, ed. and tr. *Martin Luther: Selections from His Writings.* Garden City, NY: Doubleday Anchor Books, 1961.

Dodd, C. H. *The Apostolic Preaching and Its Developments.* New York: Harper and Row, 1964 [sic; but apparently a reprint of the original 1956 edition].

Du Bois, W. E. B. *The Souls of Black Folk.* New York: The New American Library, and London: The New English library, Limited, 1963.

Du Buc [Bucanus], Guillaume. *Institutiones Theologicae seu Locorum Communium Christianae Religionis ex Dei Verbo et Praestantissimorum Theologorum Orthodoxo Consensu Expositorum Analysis.* Geneva: 1609.

Duensing, Hugo, ed. *Epistula Apostolorum nach dem Äthiopischen und Koptischen Texte.* Bonn: A. Marcus and E. Webers Verlag, 1925.

Duffy, Eamon, *The Stripping of the Altars: Traditional Religion in England, c. 1400– c. 1580.* New Haven, CT: Yale University Press, second edition revised, 2005.

Ebeling, Gerhardt. *Word and Faith*. London: SCM Press, 1963.
Edwards, O. C., Jr. *A History of Preaching*. Nashville, TN: Abingdon Press, 2004.
Ehrman, Bart D. *Lost Christianities: The Battles for Scripture and the Faiths We Never Knew*. New York: Oxford University Press, 2003.
———. *The Orthodox Corruption of Scripture: The Effect of Early Christological Controversies on the Text of the New Testament*. New York: Oxford University Press, 1993.
Enchiridion Biblicum: Documenta Ecclesiastica Sacram Scripturam Spectantia. Fourth edition. Naples: M. D'Auria, and Rome: A. Arnoldo, 1961.
Epistula Apostolorum. See entries under Schmidt and Duensing.
Evagrius Scholasticus. *Ecclesiastical History*. See entry under Whitby.
Evangelisches Gesangbuch: Ausgabe für die Evangelisch-Lutherischen Kirchen in Niedersachsen und für die Bremische Evangelische Kirche. Bremen: Verlagsgemeinschaft für das Evangelische Gesangbuch Niedersachsen, 1994.
Flew, R. Newton, and Rupert E. Davies, eds. *The Catholicity of Protestantism: Being a Report Presented to His Grace the Archbishop of Canterbury by a Group of Free Churchmen*. London: Lutterworth Press, 1950.
Fortin, Denis. "Nineteenth-Century Evangelicalism and Early Adventist Statements of Belief." *Andrews University Seminary Studies* 36:1 (Spring 1998): 51–67.
"Four Spiritual Laws." See entry under Campus Crusade for Christ.
Gassmann, Günther, ed. *Documentary History of Faith and Order, 1963–1993*. Faith and Order paper no. 159. Geneva: World Council of Churches, 1993.
Gelston, A. *The Eucharistic Prayer of Addai and Mari*. Oxford: Clarendon Press, 1992.
General Council of the Assemblies of God. "Statement of Fundamental Truths." Available at http://www.ag.org/top/Beliefs/Statement_of_Fundamental_Truths/sft_full.cfm. This material was accessed December 2006.
Gilley, Sheridan, and Brian Stanley, eds. *World Christianities, c. 1815–c. 1914*. Cambridge, UK: Cambridge University Press, 2006.
Goen, C. C. *Broken Churches, Broken Nation: Denominational Schisms and the Coming of the American Civil War*. Macon, GA: Mercer University Press, 1985.
Gospel of Thomas. See entry under Meyer.
The Greek New Testament. Ed. by Kurt Aland, Matthew Black, Bruce M. Metzger, and Allen Wikgren. London: United Bible Society, 1966.
Gregg, Robert C., and Dennis E. Groh. *Early Arianism: A View of Salvation*. Philadelphia: Fortress Press, 1981.
Griffiths, David N. *The Bibliography of the Book of Common Prayer, 1549–1999*. London: The British Library, and New Castle, DE: Oak Knoll Press, 2002.
Groh, Dennis E. See entry under Robert C. Gregg.
Gros, Jeffrey, FSC, Harding Meyer, and William G. Rusch, eds. *Growth in Agreement II: Reports and Agreed Statements of Ecumenical Conversations on a World Level, 1982–1998*. Faith and Order Paper no. 187. Geneva: WCC, and Grand Rapids, MI: William B. Eerdmans, 2000.

———. See also entry under Joseph A. Burgess.

The Ground of the Unity: A Doctrinal Statement Adopted by the Unity Synod of the Unitas Fratrum, or Moravian Church, Held at Herrnhut, German Democratic Republic, August 30 to September 12, 1981. Printed by the Moravian Church, n.p., [1981].

Gumbel, Nicky, *Questions of Life: A Practical Introduction to the Christian Faith.* Colorado Springs: Cook Ministry Resources, second edition, 1996.

Hadjiantonious, George A. *Protestant Patriarch: The Life of Cyril Lucaris, 1572– 1638, Patriarch of Constantinople.* Richmond, VA: John Knox, 1961.

Hansen, Günther Christian, ed., *Theodoros Anagnostes: Kirchengeschichte.* Berlin: Akademie Verlag, 1995.

Hauler, E., ed. *Didascalia Apostolorum Fragmenta Veronensia Latina.* Leipzig, 1900.

Hengel, Martin. *The Four Gospels and the One Gospel of Jesus Christ: An Investigation of the Collection and Origin of the Canonical Gospels.* John Bowden, tr. Harrisburg, PA: Trinity Press International, 2000.

Heppe, Heinrich. *Reformierte Dogmatik.* Kreis Moers: Buchhandlung des Erziehungsvereins, 1935. Ernst Bizer, ed., and G. T. Thompson, tr., *Reformed Dogmatics: Set Out and Illustrated from the Sources.* London: Allen and Unwin, 1950.

[Hippolytus of Rome]. *The Apostolic Tradition.* See entries under Bradshaw and Botte.

Holmes, Michael W., ed. and tr. *The Apostolic Fathers: Greek Texts and English Translations.* Grand Rapids, MI: Baker Academic, third edition, 2007.

Hopkins, Mary Alden. *Hannah More and Her Circle.* New York and Toronto: Longmans, Green, and Co., 1947.

Hordern, William E. *A Layman's Guide to Protestant Theology.* New York: Macmillan, and London: Collier-Macmillan Ltd., 1957; second edition revised, 1968.

Hurtado, Larry W. *Lord Jesus Christ: Devotion to Jesus in Earliest Christianity.* Grand Rapids, MI: William B. Eerdmans, 2003.

International Consultation on English Texts. *Prayers We Have in Common.* Philadelphia: Fortress Press, second edition revised, 1975.

Irenaeus, *Adversus Haereses.* See entry under Brox.

———, *Demonstration of the Apostolic Preaching.* See entries under Rousseau and Behr.

Jackson, George Pullen. *White and Negro Spirituals: Their Life Span and Kinship: Tracing 200 Years of Untrammeled Song Making and Singing among Our Country Folk.* Locust Valley, NY: J. J. Augustin, 1943. Reprint edition of 1970.

Jackson, Thomas, ed. *The Works of the Reverend John Wesley, A.M.* 14 vols. London: Wesleyan Conference Office, 1873.

Jenkins, Philip, *The Next Christendom: The Coming of Global Christianity.* Oxford: Oxford University Press, 2002.

Jeremias, Joachim. *The Eucharistic Words of Jesus.* Philadelphia: Fortress Press, 1966.

Jewett, Robert. *Romans: A Commentary.* Hermeneia Commentary series. Minneapolis, MN: Fortress Press, 2007.

John Cassian, *Conferences.* See entries under Luibheid and Petscheinig.

Johnson, Luke Timothy. *The Creed: What Christians Believe and Why It Matters.* New York: Doubleday Image Books, 2003.
Johnson, Maxwell E. See entry under Paul F. Bradshaw.
Jones, Scott J. *John Wesley's Conception and Use of Scripture.* Nashville, TN: Kingswood Books imprint of the Abingdon Press, 1995.
Jungmann, Josef, SJ. *The Mass: An Historical, Theological and Pastoral Survey.* Julian Fernandes, SJ, tr., Mary Ellen Evans, ed. Collegeville, MN: Liturgical Press, 1976.
Kelly, J. N. D. *Early Christian Creeds.* Burnt Mill, Harlow, UK: Longman Group Ltd., third edition, revised, 1972.
———, tr. and ed. *Rufinus: A Commentary on the Apostles' Creed.* Ancient Christian Writers series. Westminster, MD: the Newman Press, and London: Longmans, Green, and Co., 1955.
Kelsey, David H. *To Understand God Truly: What's Theological about a Theological School.* Louisville, KY: Westminster/John Knox, 1992.
Ken, Thomas. *A Manual of Prayers for the Use of the Scholars of Winchester College and All Other Devout Christians, to Which are Added Three Hymns: for Morning, Evening, and Midnight.* Originally published in 1695. London: J. Hazard, 1735.
Kinnamon, Michael. "The Place of an Authoritative Teaching Office in the Christian Church (Disciples of Christ)." In Campbell, Riggs, and Stafford, eds., *Ancient Faith and American-Born Churches: Dialogues Between Christian Traditions,* pp. 213–222.
Kittel, Gerhard, ed. *Theological Dictionary of the New Testament.* Geoffrey W. Bromiley, tr. and ed. Grand Rapids, MI: William B. Eerdmans, 1964.
Klotsche, E. H. *Christian Symbolics, or, Exposition of the Distinctive Characteristics of the Catholic, Lutheran and Reformed Churches as Well as the Modern Denominations and Sects Represented in This Country.* Burlington, IA: Lutheran Literary Board, 1929.
Kolb, Robert, and Timothy J. Wengert, eds. Charles Arand, Eric Gritsch, Robert Kolb, William Russell, James Schaaf, Jane Strohl, and Timothy J. Wengert, trs. *The Book of Concord: The Confessions of the Evangelical Lutheran Church.* Minneapolis, MN: Fortress Press, 2000.
Kroymann, Aem., ed. *Tertullian: De Corona Militis. Corpus Christianorum: Series Latina,* vol. 2.
Lehman, Helmut T., general editor. *Luther's Works.* 55 vols. Philadelphia: Muhlenberg, 1960.
Leith, John, ed. *Creeds of the Churches: A Reader in Christian Doctrine from the New Testament to the Present.* Atlanta, GA: John Knox, third edition, revised, 1982.
———. *Introduction to the Reformed Tradition.* Atlanta, GA: John Knox, 1977.
Levine, Amy Jill. "Jewish-Christian Relations from the 'Other Side': A Response to Webb, Lodahl, and White." *Quarterly Review* 20:3 (Fall 2000).
Lewis, C. S. *Broadcast Talks.* London: Centenary Press, 1942.
———. *Mere Christianity.* New York: Macmillan, 1960.

Lindbeck, George A. *The Nature of Doctrine: Religion and Theology in a Postliberal Age.* Philadelphia: Westminster, 1984.

Linyard, Fred, and Phillip Tovey. *Moravian Worship.* Grove Worship series, no. 129. Bramcote, Nottingham: Grove Books, 1994.

Lochman, Jan Milič. *The Faith We Confess: An Ecumenical Dogmatics.* Translated by David Lewis. Philadelphia: Fortress Press, 1984.

Luibheid, Colm, tr., *John Cassian: Conferences.* Classics of Western Spirituality series. New York: Paulist Press, 1985.

Luther, Martin. *D. Martin Luthers Werke: Kritischen Gesamtausgabe.* Weimar: Hermann Böhlaus Nachfolger, 1926.

———. *Works* (English). See entries under Dillenberger and Lehman.

Macquarrie, John. *Principles of Christian Theology.* Second edition. New York: Charles Scribner's Sons, 1977.

Mansi, J. D., ed. *Sacrorum Conciliorum Nova et Amplissima Collectio.* Florence: 1758; reprint edition of 1901.

Manual/1989. Kansas City, MO: Nazarene Publishing House, 1989.

Marsden, George M. *Reforming Fundamentalism: Fuller Seminary and the New Evangelicalism.* Grand Rapids, MI: William B. Eerdmans, 1987.

———. *Understanding Fundamentalism and Evangelicalism.* Grand Rapids, MI: William B. Eerdmans, 1991.

Marshall, Bruce. *Trinity and Truth.* Cambridge University Press, 2000.

Maugham, W. Somerset. *Of Human Bondage.* New York: The Modern Library, 1915.

McLaren, Brian D. *A Generous Orthodoxy: Why I am a missional + evangelical + post/protestant + liberal/conservative + mystical/poetic + biblical + charismatic/ contemplative + fundamentalist/calvinist + anabaptist/anglican + methodist + catholic + green + incarnational + depressed-yet-hopeful + emergent + unfinished Christian.* El Cajon, CA: Youth Specialties Books, an imprint of Zondervan Press, 2004.

McLeod, Hugh, ed. *World Christianities, c. 1914–c. 2000.* Cambridge, UK: Cambridge University Press, 2006.

McNeill, John T. ed. *Calvin: Institutes of the Christian Religion.* 2 vols. Library of Christian Classics series. Philadelphia: Westminster Press, 1960.

McWilliams, Warren. "'Rooted and Grounded in Jesus Christ': Christology and Soteriology in *The Baptist Faith and Message (1963)*." In Jeff B. Pool, ed., *Sacred Mandates of Conscience: Interpretations of The Baptist Faith and Message.* Macon, GA: Smith and Helwys, 1997, pp. 133–135.

Megill, Allan, ed. *Rethinking Objectivity.* Durham, NC: Duke University Press, 1994.

Meijering, E. P., ed. and tr. *Athanasius: De Incarnatione Verbi: Einleitung, Übersetzung, Kommentar.* Amsterdam: J. C. Gieben, 1989.

———, ed. and tr. *Augustine: De Fide et Symbolo.* Amsterdam: J. C. Gieben, 1987.

Meinhold, Peter. *Geschichte der kirchlichen Historiographie.* 2 volumes. Munich: Verlag Karl Albert Freiburg, 1967.

Melito of Sardis, *Paschal Homily* (or *On Pascha*). See entry under Stewart-Sykes.

Merz, Annette. See entry under Theissen.

Metzger, Bruce M. See entry under *The Greek New Testament.*
Methodist Church. *Methodist Hymnal: Official Hymnal of the Methodist Church.* Nashville: Methodist Publishing House, 1964, 1966. This volume was subsequently renamed *The Book of Hymns* of The United Methodist Church (after a church union in 1968).
Meyer, Harding, and Lucas Vischer, eds. *Growth in Agreement: Reports and Agreed Statements of Ecumenical Conversations on a World Level.* Faith and Order Paper no. 108. New York: Paulist Press, and Geneva: World Council of Churches, 1984.
———. See entry under Jeffrey Gros.
Meyer, Marvin, tr. and ed. *The Gospel of Thomas: The Hidden Sayings of Jesus.* San Francisco: HarperSanFrancisco, 1992.
Meyer, Harding, and Lucas Vischer, eds. *Growth in Agreement: Reports and Agreed Statements of Ecumenical Conversations on a World Level.* Faith and Order Paper no. 108. New York: Paulist Press, and Geneva: World Council of Churches, 1984.
Migne, Jean-Paul, ed. *Patrologiae Latinae Cursus Completus Omnium SS. Patrum, Doctorum Scriptorum Ecclesiasticorum.* 217 vols. Turnholti: Typographi Brepols Editores Pontificii, 1844–55.
Mingana, A., ed. and tr. *Commentary of Theodore of Mopsuestia on the Nicene Creed.* Woodbrooke Studies: Christian Documents in Syriac, Arabic, and Garshuni, vol. 5. Cambridge, UK: W. Heffer and Sons, 1932.
Missale Parvum ad Usum Sacerdotis Itinerantis. Vatican City: Typis Polyglottis Vaticana, 1970.
Mommsen, Theodor, ed. *Chronica Minora Saec. IV. V. VI. VII.* Monumenta Germaniae Historica series, vol. 9. Berlin: Weidmann, 1892.
Moravian Church. *Hymnal and Liturgies of the Moravian Church.* Bethlehem, PA: Moravian Church in America, Northern and Southern Provinces: 1969.
More, Hannah. *The Works of Hannah More.* New York: Harper and Brothers, 1868.
Moule, C. F. D. *The Sacrifice of Christ.* London: Hodder and Stoughton, 1956.
Moxon, Reginald Stewart, ed. *The Commonitorium of Vincentius of Lerins.* Cambridge, UK: Cambridge Patristic Texts, 1915.
Musurillo, Herbert, ed. *The Acts of the Christian Martyrs.* Oxford: Oxford University Press, 1972.
Mynors, R. A. B., ed. *C. Plini Caecili: Epistularum Libri Decem.* Oxford: Clarendon Press, 1963.
Nassif, Bradley. "Eastern Orthodoxy and Evangelicalism: The Status of an Emerging Global Dialogue" in Daniel B. Clendenin, ed., *Eastern Orthodox Theology: A Contemporary Reader.* Grand Rapids, MI: Baker Academic/Paternoster Press, second edition, 2003, pp. 211–248.
Nersoyan, Tiran, tr. and ed. *Divine Liturgy of the Armenian Apostolic Orthodox Church: With Variables, Complete Rubrics, and Commentary.* London: Saint Sarkis Church and Society for Promoting Christian Knowledge, fifth edition, revised, 1984.

New International Version of the Bible. Copyright © 1973, 1978, and 1984 by the International Bible Society.

New Revised Standard Version of the Bible. Copyright © 1989 by the Division of Christian Education of the National Council of Churches of Christ in the USA.

New Testament. See entries under *The Greek New Testament* and under specific versions of the Bible consulted here: the New Revised Standard Version and the New International Version.

Newman, John Henry. *The Arians of the Fourth Century*. London: Longmans, Green and Co., fourth edition, 1901.

Origen, *De Principiis [Peri Archon]*. See entries under Butterworth and Crouzel.

Outler, Albert C. "History as an Ecumenical Resource: The Protestant Discovery of 'Tradition,' 1952–1963." Presidential Address, American Catholic Historical Association, 28 December 1972. In *Catholic Historical Review* 59:1 (1973).

———, ed. John Wesley, *Sermons*. Bicentennial Edition of the Works of John Wesley; 4 vols. Nashville, TN: Abingdon Press, 1984–1987.

Pelikan, Jaroslav. *The Christian Tradition: A History of the Development of Doctrine*. 5 vols. Chicago: University of Chicago Press, 1971–1989.

———. *Credo: Historical and Theological Guide to Creeds and Confessions of Faith in the Christian Tradition*. New Haven, CT: Yale University Press, 2003.

Pelikan, Jaroslav, and Valerie Hotchkiss, eds. *Creeds and Confessions of Faith in the Christian Tradition*. 3 vols., with a collection of source material in original languages on CD ROM. New Haven, CT: Yale University Press, 2003.

Pentecostal Church of the Nazarene. *Manual of the Pentecostal Church of the Nazarene*. Los Angeles: Nazarene Publishing Co., 1908.

Petscheinig, Michael, ed. *Cassiani Opera: Collationes XXIIII*. Corpus Scriptorum Ecclesiasticorum Latonorum series, vol. 13. Vienna: Verlag der Österreicher Akademie der Wissenschaft, 2004.

Phillips, L. Edward. See entry under Paul F. Bradshaw.

Pliny the Younger, *Epistulae*. See entry under Mynors.

Pool, Jeff B., ed. *Sacred Mandates of Conscience: Interpretations of* The Baptist Faith and Message. Macon, GA: Smith and Helwys, 1997.

The Potter's House. "Belief Statement." Available at http://www.thepottershouse.org/PH_beliefs.html. The material on this Web site was accessed December 2006.

Power, David N. *The Sacrifice We Offer: The Tridentine Dogma and Its Reinterpretation*. New York: Crossroad, 1987.

Praise Evangel: For Sunday-Schools, Revivals, Singing Schools, Conventions, and General Use in Christian Work and Worship. Lawrenceburg, TN: James D. Vaughn, 1919.

Ratzinger, Joseph (Pope Benedict XVI). *Introduction to Christianity (Einführung in das Christentum)*. Tr. J. R. Foster. New York: Seabury Press, 1970. I have also consulted a more recent Spanish translation: *Introducción al Cristianismo*. Eighth edition. Salamanca: Ediciones Sígueme, 1996.

Reifferscheid, A., and G. Wissowa, eds. *Tertullian: De Ieiunio adversus Psychicos. Corpus Christianorum: Series Latina.* Turnhout: Brepols, 1954.

The Revivalist: A Collection of Choice Revival Hymns and Tunes. Troy, NY: Joseph Hillman, revised and enlarged edition, 1872.

Riedl, Wilhelm, and W. E. Crum, eds. and tr. *The Canons of Athanasius of Alexandria: The Arabic and Coptic Versions Edited and Translated with Introductions, Notes, and Appendices.* London: Williams and Norgate, 1904. Reprint edition of the American Theological Library Association in microfiche format.

The Rites of the Catholic Church: As Revised by Decree of the Second Vatican Ecumenical Council and Published by the Authority of Pope Paul VI. English translation prepared by The International Commission on English in the Liturgy. New York: Pueblo, 1983.

Rivière, J., ed. and tr. *Exposés généraux de la Foi.* Bibliothèque augustinienne: Oeuvres de Saint Augustin series, no. 9. Paris: Desclée, de Brouwer, et Cie, 1947.

Roberts, Alexander, James Donaldson, and Cleveland Coxe, eds. *The Ante-Nicene Fathers.* 10 volumes. Buffalo: Christian Literature, 1885–1887.

Roberts, C. H., and Dom B. Capelle. *An Early Euchologium: The Dêr Balyzeh Papyrus.* Louvain: 1949.

Robinson, Kim Stanley. *Red Mars.* New York: Bantam Books, 1993.

Roman Catholic Church. See entries listed under Catholic Church.

Rousseau, Adelin, ed. *Irénée de Lyon: Démonstration de la Prédication apostolique.* Sources chrétiennes series, no. 406. Paris; Éditions du Cerf, 1995.

Rufinus of Aquileia. *Commentarius in Symbolum Apostolorum.* See entry under Kelly.

Rusch, William G. *Reception: An Ecumenical Problem.* Philadelphia: Fortress Press in cooperation with the Lutheran World Federation, 1988.

———. See also entry under Jeffrey Gros.

The Sacramentary: Approved for Use in the Dioceses of the United States of America by the National Conference of Catholic Bishops and Confirmed by the Apostolic See. Collegeville, MN: Liturgical Press, 1974.

The Sacramentary: Approved for Use in the Dioceses of the United States of America by the National Conference of Catholic Bishops and Confirmed by the Apostolic See. English translation prepared by the International Committee on English in the Liturgy. Collegeville, MN: Liturgical Press, 1985.

Saddleback Church (Lake Forest, California). Statement on "What We Believe." Available at http://www.saddleback.com/flash/believe2.html. The material on this Web site was accessed December, 2006.

Salvati, M., ed. and tr. *Sant' Ambrogio: Scritti sulla Verginità.* Corona Patrum Salesiana series, vol. 6. Turin: Società Editrice Internazionale, 1955.

Schaff, Philip. *History of the Christian Church.* 5 volumes. New York: Charles Scribner's Sons, 1892.

Schleyer, Dietrich, tr. and ed. *Tertullian: De Baptismo: De Oratione.* Fontes Christiani series. Turnhout: Brepols Publishing, 2006.

Schlink, Edmund. *Ökumenische Dogmatik: Grundzüge.* Göttingen: Vandenhoeck & Ruprecht, 1993.

Schmidt, Carl, and Isaak Wajnberg, eds. *Gespräche Jesu mit seinen Jüngern nach der Auferstehung: Ein Katholisch-Apostolisches Sendschreiben des 2. Jahrhunderts. Texte und Untersuchungen* series, vol. 36; Leipzig and Berlin: Hinrichs Verlag, 1919.

Sernett, Milton G. "Black Religion and the Question of Evangelical Identity." In Donald W. Dayton and Robert K. Johnson, eds., *The Variety of American Evangelicalism.* Downers Grove, IL: InterVarsity Press, 1991, pp. 135-147.

Seventh-day Adventist Church. Statement of 28 "Fundamental Beliefs" (revision of 2005). Available at http://www.adventist.org/beliefs/fundamental/index.html. The document consulted was accessed December 2006.

Shannon, David T., and Gayraud S. Wilmore, eds. *Black Witness to the Apostolic Faith.* Grand Rapids, MI: William B. Eerdmans Publishing Company, for the Commission on Faith and Order of the National Council of the Churches of Christ in the USA, 1985.

Sieben, Hermann-Josef, ed. *Tertullian: Adversus Praxean/Gegen Praxeas.* Fontes Christiani series, no. 34. Freiburg: Herder, 2001.

Simonetti, Manlio. See entry under Henri Cruzel.

Sims, Walter Hines, ed. *Baptist Hymnal.* Nashville, TN: Convention Press, 1956.

Skibbe, Eugene. *A Quiet Reformer: An Introduction to Edmund Schlink's Life and Ecumenical Theology.* Minneapolis, MN: Kirk House Publishers, 1999.

Smith, Jonathan Z. *Divine Drudgery: On the Comparison of Early Christianities and the Religions of Late Antiquity.* Chicago: University of Chicago Press, 1990.

Southern Baptist Convention. "The Baptist Faith and Message" (2000). Available at http://www.sbc.net/bfm/bfmpreamble.asp. This material was accessed December 2006.

Stead, G. Christopher. "The Concept of Divine Substance." *Vigiliae Christianae* 29:1 (March 1975), pp. 1-14.

———. *Divine Substance.* Oxford: Clarendon Press, 1977.

Stewart-Sykes, Alistair, ed. and tr. *On Pascha: With the Fragments of Melito and Other Material Related to the Quartodecimans.* Crestwood, NY: St. Vladimir's Theological Seminary Press, 2001.

Stout, Harry S. *Divine Dramatist: George Whitefield and the Rise of Modern Evangelicalism.* Grand Rapids, MI: William B. Eerdmans, 1991.

Sweney, John O., C. C. McCabe, T. C. O. Kane, and William J. Kirkpatrick. *Songs of Redeeming Love.* Philadelphia: Perkinpine and Higgins, 1882.

Tanner, Kathryn. *Jesus, Humanity and the Trinity: A Brief Systematic Theology.* Minneapolis, MN: Fortress Press, 2001.

Tanner, Norman P., SJ, ed. *Decrees of the Ecumenical Councils.* 2 vols. London: Sheed and Ward; and Washington, DC: Georgetown University Press, 1990.

Tertullian, *Adversus Praxean.* See entry under Sieben.

———, *De Baptismo.* See entry under Schleyer.

———, *De Corona Militis.* See entry under Kroymann.

———, *De Ieiunio.* See entry under Reifferscheid.

Thacker, J. Ernest, George A. Fisher, and R. E. Magill, eds. *Assembly Songs.* Richmond, VA: Presbyterian Committee for Publication, 1910.

Theissen, Gerd, and Annette Merz. *The Historical Jesus: A Comprehensive Guide.* London: SCM Press, 1998. Translation by John Bowden from *Der historische Jesus: Ein Lehrbuch* (Göttingen: Vandenhoek & Ruprecht, 1996).
Theodore Lector (or Theodore Anagnostes), *Ecclesiastical History.* See entry under Hansen.
Theodore of Mopsuestia, *Commentary on the Nicene Creed.* See entry under Mingana.
Thompson, Bard, ed. *Liturgies of the Western Church.* Cleveland, OH, and New York: World Publishing Company, 1961.
Tovey, Phillip. See entry under Fred Linyard.
The United Methodist Church. *The United Methodist Hymnal: Book of United Methodist Worship.* Nashville, TN: Abingdon Press, 1989.
———. See entry under Methodist Church.
Van Buren, Paul. *According to the Scriptures: The Origins of the Gospel and of the Church's Old Testament.* Grand Rapids, MI: William B. Eerdmans Publishing Company, 1998.
Vincent of Lérins. *Commonitorium.* See the entry under Moxon.
The Vineyard USA. "Statement of Faith." Available at http://www.vineyardusa.org/about/beliefs.aspx. Material on this Web site was accessed December, 2006.
Vischer, Lucas, ed. *A Documentary History of the Faith and Order Movement, 1927–1963.* St. Louis, MO: Bethany Press, 1963.
———. See entry under Harding Meyer.
The Voice of Praise: A Compilation of the Very Best Sacred Songs for Use in Sunday Schools and Praise Services. Philadelphia and New York: Hall-Mack Company, 1904.
Vööbus, Arthur, tr. *The Didascalia Apostolorum in Syriac.* Corpus Scriptorum Ecclesiasticorum Orentalium series. Louvain: Secrétariat du CorpusSCO, 1979.
Wajnberg, Isaak. See entry under Carl Schmidt.
Waldensian Church. *Confessione di Fede del 1655.* Available at http://www.chiesavaldese.org. The material in this Web site was accessed December 2006.
———. "L'ecumenismo e il dialogo interreligioso." Consultative Commission on Ecumenical Relations of the Waldensian Church, 1998.
Ware, Timothy [Kallistos]. *The Orthodox Church.* Second edition, revised. London: Penguin, 1993.
Watson, J. R. *The English Hymn: A Critical and Historical Study.* Oxford: Oxford University Press, 1997.
Watts, Isaac. *Hymns and Spiritual Songs.* Originally published in 1707. London: T. Hawes and Co., T. Longman, C. and R. Ware, H. Woodfall, J. Buckland, J. Waugh, T. Field, E. and C. Dilly, W. Strahan, J. Fuller, and G. Leith, 1766.
Wengert, Timothy J. See entry under Robert Kolb.
Wesley, Charles. *Hymns and Sacred Poems.* London: William Strahan, 1739.
———. *Hymns for Ascension-Day.* Bristol: Felix Farley, 1747.
———. *Hymns for Our Lord's Resurrection.* London: W. Strahan, 1746.
———. *Hymns for the Nativity of Our Lord.* [No publisher indicated], 1745.
———. *Hymns of Petition and Thanksgiving for the Promise of the Father: Hymns for Whitsunday.* Bristol: Felix Farley, 1746.

Wesley, John. See entries under Jackson, Outler, and White.

White, James F., ed. *John Wesley's Sunday Service of the Methodists in North America*. Nashville, TN: United Methodist Publishing House, 1984. Currently available in reprint form from Order of St. Luke Publications. This is a reprint edition of the 1784 *Sunday Service of the Methodists in North America* with an introduction by James F. White.

Whitby, Michael, tr. *The Ecclesiastical History of Evagrius Scholasticus*. Translated Texts for Historians series, vol. 33. Liverpool: Liverpool University Press, 2000.

Wikgren, Allen. See entry under *The Greek New Testament*.

Wilken, Robert L. "The Christians as the Romans (and Greeks) Saw Them." In *Jewish and Christian Self-Definition*. Ed. E. P. Sanders. 3 vols. Philadelphia: Fortress Press, 1980ff.

Williams, Rowan. *Eucharistic Sacrifice—The Roots of a Metaphor*. Grove Liturgical Studies, no. 31. Bramcote, Nottinghamshire: Grove Books, 1982.

Wilmore, Gayraud T. See entry under David T. Shannon.

Willow Creek Community Church (South Barrington, Illinois). Statement of "What We Believe." Available at http://www.willowcreek.org/what_we_believe.asp. Material on this Web site was accessed December 2006.

Wills, Garry. *Head and Heart: American Christianities*. New York: Penguin, 2007.

Wissowa, G. See entry under A. Reifferscheidt.

World Council of Churches, Faith and Order Commission. *Confessing the One Faith: An Ecumenical Explication of the Apostolic Faith as it is Confessed in the Nicene-Constantinopolitan Creed (381)*. Faith and Order paper no. 153. Geneva: WCC, 1991.

Yinger, J. Milton. *The Scientific Study of Religion*. London: Macmillan, 1970.

Yoido Full Gospel Church. Statement on "Understanding the 'Full Gospel' Theology." Available at http://english.fgtv.com/Gospel/main.asp. Material on this Web site was accessed December 2006.

Young, Frances. *Sacrifice and the Death of Christ*. London: SPCK, 1975.

———. *Virtuoso Theology*. Cleveland, OH: Pilgrim Press, 1993.

Index

Abraham, William: 6
adoptionism: 36–37
Advent (season): 48, 69, 96, 117
Adventism, Adventist churches: *see* Seventh-day Adventist Church
African American churches: *see* black churches in the USA
altar call: *see* invitation
Anabaptist theologians: 60
"analogy of faith" (term): 64–65, 72, 117, 159
anamnesis (remembrance) of the work of Christ: 42–44, 67–68, 109, 112, 113
Anglicanism, Anglican churches: 6–8, 57, 58–59, 60, 61–62, 64, 66, 67–68, 68–69, 71, 76, 77, 108, 109
apocrypha: 31
Apollinaris of Laodicea, Apollinarianism: 38
Apostles' Creed: 23, 58, 59, 60, 61, 65, 85, 87, 96, 97, 107, 108, 110, 112, 113, 132
Apostolic Fathers: 18–20, 144, 145
Apostolic Tradition: 22–23, 24, 43, 108
Arius, Arianism: 33–34, 36, 50

Armenian Apostolic Orthodox Church: 38, 48
Assemblies of God: 84
Assyrian Church of the East: 8, 10, 31, 41–42, 43–44, 48, 52, 53, 55–56, 65–66, 102, 104, 107–108, 108–109, 110, 111, 117, 122, 148, 152
Athanasian Creed: 50, 58–59, 60
Athanasius: 27, 59
Augsburg Confession: 55, 60, 61, 62, 66, 68
Augustine of Hippo: 23, 108

baptism: 20, 22–23, 35–36, 108–109, 113, 124
baptism of the Holy Spirit (Pentecostal): 77, 81, 89, 136
Baptist churches: 11, 78, 79, 82–83
Barnabas, Greek letter attributed to: 18
Barth, Karl: 5–6
Benedict XVI, Pope: *see* Ratzinger, Joseph
Bible-teaching churches: 163, 166
Billy Graham Evangelistic Association: 78
binitarian formulae: 20

INDEX

bishops: 31, 35, 104, 129
black churches in the USA: 79–80, 89, 90–91, 162, 166–167
blessings and curses to protect oral texts: 16, 17
Bonjean, Christophe: 132–133
Brown, Dan, The Da Vinci Code: 4
Bucanus: *see* Du Buc
Bucer, Martin: 60

Calvary Chapel: 79
Calvin, John: 60
camp meetings: 88
Campus Crusade for Christ: 78, 94–95
canon of Christian scripture: 2, 4, 18, 24–28, 30, 31, 63–64, 65, 66, 72, 104, 116, 117, 118–119
carols: 45, 70, 93
catechisms and catechetical processes: 8, 23, 35–36, 53, 56–57, 59, 62–63, 94–95
"catholic" (term): 97, 113, 127, 155
Catholic Church: 2, 8, 9, 10, 31, 37, 38–39, 41–42, 43, 48, 66, 102, 104, 108, 109, 132
centrifugal and centripetal tendencies: viii, 80–82, 85–87, 96–97, 98–99, 121, 124, 163
Chalcedon, council of (451 C.E.): 36, 37, 59, 60, 83, 85, 122
Charry, Ellen: 6
"Christ" (term): 17, 29. *See also* Jesus Christ
Christmas: 48, 69–70, 93–94, 96, 153–154
Clement of Rome: 18, 144, 145
commensurability of language and meaning: 111–112, 132–136
Congregational churches: *see* Reformed churches
Constantinople, first council of (381 C.E.): 32, 37, 59, 148
Constantinople, third Council of (680–681 C.E.): 37, 150
Contemporary Christian music: 70, 78, 93–94, 98, 113

conversion experience: 75, 77, 98, 161–162
creation of the material world: 26, 29, 31, 34–35, 50–51, 116
Crosby, Fanny J.: 92
Crouch, Andraé: xii, 92
crucifix: 45–46
Crusades: 46
Czech Reformation: 56

deification: *see* divinization or deification of humanity
Delumeau, Jean: 66, 138, 154
denominations and denominationalism: vii–viii, 3, 8, 76, 77–79, 81, 141, 162
deuterocanonical scriptures: 31
dispensationalism: 76, 163
diversity of early Christian communities: 1, 3–5, 13–14
divinization or deification of humanity: 51
divisive issues in contemporary Protestant and Anglican churches: 6–8, 120–121
divorce and remarriage: 7
docetism: 19
doctrine: 11, 58–63, 82–87, 129–131. *See also* reception of doctrine
Du Bois, W. E. B.: 80
Du Buc (Bucanus), Guillaume, of Lausanne: 64–65

Easter: 46–49, 60–61, 65, 70, 96, 114, 161
Eastern Orthodox churches: xi, 8, 9, 31, 38, 41–42, 104, 136, 148
Eaton, Chris: xii, 93
ecumenical movement: viii–ix, xi, 2–6, 8, 9–10, 11–12, 31–32, 53, 57, 61, 101 (defined), 101–110 (more generally), 111, 113, 115, 120, 122, 128–129, 132, 133
Ehrman, Bart D.: xii, 27, 138
"Emergent" churches: 10, 97
Enlightenment: 29, 77, 119

INDEX 193

entertainment culture: 78
entire sanctification (holiness): 77, 81, 88, 89
Epiphany or Theophany (season): 46, 48, 70, 153
eucharist ("the Lord's supper" or mass): 16, 25, 29, 35–36, 39–45, 49, 51, 66, 67–68, 71, 88, 106, 109, 112, 113, 114, 124, 151 (term)
Euhemeranism: 29
evangelical churches and communities: 8–10, 72, 75–78 (defined), 75–99 (generally), 161
evangelistic associations: 78
extracanonical gospels: 4, 29, 118

Faith and Order: xi, 2–3, 9–10, 101–110, 111, 120, 128, 135–136
filioque clause: 37, 38, 39, 58, 59, 97, 130, 140
First Things: 9
Florence, Council of: 130
Ford, John: 135
formulae of tradition: 15–16, 20, 25, 39
Fortin, Denis: xii, 165
Founds, Rick: xii, 93
free churches: 77, 162
Fundamentalism and Fundamentalist churches: 16, 76–77, 117

gay and lesbian persons: *see* sexuality, contemporary issues about
Geertz, Clifford: 122–123
Gelasian Sacramentary: 48
Gerhardt, Paul: 68
Gnosticism: 24, 35, 147
"gospel" (term): xi, 13, 25–26, 29, 56–57, 75, 98, 155
Gospel music: 78, 91–92, 94, 115
Grant, Amy: xii, 93
Gros, Jeffrey: xii
Gumbel, Nicky: 95

Handel, George Frederick: 70
Hankey, Katherine: 75, 92

Hebrew scriptures: *see* Old Testament
heresies and heterodox teachings: 38, 50, 131
Hippolytus: *see* Apostolic Tradition
Holiness churches: 11, 77, 78, 81, 83–84, 121
Holy Spirit: 19–24, 25, 33, 34–35, 37, 38–39, 42, 43, 46, 48, 50, 76, 77, 81, 83, 85, 86, 87, 88, 89, 93–94 ("breath of heaven"), 101, 102, 105, 108, 136
homosexuality: *see* sexuality, contemporary issues about
hymns and hymnals: 68–70, 87, 89–90

idolatry: 34
Ignatius of Antioch: 18, 19
"in accordance with the scriptures": 14, 17, 22, 25, 27, 35, 50, 103, 110, 116–117
inerrancy or infallibility of scripture: 76–77, 117
institution narrative (of eucharist): 42, 43
intention to believe as other Christian communities believe: 63, 70, 113, 134
invitation: 88, 89
Irenaeus of Lyons: 19–21, 24, 25, 28, 51, 104
Islam: 36, 46, 47, 123, 133–134

Jehovah's Witnesses: 121
Jesus Christ:
  ascension into heaven: 20–23, 33, 44, 61, 69, 83, 84, 85, 86, 87
  birth: 20–21, 46, 48, 70, 83, 84, 93–94, 113, 153
  blood: 39–40, 62, 67, 83, 85, 91–92, 115
  burial: 13–15, 17, 21, 22, 23, 28, 31, 33, 34, 40, 61, 62, 71, 93, 112–114
  contemporary issues about: 3–4, 118–119

Jesus Christ (*continued*)
  cross (crucifixion) and death: 15, 17, 18, 19, 21, 22, 26, 28, 29, 41, 42, 44, 45, 49, 56, 62, 67, 69, 71, 83, 84, 85, 86, 90, 91, 93, 95, 97, 98, 102, 103, 106, 107, 110, 112–114
  descent into hell: 61–62, 113, 157
  incarnation: 19, 20, 33, 39, 50, 58, 61, 62, 83, 86–87, 93, 98, 113
  life: 21, 22, 24, 25, 26, 29, 40, 41, 44, 46, 48, 50–52, 61, 62, 70, 71, 83, 84, 86, 92, 97, 102, 103, 106, 110, 112, 113, 115–116, 117
  "Lord" (title): 18, 20, 29, 32, 40, 44, 58, 67, 68, 84, 85, 90, 93, 103, 109, 116
  mediation and intercession: 83, 84, 85–86
  messiah: 17, 85, 86
  miracles: 84, 86, 98, 113
  priesthood: 85
  resurrection: 15, 17, 18, 19, 20, 21, 22, 26, 28, 29, 34, 41, 42, 45, 49, 56, 62, 71, 83, 84, 85, 86, 91, 93, 95, 98, 102, 103, 106, 107, 110, 112–114
  second coming or second advent: 20, 41, 44, 68, 81, 86, 103, 113, 165
  suffering or passion: 18, 20–21, 62, 68, 86, 102, 107, 113
  teachings: 98, 102, 103, 113
  worship of: 34
Judaism: 123, 133–134

Kelsey, David: 5
Ken, Thomas: 96
kerygma: 1 (defined), 17, 20, 25, 27, 28, 40, 103, 105, 118, 170
Kinnamon, Michael: 76

laity: 130
Lent: 47–48, 70
Lérins, Vincent of: 127

Lindbeck, George: 6, 128–129, 131–132
linguistic study: 135
liturgical renewal: 107–109, 134
liturgical year or cycle: 46–49, 49–50, 117, 161
Liturgy of Addai and Mari: 43–44
Liturgy of St. John Chrysostom: 44
Lord's supper: *see* eucharist
Luther, Martin: 55, 56, 57, 63–64, 65, 125
Lutheran churches: 11, 55–57, 58, 59, 60, 61, 62–64, 66, 68, 71, 77, 132

Mackay, William: 91
Macquarrie, John: 139
McLaren, Brian: vii–ix, xii, 10, 97
Mar Thoma Church: 57–58, 65, 148
Marcion and Marcionitism: 24, 25, 26, 29, 50, 104, 116
Marshall, Bruce: 6
Matthias of Janow: 56
Marsden, George M.: 77
Mary the mother of Jesus: 23, 33, 39, 45, 83, 85, 86, 87, 93–94
mass: *see* eucharist
material world: *see* creation of the material world
megachurches: 11, 79, 81, 84, 85
Melito of Sardis: 47
memorial acclamations in the eucharist: 1, 109, 113
Merz, Annette: *see* Theissen, Gerd
Methodist churches: 11, 57, 61, 71, 76, 79, 108, 121, 132, 134, 162, 163
Methodologies used in this book: 3, 11–12, 127–136
Montanus and Montanism: 24
monasticism: 33–34, 98
monophysite: 36, 150 (term)
Moravian Church: 11, 57, 59, 60–61, 65, 70
More, Hannah: 94
Morley, Frederick B.: xii, 103
Mormons: 121

Muratorian fragment: 26, 27
Muslim: *see* Islam
mystery: 41, 45, 58, 69, 90–91, 109, 111, 124 (term), 124–125
narrative of the gospel: 112–114
Nassif, Bradley: xii, 142
National Council of the Churches of Christ (USA): xi, xii, 9–10, 135–136, 162, 163
Nazarene, Church of the: 83–84
New Testament: *see* canon of Christian scripture
Nicaea, first council of (325 C.E.): 35, 47, 59
Nicaea, second council of (787 C.E.): 38
Nicene (Nicene-Constantinopolitan) Creed: 32–39, 42, 50, 58, 60, 61, 71, 97, 107, 112, 113, 130, 132, 134
non-creedal churches: 107

Old Testament: 17, 22, 25, 29, 34–35, 42, 51, 113–114, 116–117, 147 (term)
old-line Protestant churches: 6–8, 141
oral traditions before Paul or the canonical gospels: 4, 14–18, 105–106
Oriental Orthodox churches: 8, 10, 21, 31, 38, 41, 46, 111, 122, 141, 148 (term)

passion plays: 45, 70
Passover: 46–47, 113, 114
Pelikan, Jaroslav: 24, 28, 39, 152
Pentecost: 46
Pentecostal churches, Pentecostalism: xi, 77, 78, 79, 80, 81, 84, 96, 102, 121, 136
performed music: 70, 87–88, 93
Pliny the Younger: 34
Pneumatomachianism: 50
Polycarp of Smyrna: 18
popular culture, expressions of the gospel in: 45–46

popular religious beliefs: 130
postil: 52, 66
postmillennial understanding of biblical history: 76
The Potter's House: 79, 165
"prayers" addressed to saints: 42, 151–152
premillennial understanding of biblical history: 76
pre-Pauline kerygma: *see* oral traditions before Paul or the canonical Gospels
preaching: *see* sermons and preaching
Presbyterian churches: *see* Reformed churches
Protestant and related churches: 11, 55–73, 76, 119, 120–121. *See also* old-line Protestant churches
proto-orthodox Christian communities: 2, 13, 13–30 (more generally)

"Q" source: 25

Ratzinger, Joseph (Pope Benedict XVI): 6, 129, 174
recapitulation: 51, 115
reception of doctrine: 11, 35, 87, 129–130, 174
Reformed churches: 11, 57, 58–59, 60, 61, 63, 64–65, 66–67, 68–69, 71, 77, 108, 161
"religion" (definition): 122–123
Restoration movement (Stone-Campbell): 76, 163, 166
revivals: 88
Rolle, Johann Heinrich: 70
Roman Catholic Church: *see* Catholic Church
rule of faith (*regula fidei*): 21, 29, 63, 65

sacrifice and sacrificial meanings of Christ's work: 29, 40–41, 51, 62, 71–72, 84, 85, 91–92, 107, 110, 114–116
Saddleback Church: 79, 84, 164–165

salvation: 114–116
Satlow, Michael L.: 173
Schleiermacher, Friedrich: 131–132, 175
Schlink, Edmund: 6
sermons and preaching: 7, 43, 65–67, 88–89, 166
Seventh-day Adventist Church: 11, 79, 80–81, 85–87, 121, 134, 165
sexuality, contemporary issues about: 6–8, 73, 121
sin: 7, 114
slavery: 7
spirituals: 90–91
Stamm, Mark: xii
Status confessionis: 6
Strong, Douglas M.: xii
substitutionary atonement: 71–72, 83–84, 89, 93, 95, 98, 115–116
supercessionism: 29–30
systematic theology: 128

Tanner, Kathryn: 139
Tertullian: 21–22, 24, 25,47
testimonies in Evangelical worship: 88
Theissen, Gerd, and Annette Merz: 17, 118–119, 143
Theodore of Mopsuestia: 35–36
"theology" (term): 130, 174–175
Theophany: *see* Epiphany
Thomas, Gospel of: 29, 118
toleration, religious: 77
"tradition" (term): 16, 104–105
Triduum: 47
Trinity and trinitarian formulae: 20–24, 34, 42, 79, 80–81, 83, 86, 102

Union churches and United or Uniting churches: 57, 63
unity of Christian churches: *see* visible unity of churches
unmediated authority of scripture: 76

Valentinus and Valentinianism: 24, 25, 26, 29, 50, 104, 116
Vatican Council, second: 53, 108
Victimae paschali laudes: 49
victory over evil: 49, 62, 72, 84, 95, 110, 115–116
Vineyard Christian Fellowship: 79, 84–85, 165
visible unity of churches: 2, 121–124
voluntary organization of Evangelical communities: 77

Waldensian church: 11, 57
Watts, Isaac: 69, 89, 91
Wesley, Charles: 69, 89, 135
Wesley, John: 166
Wheeler: Sondra E.: xii
White, Ellen G.: 86
Whitefield, George: 78
Wilken, Robert: 5
Williams, Rowan: 151
Willow Creek Community Church: 79, 165
Wipo: 49
witnesses to oral traditions: 15–16
World Council of Churches (WCC): 101, 103, 111, 112
"Word of God" (term): 64, 158, 159

Yoido Full Gospel Church: 79, 96, 165, 169
Young, Frances: 28

Zwingli, Ulrich: 60